T0301679

Economic Diplomacy and the Geography of International Trade

To Doris, Vera, Eva and Hanneke

Cover illustration based on Peeter Burgeik, 'Homo Globalicus', 2008, wood cut and lithography, printed on the KARL KRAUSE press at Steendrukkerij Aad Hekker, Amsterdam

Economic Diplomacy and the Geography of International Trade

Peter A.G. van Bergeijk

Professor of International Economics/Macroeconomics, Institute of Social Studies, The Hague, The Netherlands

Edward Elgar
Cheltenham, UK • Northampton, MA, USA

Published by
Edward Elgar Publishing Limited
The Lypiatts
15 Lansdown Road
Cheltenham
Glos GL50 2JA
UK

Edward Elgar Publishing, Inc.
William Pratt House
9 Dewey Court
Northampton
Massachusetts 01060
USA

A catalogue record for this book
is available from the British Library

Library of Congress Control Number: 2009925930

ISBN 978 1 84844 463 8

Contents

Figures and Tables   *vii*
Preface and Acknowledgements   *xi*

1. Introduction: New Challenges to Economic Diplomacy   1

PART I   ECONOMIC DIPLOMACY AND TRADE UNCERTAINTY

2. Trade and Conflict (and *Vice Versa*)   23
3. Trade Uncertainty and Trade Disruption   47

PART II   ECONOMIC DIPLOMACY AND COMMERCIAL POLICY

4. Commercial Policy and Economic Diplomacy: Why?   69
5. The Weight of Bilateral Economic Diplomacy and Commercial
     Policy Revisited   93

PART III   ECONOMIC STATECRAFT: THE CASE OF SANCTIONS

6. Failures and … Successes of Economic Sanctions   115
     Appendix 6A.1: Data Sources and Methodology   138
7. The Expected Utility of Positive and Negative Economic Sanctions   147

PART IV   POLICY CONCLUSIONS AND FURTHER RESEARCH

8. An Agenda for Economic and Commercial Diplomacy   173

References   *187*
Index   *211*

Figures and Tables

FIGURES

1.1	Trends in economic diplomacy 1950–1999	3
1.2	Change in distance parameter 1995–2004	12
2.1	Contribution to the explanation of the variance of bilateral trade of 40 countries in 1985–6	40
3.1	Production, consumption and specialization at different stages of international trade	49
3.2	The free trade and no-trade utility functions	52
3.3	Prices and quantities that play a role in the consumers' and producers' decisions	56
3.4	Optimal specialization and trade inclination parameter	59
3.5	Time path of utility (economy moves from autarky to free trade)	60
3.6	Time path of utility (economy disrupted from free trade to autarky)	61
3.7	Anticipation of trade disruption	62
4.1	Elasticity of trade with respect to a decrease of policy variables	73
4.2	Export premium in per cent (United Kingdom)	74
4.3	Development of employment (right axis) and labour productivity (left axis) for Dutch locally operating firms and international firms in the Netherlands (1995–2005)	76
4.4	Exports *per capita* and export promotion *per capita* (2005)	90
5.1	Development of the number of export promotion agencies in the sample (1915–2005)	94
5.2	Diplomatic network (share of embassies and consulates in relation to bilateral distance in kilometres, 2006)	95
5.3	Percentage of data set covered below a level of *per capita* GDP	105
5.4	Estimated co-efficients and two standard errors confidence intervals for (sub) samples by *per capita* GDP (in 1000 US$) a. Embassies and consulates b. Export promotion agency staff (100s)	107

5.5   Relative importance of the explanatory variables in two
       gravity models (absolute values β co-efficients of the
       estimated parameters)   109
5.6   Indexes of aggregate hostility and co-operation for 40
       countries in the mid-1980s   110
6.1   Success rate and proportional trade linkage (1946–2000)   118
6.2   The political market for misconduct   121
6.3   Democratic and autocratic institutions and success of sanctions   122
6.4   Duration of unsuccessful sanctions 1945–2005 (excluding
       ongoing sanctions)   128
6A.1   Comparison of the 2nd and 3rd edition of Hufbauer et al.   139
7.1   Indifference curves for risk aversion (v_2), risk neutrality (v_1)
       and risk preference (v_0)   155
7.2   Increase in π (case of risk preference)   159
7.3   Unconditional increase in the yield of neutral activities for the
       case of risk aversion   161
7.4   The impact of a positive sanction   164
8.1   Available empirical knowledge   181

TABLES

1.1   Trade shares by major countries and country groupings for the
       years 1995 and 2025 (in %)   4
1.2   Summary of empirical studies on the relationship between
       trade, conflict and instruments of international politics and
       commercial policy   6
1.3   Summary statistics for recent empirical investigations into the
       effectiveness of economic sanctions   8
1.4   Impact of a one standard deviation change in intangible trade
       barriers (% change)   10
1.5   Empirical results of the OLS estimation of the bilateral trade
       to GDP ratios for individual countries 1995 and 2004 ($N =$
       2994)   13
2.1   Percentage reduction in net conflict due to a 1% increase in
       trade   33
2.2   Gravity equations including non-binary indicators of
       diplomatic and political interaction   38
3.1   Choice set   53
4.1   Impact of a 1 percentage point increase in multilateral trade   72
       linkage on annual long-run GDP growth
4.2   Results of gravity equations that include the number of
       embassies and consulates amongst the explanatory variables   84

4.3	Co-efficient for embassies and consulates in gravity equations for sub-samples distinguished by income level	85
5.1	Countries included in the empirical investigation, GDP *per capita* level and relation to the other data sets on export promotion and embassies and consulates	102
5.2	Empirical results of the OLS estimation of the gravity equation for 36 countries in 2006 (N=1242)	104
6.1	The success rate of economic sanctions (1946–2000)	117
6.2	Distribution of duration of post-1945 sanctions	124
6.3	Summary of explanatory variables (excluding ongoing cases)	129
6.4	Success of sanctions: LOGIT estimates for the quasi-reduced form equation of the success score of sanctions 1946–2000	131
6.5	Extending the core equation	132
6.6	Key characteristics pre-1990, post-1990 and for 1946–2002	134
6A.1	The construction of the success score of economic sanctions	141
6A.2	The construction of democracy and autocracy indicators in the Polity data set	144
7.1	Choice set	152
7.2	Impact of the economic instruments on misconduct	165
8.1	Reported heterogeneity in international economic relations	176

Preface and Acknowledgements

In early 2006 Edward Elgar surprised me with an invitation to make a second edition of my PhD thesis – which he had published as *Economic Diplomacy, Trade and Commercial Policy* in 1994; the original thesis was published in 1990 at Groningen University as *Handel en diplomatie* (Trade and diplomacy, in Dutch). I gratefully accepted the challenge of a comeback to a subject that I left in the mid-1990s. Of course I did: who gets a second chance in the scientific world? Moreover, a number of publications written after 1994 provided a good basis for a revised edition.

Eventually, however, the project became too intensive and we had to settle for a fully new title. The main reason was that too much new knowledge had been developed, new theories had emerged and important data sources had been updated (such as the Hufbauer *et al.* data set on economic sanctions published in April 2008). Indeed, both the scientific and the real policy world had dramatically changed, especially since the turn of the millennium. Thus a second edition could not ignore how much has changed and a new title was needed.

In comparison with *Economic Diplomacy, Trade and Commercial Policy*, three chapters by and large survived the editing: Chapter 2 which contains a review of literature and history of thought, Chapter 3 on modelling uncertain trade and Chapter 7 on the use of positive and negative sanctions. These chapters have been updated; references to new literature have of course been included and wherever publications since 1994 were relevant I included parts and pieces. Chapters 5 and 6 have been completely revised because I used a different research strategy although the empirical design of the original book can still be recognized in these two chapters. Anyhow, the analyses now cover data up to the mid-2000s and thus – compared with the original work – the data and findings have been moved forward by about 20 years. Chapters 1, 4 and 8 are completely new.

Edward Elgar's interest in my book was not the only signal for renewed interest in the topic of my thesis. Firstly, I am really happy to have been invited to the conference 'New Frontiers of Economic Diplomacy' in Lisbon in May 2007 (where I presented what has become the first chapter of the present book). Secondly, I met great enthusiasm when I was co-organizing with Steven Brakman the conference 'The Gravity Equation or: Why the World is not Flat' (Groningen, October 2007, where I presented the work with Mina Yakop that eventually developed into Chapter 5 of this book). Thirdly, Chapter 6 was presented at a special economics of development seminar at the Institute of Social Studies (The Hague, September 2008). Both the deadlines of these events and the discussions with the participants helped me to further this project.

On the Structure of the Book

This book is divided into four parts and an introductory chapter. The introduction sketches the trends and shifts in the world economic system influencing the impact and importance of economic diplomacy and at the same time gives a broad overview of recent theories and empirical findings. The Parts can be read independently (although they contain cross-references, of course). Readers that are, for example, only interested in economic sanctions can limit themselves to Part III; readers that want to know more about the economics of commercial diplomacy can focus on Part II. One benefit of this structure is that Parts can thus be used as *capita selecta* in courses in international economics and international political science.

Part I provides the scientific background for the discussions in later chapters. It contains an overview of the history of economic analysis of the interaction between economic and political variables in the field of international relations (Chapter 2) and a discussion of a neoclassical model of trade uncertainty which is one of the key analytical tools in this book. Non-technical readers may wish to skip Chapter 3 as it contains mathematics.

Part II deals with bilateral economic diplomacy and commercial policy. It investigates the reasons for government intervention. Chapter 4 critically discusses the available empirical evidence regarding the relation between international economics and productivity, both at the macro and the micro level, and the influence that governments can and cannot exercise thereon. Chapter 5 econometrically investigates two typical instruments of bilateral economic diplomacy. The chapter is accessible for non-technical readers provided that they are willing to skip an occasional equation.

Part III deals with economic sanctions. Chapter 6 deals with negative economic sanctions – that is with (threats of) punishment – and brings together the many literatures on the effectiveness of this instrument of economic diplomacy. Data issues are important in this field, especially since data sources from different scientific disciplines are combined, but in order to keep the discussion transparent and focussed, measurement issues have been contained in a data appendix. Chapter 7 is by necessity theoretical in nature: data on positive economic sanctions (rewards) are not available and thus only theory can provide a guide.

Finally, Part IV deals with policy issues and clarifies where new knowledge needs to be developed. In a sense, Chapter 8 answers the self-posed question of what topic I would choose for my PhD if I had to write the thesis at this moment.

ACKNOWLEDGEMENTS

This book is based on material that over the years has been published in *De Economist, Economic Modelling, ESB, Internationale Spectator, Journal of World Trade, Kyklos, Peace Economics, Peace Science, and Public Policy, Regional Science and Urban Economics* and *World Economy*. I have benefited a lot from comments by editors and anonymous references.

I am also indebted to a great many colleagues and friends that since 1986 gave me the opportunity to do research on this topic, provided research assistance, helped me to improve on my investigations, commented on drafts of (parts of) the manuscript, were co-authors and/or stimulated me to 'make the difference': (in alphabetical order and without any implication) Marten van den Berg, Jenny Boelens, Shane Bonetti, Steven Brakman, Gerrit Faber, Bart van de Gevel, Richard Gigengack, Heleen van Gorcum, Henri de Groot, Henk de Haan, Robert Haffner, Dick Kabel, Frank Kalshoven, Astrid Kampen, Pieter Karsdorp, Ger Lanjouw, Robert Lensink, Hans Linnemann, Charles van Marrewijk, Selwyn Moons, Ruud de Mooy, Harry Oldersma, Pedro Conceição Parreira, Jan Pen, Roderick van Schreven, Jarig van Sinderen, Jan Veenbergen, Marie-Lise van Veenstra, Pieter Waasdorp, Robert Went, Ed Westerhout, Mina Yakop and (of course) Hanneke Sassenburg.

Nieuw Vennep,
March 2009

1. Introduction: New Challenges to Economic Diplomacy

Economists and diplomats are different specimen. For long they could neglect each other's existence. Typically economic and commercial policies were labelled 'low politics' by statesmen and diplomats. At first sight the tough dynamic world of commerce and the subtle glamour of diplomacy do not have much in common, but as any newspaper reader knows, international economic relationships are an important factor in the diplomatic sphere of influence and *vice versa*. 'No matter who reigns, the merchant reigns.' 'Trade follows the flag.' This book takes a closer look at international economics and politics. Economic diplomacy (of which commercial policy is an important element) is at the interface between these subject fields as its aim is to influence decisions about cross-border economic activities (export, import, investment, lending, aid and migration) pursued by governments and non-state actors. A closer study of the interrelationships between, on the one hand, diplomacy and politics and, on the other hand, trade, investment and capital is warranted from a broader theoretical perspective. Mainstream neoclassical economic theory typically tends to pay little if any attention to public policy in the context of bilateral economic relationships. This is an undesirable situation and one can only agree with Bhagwati (1991, p. *xvi*) when he complains 'How can we possibly explain what happens unless we bring in the political equations into our modelling at the same time?' The lack of attention may be due to the fact that the economic recipe is to specialize according to comparative advantage and to avoid subsidies and other distorting government policies that reduce welfare. Indeed, most textbooks in international economics do not pay attention to the inherent political character of international economic exchange. A case in point is Ricardo's *Principles of Political Economy and Taxation* ([1817] 1962, para. 7.1) which develops the theory of comparative advantage as an explanation for the 'natural trade' that leads Portugal to export wine and England to export cloth:

> Under a system of perfectly free commerce, each country naturally devotes its capital and labour to such employments as are most beneficial to each. This pursuit of individual advantage is admirably connected with the universal good of the whole. By stimulating industry, by regarding ingenuity, and by using most efficaciously the peculiar powers bestowed by nature, it distributes labour most

effectively and most economically: while, by increasing the general mass of productions, it diffuses general benefit, and binds together by one common tie of interest and intercourse, the universal society of nations throughout the civilized world.

The issue, however, that is relevant for our discussion is that the trade in wine and cloth between Portugal and England had not been the outcome of free trade at all. It was the result of economic diplomacy and arranged in the context of the Methuen Treaty, a military and commercial treaty between Portugal and England signed in 1703 as part of the War of the Spanish Succession.[1] In addition, the treaty helped to establish trading relations between England and Portugal. The trade agreement that formed part of the treaty set a zero tariff on English woollen cloth and reduced the duties on Portuguese wines by a third giving Portugal a clear competitive edge *vis-à-vis* France.[2] The upshot clearly is that comparative advantage is only one side of the coin and that economic diplomacy and economic security can be drivers of trading patterns. Indeed, as pointed out by Adam Smith ([1776] 1976, p. 179), the treaty diverted potential imports from France towards Portugal:

> By the famous treaty of commerce with Portugal the consumer is prevented by high duties from purchasing of a neighbouring country, a commodity which our own climate does not produce, but is obliged to purchase it of a distant country, though it is acknowledged, that the commodity of the distant country is of a worse quality than that of the near one.

According to O'Brien (1976, 544–48) the trade diversion element became a standard objection against commercial treaties and was included in the major works of Classical economists (including Hume, McCullogh and Say).[3] Actually, this negative verdict of commercial treaties may very well be one of the explanations why modern trade economists have tended to shy away from the interrelated issues of commercial policy and economic diplomacy.

1   A BRIEF HISTORY OF ECONOMIC DIPLOMACY

Since the start of the third millennium the interrelated issues of economic diplomacy and economic security have risen to the top of the international policy agenda. A mix of political and economic drivers can be discerned behind this rise: the integration of formerly communist countries into the world economy, the 'new' scarcity (reflected by unprecedented increases in the prices of oil, raw materials and other essential goods and products), global warming and the occurrence of new forms of conflict such as transnational terrorism. Characteristic of the present era is the intensity of multi-dimensional relations between nations and people around the globe. This creates tremendous commercial opportunities in newly emerging markets and this economic potential is one reason for the increased interest amongst scientists and policy makers in economic diplomacy and commercial policy.

Figure 1.1 illustrates the increasing intensity of international interaction for the field of economic diplomacy in the second half of the twentieth century, charting two visible aspects in the arena of international politics: state visits and economic sanctions (such as boycotts and embargoes). By the year 2000 the deployment of economic sanctions that aimed to achieve foreign policy goals was four times as high as the 1950s level; in the same period typical foreign policy activities related to commercial policy increased even stronger as shown by the eightfold increase in the number of state visits by Heads of State of the US, Germany and France.

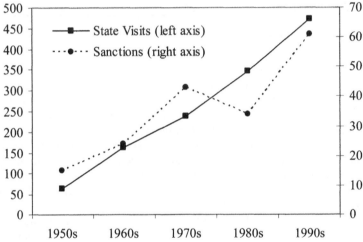

Sources:
Nitsch (2007, p. 1800, Table 1); all visits by Heads of State from France, Germany and the United States.
Hufbauer *et al.* (2008), database on CD-ROM.

Figure 1.1 Trends in economic diplomacy 1950–1999

One of the most important aspects of the present phase of the globalization process is the fact that the formerly communist states have become more market-oriented economies and participate to a much larger extent in the world economic system than previously. Although their performance is already impressive, much is still in the pipeline and by 2025 the OECD's latest world model (Hervé et al. 2007) predicts that the old group of trading nations (Europe and North America) will have lost their majority position in terms of trade shares; see Table 1.1.

Table 1.1 Trade shares by major countries and country groupings for the years 1995 and 2025 (in %)

	1995	2025
United States	16	11
Euro Area	29	18
Non-euro Europe	11	5
Japan	7	4
China	2	17
Rest of Asia	14	15
Rest of the World	21	30

Source: Hervé et al. (2007)

In particular the trade share of Asia would increase from 23% in 1995 to 36% in 2025 whereas the share of the European Union over the same period would decrease from 40% to 23%. This development is relevant for two reasons. First, many firms in the newly emerging economies are state-owned and trade and investment relations often require government to government contacts. Second, the combined share of the United States and the European Union will reduce to about one third of world trade in 2025. This will clearly have consequences, because an increase in the number of countries that participate in international trade negotiations will complicate and slow international consensus building.[4] Moreover, the emergence of new economies with very different institutions and cultural background will influence global norms and values and this will undoubtedly have an impact on the rules of international trade and investment. In particular the historical, cultural and institutional background of China and India may in the long run exert an influence on the ways the world defines and settles international conflicts.

The emergence of these new players offers a challenge for economic diplomacy and to a large extent explains why interest of economic scholars in commercial policy has increased following seminal work by Strange (1998) on new modes of diplomacy. One relevant result of academic research has been a strengthening of the empirical base regarding the mutual impact of trade and politics, which we consider in the next section.

2 EMPIRICAL EVIDENCE

Econometric investigations since the early 1990s consistently show that economic diplomacy is empirically relevant. The empirical basis is illustrated in Table 1.2 (the studies are discussed in Chapter 2). The table summarizes empirical studies that deal with both the conflict–trade relationship (that is the questions of how conflicts hinder international trade or how the reduction of conflict increases trade) and the trade–conflict relationship (that is how does international trade influence conflict and co-operation between nations). The table lists 18 studies, starting with Polachek's seminal 1980 article on the impact of trade on international conflict regarding 30 countries and the period 1958–67 and ending with a number of studies that followed up on Rose's (2007) investigation of the influence of the embassies and consulates of 20 exporting countries regarding 220 export destinations. The studies together provide a rich sample that covers the post-Second World War period and includes the 1990s (this is relevant since this decade is often seen as the start of a new phase of the globalization process).[5] Indeed, it is important that the relationships have been established both prior to 1990 and after 1990 (when the Iron Curtain fell and *détente* set in).

Box 1.1 Gravity in a nutshell

The gravity model (which will be discussed in more detail in Chapter 5) is an applied empirical trade model that describes bilateral trade flows. The key drivers in this model are economic mass and distance. Just as in the Newtonian gravity model this trade model assumes that interaction is weaker if distance is larger and stronger when masses are larger. Thus a large country that has substantial production and population will *ceteris paribus* trade more than a small country. Likewise countries that are closer to each other trade more. Often the model also includes a great number of trade resistance factors (such as import tariffs) and trade enhancement factors (such as a common language) that are relevant at the bilateral level.

Typically the empirical investigations use a gravity model approach in which distance and economic or political mass (proxied by GDP, population and so on) are the drivers for the dependent variable which is listed in the second column of Table 1.2. The third column reports the main explanatory variable of interest. The fourth and fifth column report the number of countries N and the period that has been investigated.

Table 1.2 Summary of empirical studies on the relationship between trade, conflict and instruments of international politics and commercial policy

Study	Dependent variable	Exogenous variable[a]	N[b]	Period	Elasticity
Polachek 1980	Conflict	Export, Import	30	1958–67	0.15/0.31
Gasiorowski 1986	Conflict	Trade	44	1960–77	0.33
Pollins 1989b	Trade	Conflict	25	1960–75	0.04/0.37
Summary 1989	US trade	Conflict	66	1978–82	0.2/0.3
Bergeijk 1989b	Trade	Co-operation	25	1966–70	0.2/0.49
Polachek et al. 1992	Conflict	Trade	105	1948–78	0.12/0.50
Bergeijk 1994a	Trade	Co-operation	40	1985–86	0.23/0.60
Mousseau et al. 2003	Military conflict	Trade	n.a.	1885–1992	-0.3/-0.4
Nitsch et al. 2004	Trade	Terrorism	200	1960–93	0.01/0.10
Li et al. 2004	Terrorism	Trade	112	1975–97	0.001
Blomberg et al. 2006	Trade	Terrorism	177	1968–99	0.04/0.05
Freytag et al. 2006	Terrorism	Trade	96	2000–02	u–shaped
Fratianni et al. 2006a	Trade	Terrorism	n.a.	1980–99	0.01/0.10
Lederman et al. 2006	Export	Export Promotion	104	2002–04	0.07/0.11
Rose 2007	Trade	Embassies	20[c]	2002	0.08/0.11
Gil-Pareja et al. 2007	Tourism	Embassies	7[d]		0.15/0.30
Maurel et al. 2007	Trade	Embassies	56	1997–2005	0.07/0.17[e]
Yakop et al. 2007	Trade	Embassies	63	2006	0.06/0.13
Nitsch 2007	Trade	State visits	3[c]	1948–2003	0.08/0.13

Notes:
a. This column reports only the result for the most important explanatory variable in the multiple regressions.
b. Number of countries included in the study.
c. Number of exporting countries; number of export markets amount to 220.
d. G7 *vis-à-vis* 156 countries.
e Estimates according to the specification by Rose (2007).

Finally, the table reports in the penultimate column the (range for the) relevant elasticity between on the one hand, the political (or diplomatic) variables and on the other hand, the trade variables (import, export). Generally speaking, this elasticity is significantly different from zero and in the range of 0.001 to 0.5 with an average of 0.17 (the standard deviation of the reported co-efficient in Table 1.2 is 0.16).

The econometric studies summarized in Table 1.2 are conclusive regarding the three key theoretical propositions that have been developed in the conflict–trade and trade–conflict literatures.

- An increase in conflict (for example, negative military and diplomatic exchange, international terrorism) significantly reduces bilateral trade.
- An increase in co-operative behaviour (for example, positive and constructive diplomatic exchanges and agreements) increases bilateral trade.
- An increase in international economic exchange (export, import, foreign investment, aid and so on) reduces conflict (wars, transnational terrorism and so on).

The rise of economic diplomacy and international security on the policy agenda since the turn of the century is also reflected in the increase in the number of studies that have become available. A number of researchers (Nitsch et al. 2004, Li et al. 2004, Blomberg et al. 2006 and Fratianni et al. 2006a) have recently dealt with the new issues of the impact of terrorism on trade and *vice versa*. Transnational terrorism is a substitute for traditional violence between nations and thus offers an additional challenge to international security. It reduces trust between and within trading nations and their populations and has a measurable negative impact on trade. The bright side is that the empirical evidence suggests that both increasing economic ties and economic development tend to reduce the very basis from which terrorism emerges.

A second, relatively recent, line of research emerges in Table 1.2, namely the empirical research into the impact of export promotion agencies, state visits, embassies and consulates on trade in goods and services. This strand of the literature includes studies by Lederman et al. (2006), Nitsch (2007), Rose (2007), Gil-Pareja et al. (2007), Maurel and Afman (2007) and Yakop et al. (2007). These studies consistently find significant and empirically relevant indications for trade creation by means of economic diplomacy. Maurel and Afman (2007), for example, estimate that the opening of an embassy is equivalent to an *ad valorem* tariff reduction of 2% to 8%.

Obviously, the issue of causality is not completely settled given the different research approaches and theories so there is – as yet – no definite scientific proof whether international trade determines political and diplomatic relationships between countries or *vice versa*.[6] The correlation, however, is robust so it would seem to be beyond scientific doubt that the interrelationship between international politics and economics is a topic worth of further investigation.

The empirical evidence on the relationship between international politics and economics is further strengthened by econometric investigations into the determinants of success and failure of economic sanctions. This line of research has been stimulated by the study *Economic Sanctions Reconsidered* (Hufbauer and Schott 1985) which was first published in 1985 by the Peterson Institute for International Economics. Table 1.3 summarizes empirical research into the determinants of failure and success related to the 1985 and 1990 data set as well as the econometric estimates that are included in or relate to the third edition of this study (Hufbauer et al. 2008). The empirical analyses that were carried out by Hufbauer et al. have on different accounts been criticised. Indeed, also their latest econometrics have some serious flaws. We will re-analyse their data sets in Chapter 6.

Table 1.3 Summary statistics for recent empirical investigations into the effectiveness of economic sanctions

Study	N	Period	Trade parameter	Estimate
Investigations based on the 1985 data set				
Hufbauer et al. (1985)	108	1914–83	ATL	0.031
Bergeijk (1989a)	80	1946–83	PTL	$0.21^{\$}$
Lam (1990)	98	1914–83	ATL	0.008
Investigations based on the 1995 data set				
Dehejia and Wood (1992)	115	1914–89	ATL	0.002
Bergeijk (1994a)	103	1946–89	ATL	$0.036^{\#}$
	92	1946–89	PTL	$0.15^{\$}$
Bonetti (1998)	104	1946–89	ATL	$0.10^{\$}$
			ATL^2	$-0.002^{\$}$
Investigations based on the 2008 data set				
Hufbauer et al. (2008)	174	1914–99	ATL	0.01
Bergeijk and Fenthur (2008)	150	1946–99	PTL	$0.06^{\$}$

Notes: $ significant at 99%,
          # significant at 95%,
          ATL is average trade linkage
          PTL is proportional trade linkage

The economic researchers that have investigated the Hufbauer et al. data sets have used different econometric methods and have applied judgement both regarding the reliability of data in specific sanction cases and the need to consider different sets of explanatory variables. Sometimes variables that were not included in the Hufbauer et al. data sets have also been used; in contrast other researchers have completely relied on the Hufbauer et al. data sets. So while all studies in Table 1.3 start from the same data set and use the judgement of Hufbauer et al. on the outcome of sanctions, different research designs led to different numbers of observations N for the reported studies.

The relevant mirror question (do sanctions influence bilateral trade?) has also been investigated. Deploying a gravity model Hufbauer et al. (2008, pp. 201–207) estimate trade elasticities of US sanctions with respect to US bilateral trade flows that are significant at the usual 95% confidence level and better and are in the range of –0.39 to –0.19. Estimates by Farmer (2000) of the costs of sanctions for the sender (that is for the country that imposes the sanctions) reveal meaningful but smaller impacts.

All in all sufficient empirical evidence is available to substantiate the claim that international trade and politics mutually exerted strong influences in the post-Second World War period. Obviously this is a backward-looking answer as it is based on real world observations which by definition relate to the past. The forward-looking question asks how trade patterns may change especially in relation to the observed increasing deployment of economic diplomacy.

It is thus relevant that it has been argued that globalisation reduces the distance between countries due to the Internet, reduced transportation costs and the ease of travelling and communication. The death of distance has been announced by amongst others Cairncross (1997) and Friedman (2005). In a truly 'global village' the difference between external trade and internal trade would seem to disappear and less, if any, need exists for the state to intervene through economic diplomacy. In the flat world of Friedman no difference could after all be discerned between internal and external trade. So a nagging empirical question emerges that needs to be answered before we can proceed with our discussion of economic diplomacy. Do border effects (continue to) exist and in particular: what has happened to the distance effect in international trade?

3 DISTANCE IS NOT DEAD, IT IS HETROGENEOUS

So: does distance still matter? This is a relevant question for any student of economic diplomacy. If distance does not matter or matters much less than before, then foreign trade and domestic trade become closer (and perhaps perfect) substitutes and it becomes difficult to see a role for the public sector. Essentially, this is an empirical question and a topic of much debate among trade economists. A counterintuitive finding of the empirical literature is that the impact of distance, despite stronger globalization, has at least remained as important as it used to be in international trade. An example is provided by the meta analysis of the existing scientific literature by Disdier and Head (2008). They report on the basis of 103 scientific econometric studies for the years 1870–2000 and a good 1500 estimated distance parameters. Their analysis shows that the distance decay effect is on average one third stronger in the more recent period 1990–2000 compared to the average finding for the years 1870–1970. This result is a general finding in the empirical trade literature.[7] It implies that on average distance has become more important; indeed border effects remain substantial even within the European Monetary Union although on a downward trend (see, for example, Rae and Sollie, 2007 and Helble, 2007).

Table 1.4 Impact of a one standard deviation change in intangible trade barriers (% change)

Intangible Barrier	Export	Foreign Direct Investment (Stock)
Increase in trust	24–38 [a,b,c]	75–111 [a,c]
Decrease in cultural diversity	−14–8 [a,d,e]	16–28 [a,e]
Increase institutional quality	22–45 [d]	14–33 [e]

Source: Adapted from van den Berg et al. (2008), Table 3.6, pp. 37–38.

Notes: a. Dekker et al. (2006)
　　　　 b. den Butter and Mosch (2003)
　　　　 c. Guiso et al. (2004)
　　　　 d. Linders et al. (2005)
　　　　 e. Lankhuizen et al. (2008)

Given the reduction of transportation costs, this finding suggests that other non-economic factors related to preferences, culture and institutions may have become more important barriers to trade over the last decade or so.[8] Cultural distance has probably always been important but may have remained unnoticed under the veil of physical distance. Indeed, recent investigations have uncovered a significant impact of intangible barriers such as cultural diversity, international (dis)trust and the quality of institutions, as illustrated by Table 1.4 that summarizes the empirical literature.

Since commercial policy and economic diplomacy are especially aimed at bridging these intangible barriers it would not seem far-fetched to expect that such policies may play an important role in shaping the geographical trading patterns of nations. If so, we would expect to observe different developments for different countries since the effectiveness of and inputs available for economic diplomacy and commercial policy vary greatly between nations (see Riberio 2007, pp. 156–87 for an overview).

I will investigate this question econometrically using a small quasi-reduced form equation for the years 1995 and 2004 focussing on differences in the impact of distance both over time and between countries. In order to check for the heterogeneity of the distance parameters, I regress the distance d on the bilateral export-to-GDP ratio x. This ratio x is defined as the export from country A to country B divided by the exporter's Gross Domestic Product. The variable d represents the distance that goods have to be transported between the exporter's home market (or production facilities) and the target foreign market. In addition I take into account the extent of the export market which is proxied by the importer's Gross Domestic Product y. The equation to be estimated is:

$$x_t = \alpha\,(1 + \delta_{2004})\,d + \beta\,y_t + c + u, \qquad (1.1)$$

where x is the bilateral export-to-GDP ratio, d is distance, δ_{2004} is a dummy variable that is 1 in 2004 (else 0), y is the importer's GDP, $t = 1995$ or 2004, c is the constant term, u is an error term and x, d and y have been expressed in natural logarithm. *A priori* one expects a negative sign for α (one trades less with more distant countries) and a positive sign for β (one trades more with bigger countries). The parameter of particular interest in this investigation is δ_{2004}. If δ_{2004} is positive then distance has become more important and if it is negative then distance has become less important in shaping the geographical trading pattern. The empirical investigation pertains to a group of 29 exporting countries and 44 export markets. The sample covers all continents and investigates exporting countries at all levels of development. The investigation deals with almost three quarters of world trade. The number of observations is 2474. Using Ordinary Least Squares for the sample as a whole the following equation is estimated (all estimated parameters are significant at the 95% confidence level and better and adjusted-$R^2 = 0.63$):

$$\ln(x) = -0.827(1+0.0169\,\delta_{2004})\,\ln(d)+0,82\,\ln(y)-28.0 \qquad (1.2)$$

The positive co-efficient for δ_{2004} is in line with the meta analysis of Disdier and Head (2008) since we also find that distance has become more important over time (the negative trade parameter increases). An interesting question is whether this average finding for the whole population can also be discerned at the level of individual countries. Therefore Table 1.5 and Figure 1.2 report econometric results regarding 29 equations that have been individually estimated for the exporting countries, and the change in trade resistance (as measured by parameter δ_{2004}), respectively. The results of the empirical investigation are satisfactory from a statistical point of view. The estimated parameters for distance and the importer's national income are significant at the usual confidence levels of 95% and better and roughly 60 to 90% of the variance in bilateral trade to GDP ratios is explained by the estimated individual country equations.

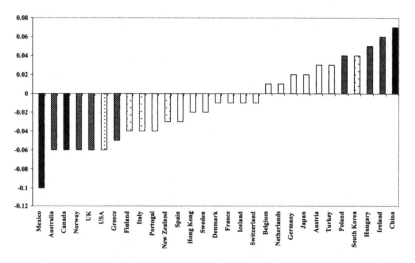

Note: Significance levels are denoted as ■ 99%, ▨ 95%, ☐ 90%

Figure 1.2 Change in distance parameter 1995–2004

The results point out significant heterogeneity in the impact of distance on national geographical trade patterns as illustrated in Figure 1.2.[9] Distance appears to have become more important for countries such as China, Hungary, Ireland, Poland and Korea; but it seems to have become a less important determinant of geographical trade patterns for the member countries of the North American Free Trade Agreement (NAFTA), Australia, Greece, Finland and Spain). Consequently, the measured reduction of the distance effect could reflect different modes of integration into the world economic system.

Table 1.5 *Empirical results of the OLS estimation of the bilateral trade to GDP ratios for individual countries 1995 and 2004 (N = 2994)*

Country	Distance (α)	Dummy (δ_{2004})	GDP$_j$ (β)	Constant	adj.-R^2	F-test
Australia	$-3.15^\$$	$-0.06^\#$	$1.09^\$$	$-13.12^\$$	0.78	104
Austria	$-0.83^\$$	0.03	$0.86^\$$	$-29.52^\$$	0.76	92
Belgium	$-0.37^\$$	0.01	$0.77^\$$	$-26.77^\$$	0.85	172
Canada	-0.27^*	$-0.06^\$$	$1.02^\$$	$-38.43^\$$	0.80	117
China	$-1.17^\$$	$0.07^\$$	$0.82^\$$	$-25.03^\$$	0.73	80
Denmark	$-0.77^\$$	-0.01	$0.69^\$$	$-25.12^\$$	0.77	95
Finland	$-0.68^\$$	-0.04^*	$0.80^\$$	$-28.37^\$$	0.77	96
France	$-0.59^\$$	-0.01	$0.70^\$$	$-27.01^\$$	0.79	155
Germany	$-0.66^\$$	0.02	$0.79^\$$	$-28.53^\$$	0.87	195
Greece	$-1.31^\$$	$-0.05^\#$	$0.70^\$$	$-22.24^\$$	0.72	73
Hong Kong	$-0.88^\$$	-0.02	$1.00^\$$	$-30.53^\$$	0.67	59
Hungary	$-1.23^\$$	$0.05^\#$	$0.89^\$$	$-27.35^\$$	0.84	155
Iceland	$-1.37^\$$	-0.01	$1.05^\$$	$-29.31^\$$	0.60	43
Ireland	$-0.73^\$$	$0.06^\#$	$0.83^\$$	$-28.22^\$$	0.72	73
Italy	$-0.65^\$$	-0.04^*	$0.72^\$$	$-26.80^\$$	0.80	112
Japan	$-1.49^\$$	0.02	$0.82^\$$	$-22.47^\$$	0.73	78
Mexico	$-1.16^\$$	$-0.10^\$$	$1.18^\$$	$-35.00^\$$	0.71	70
Netherlands	$-0.74^\$$	0.01	$0.68^\$$	$-24.72^\$$	0.86	171
N-Zealand	$-1.51^\$$	-0.03	$1.02^\$$	$-26.13^\$$	0.67	59
Norway	$-0.94^\$$	$-0.06^\#$	$0.82^\$$	$-27.13^\$$	0.64	50
Poland	$-1.24^\$$	$0.04^\#$	$0.72^\$$	$-22.97^\$$	0.86	166
Portugal	$-1.17^\$$	-0.04	$0.79^\$$	$-24.67^\$$	0.72	73
Korea	$-1.10^\$$	0.04^*	$0.52^\$$	$-17.23^\$$	0.67	57
Spain	$-0.86^\$$	-0.03^*	$0.74^\$$	$-25.90^\$$	0.82	126
Sweden	$-0.71^\$$	-0.02	$0.77^\$$	$-27.25^\$$	0.83	135
Switzerland	$-0.33^\$$	-0.01	$0.83^\$$	$-32.09^\$$	0.81	124
Turkey	$-1.36^\$$	0.03	$0.76^\$$	$-22.80^\$$	0.73	78
UK	$-0.47^\$$	$-0.06^\#$	$0.63^\$$	$-25.84^\$$	0.63	73
USA	-0.29	-0.06^*	$0.89^\$$	$-35.01^\$$	0.61	45

Notes: $ significant at 99%, # significant at 95%, * significant at 90%

The opening up of China and the former members of the Comecon (the communist country trading system) and regional integration and trade reorientation within NAFTA affect the geographic pattern of trade and thus the measured impact of distance. Diverging country experiences can even be observed within homogeneous country groups such as the European Union. Interestingly, this European heterogeneity cannot be explained by developments on the European continent such as the end of the Cold War in 1990 (Bergeijk and Oldersma, 1990) or the creation of the European Monetary Union with the euro as a common currency in 1998 (Bergeijk et al. 2000) because we have genuine European heterogeneity and this implies that the benefits that countries reap from international trade differ substantially. This is an additional indication for the continued relevancy of economic diplomacy and commercial policy in an increasingly global economy.

4   ECONOMIC DIPLOMACY AND NON-STATE ACTORS

Building on the seminal definition of Baine and Woolcock (2003, p. 3) we can define economic diplomacy as a set of activities (both regarding methods and processes for international decision making) related to cross-border economic activities (export, import, investment, lending, aid, migration) pursued by state and non-state actors in the real world. Typically economic diplomacy at the state level consists of three elements.

- The use of political influence and relationships to promote and/or influence bilateral international trade and investment, to improve on functioning of markets and/or to address market failures and to reduce costs and risks of cross-border transactions (including property rights). Typically this subfield of economic diplomacy comprises commercial policy (export promotion, state visits and so on). We will often use the term 'bilateral economic diplomacy' to indicate this subfield. This will be the topic in Part II.
- The use of economic assets and relationships to increase the cost of conflict and to strengthen the mutual benefits of co-operation and politically stable relationships, that is to increase economic security. This subfield both contains structural policies and bilateral trade and investment agreements (aimed at achieving specific geographic trading patterns) and the political distortion of trade and investment as in the case of boycotts and embargoes. This will be the topic of Part III.
- Ways to consolidate the correct political climate and international political economic environment to facilitate and institute these objectives. This subfield is also indicated as 'trade diplomacy'

(Woolcock 2002) and covers multilateral negotiations. It is the domain of the supranational organizations and institutions such as the World Trade Organization (WTO), the Organization for Economic Cooperation and Development (OECD) and the European Union (EU). We will not dwell too much on this subject in this book. One reason is that, generally speaking, the (potential) benefits of multilateral trade negotiations are well understood (see, for example, on the Uruguay Round: Hertel et al. 1999 and Brown et al. 2002 and on the Doha Round, Francois et al. 2003). Interestingly, studies also exist on the conflict reducing impact of international organisations such as the OECD (Wolfe 2003) and the success and failure factors of the diplomatic activities that are taking place within such organisations (for example, Heydon 2008 on the General Agreement on Trade in Services and the Multilateral Agreement and Investment). Also noteworthy is that the WTO (2007, pp. 35–111) provided an analysis of the political economy of trade co-operation on the occasion of the sixtieth anniversary of the multilateral trading system (that is the signing of the General Agreement on Tariffs and Trade in 1948).

The Baine and Woolwock definition rightly points towards the role of non-state actors and this offers two additional elements that need consideration in the analysis. This is especially so since the increasing role of non-state actors, such as multinational enterprises (MNEs), consumer groups and non-governmental organizations (NGOs) makes the international environment and the role and function of different types of 'diplomats' in firms and NGOs clearly different from the world in which we lived only a few decades ago (Saner and Yiu 2003).

Producers

Multinational enterprises are key players in the current phase of globalization. McCann and Acz (2008, pp. 13–14) sketch their impressive rise in the world economic system in the post-Second World War period.

> At the end of the 1960s there were approximately only 7,000 MNEs in the global economy, and the ownership of these firms was accounted for almost entirely by just fifteen countries (... and) by 2006 an estimated 78,000 MNEs in the global economy with some 780,000 foreign affiliates (...). As such, the number of MNEs in the global economy has increased by more than eleven-fold in four decades, with the number of MNEs in the global economy increasing at a rate of approximately 1000–2000 per annum, while the number of MNE foreign affiliates has been increasing by 10,000–20,000 per annum.

It is not only the increase in numbers that matters, but also the sheer size of these MNEs. According to De Grauwe and Camerman (2002) about one third of the 100 largest economies in the world are corporations. According to their ranking of nation states and corporations (based on GDP and value added, respectively), ranks 1 to 43 inclusive are occupied by nation states, but Wal Mart, an American chain of large discount department stores ranks 44. The second largest corporation is Exxon with rank 48 just above New Zealand. Clearly these corporations are important decision making institutions and their activities and interests may form an important element of the global game. Such non-state actors can counteract the plans of national governments and since they have the option to shift activities between jurisdictions, governments have less grip on what these actors do and how they do it. Interestingly, such firms are also more vulnerable to pressures from large consumer groups that (can) boycott their products. Importantly, multinational firms that bow for consumer pressure and change their behaviour may thus become vehicles through which consumers exert influence on specific government, state or country activities.

Consumers

The strength of consumer boycotts has been well documented. The instruments of these boycotts comprise the refusal to buy goods and/or services (tourism, media) and divestment actions. In a number of cases, civil groups have exerted pressure (for example as shareholders) on corporations to actually implement the boycott. Indeed, as Herz (2001) remarks:

> It would appear that people are exercising political choices not at the ballot box but by means of consumer activism. Corporations respond to consumer pressure in a way that governments do not, and are gradually assuming the role of global political actors.

Consumer boycotts have sought many goals that may even be multi-dimensional (see Grosso and Smith 2005). The first dimension concerns politics and human rights: the anti-Apartheid movement is a case in point. This was a transnational movement that included consumer boycotts of South African export products. The movement was especially effective in severing financial ties with the Apartheid government in the 1980s leading to an actual divestment from South Africa of some $20 billion (Cortright and Lopez, 2002, pp 95–6.) The second dimension (a refusal to buy goods and services from firms that endanger the natural environment) is well illustrated by the case of the Brent Spar, an oil storage and tanker loading buoy, which Shell in 1995 wanted to dispose of in deep Atlantic waters. Greenpeace organized a worldwide, high-profile media campaign against this plan. Although

Greenpeace never actually called for a boycott of Shell service stations, many customers turned to other firms. In the end Shell felt forced to dismantle the oil platform in an environmentally friendly way and recycle it. The third dimension, a relatively new one, is religion, for which the 2006 Danish cartoon crisis stands out as an example (Larsen 2006 and Andreasen 2008). Following the publication of a set of cartoons of the Prophet in a Danish newspaper in September 2005, a crisis emerged that also included violence against people, property and embassies. Many Muslims and supporters took part in protests throughout the world, but the big success was in international trade as one of the strongest consumer boycotts of all time emerged.

Terrorism

From the viewpoint of the Baine and Woolwock definition of economic diplomacy, a key distinguishing characteristic of modern terrorism *à la* Al Qaeda is that inter-country violence takes place at the non-state level (Bergeijk and Oldersma, 2006). Traditional terrorism often attacked foreign interests as well in order to put pressure on governments, but by and large such activities were limited to the geography of the nation state (or perhaps included some training facilities and bases in neighbouring countries). The 9/11 attack on US territory thus marked a new phase in transnational terrorism. It is often assumed that globalization facilitates transnational terrorism as the increasing volumes of travel, trade and finance would make detection of illegal activities much more difficult. Transnational terrorism increases uncertainty in general and reduces trust between and within trading nations and their populations. The challenge of transnational terrorism is that solutions should not be restricted to traditional state-to-state approaches but need to consider the involvement of non-state actors as well. The implications of these trend for economic diplomacy are not yet fully clear, but no doubt the decision making processes will become more complex since the number of players increases as does their heterogeneity. Also important is the fact that economic diplomacy will have to move beyond the old frontiers of government to government contacts. The new approach will have to address the needs and aspirations at decentralized levels, that is related to fuzzy groups of consumers and firms that are not represented by official bodies or governments because they live and work in a great many jurisdictions.

5 ECONOMIC SECURITY

It is tempting to investigate further how the use of economic assets and relationships can be used to increase the cost of conflict and trade disruption and also to investigate how the mutual benefits of co-operation can create politically stable relationships, that is to increase economic security. Indeed, interdependence and the mutual benefits that derive from international exchange are important economic incentives to reduce international political and military conflicts in the long run (Polachek, 1992).

Here the modern history of Europe is encouraging, both in pacifying the former belligerents France and Germany and in delivering democracy in formerly autocratically ruled countries such as Portugal and Greece (and later the countries in Eastern Europe). Indeed as Skylakakis (2006) remarks:

> Economic diplomacy is also of great importance as a long-term instrument for conflict prevention. The most obvious example, and one of the greatest success stories of the past 60 years, is the creation and astounding success of the European Union.

The successful transformation from Marx to market and democracy in the former East Bloc does of course not only reflect the success of the European Union. The institutional setup for the western aid to the restructuring economies in Central and Eastern Europe in the early 1990s also played an important role: Article 1 of the Agreement establishing the European Bank for Reconstruction and Development (EBRD) limits eligibility for loans to those countries that are committed to and applying the principles of multiparty democracy, pluralism and market economies (Menkveld 1991). Theories and successes extend well beyond recent history and the European continent, as will become clear in the next chapter that reviews the literature.

The present chapter clarified the new challenges to economic diplomacy and economic security. Economic security as it is based on and/or building on international economic relations (such as trade in goods and services and capital flows, that is foreign direct investment, lending and development aid) will need consideration of the increasing complexity that is induced by globalization and decentralized decision making by an increasing number of actors in different jurisdictions. As will become clear, economic diplomacy has a viable role to play and may provide the risk management system for critical international situations. Successful and effective economic diplomacy will have to be based in both the public and the private sector in order to build economic security on a recipe in which stronger and broader bilateral economic relations provide the anchor of mutual interests and benefits.

6   PLAN OF THE BOOK

Part I (Chapters 2 and 3) will deal with the general aspects of trade uncertainty. Trade uncertainty is a central element in the analysis of economic diplomacy. Some instruments such as sanctions increase trade uncertainty while other instruments such as multilateral trade policy aim at reducing this uncertainty. Importantly, economic subjects may react differently towards a change in the level of trade uncertainty. In order to offer a better understanding Chapter 2 first reviews the history of economic thought on this subject and offers a detailed discussion of individual empirical studies that were summarized in the present chapter. Chapter 3 develops a general model to analyse trade uncertainty at the micro level of firms and consumers and at the macro level of the trading state thus offering an analysis of policy responses and bringing the political economy aspects into the picture. Against this background the next two parts develop specific elements of economic diplomacy: commercial policy and economic sanctions, respectively.

Part II deals with commercial policy and bilateral economic diplomacy. Chapter 4 deals with the economic rationale for public intervention in international activities, discussing the benefits from trade both in the context of macroeconomic analysis (economic growth) and in a microeconomic setting (that is firm-level data analysis). Next we will discuss the occurrence of border effects and investigate whether market failure might provide an explanation and see what instruments are available to solve the problems at hand without committing government failure. Particular attention is paid to recent empirical research on the international network of nation states, so as to provide a basis for comparison for Chapter 5 that investigates how trade and bilateral economic diplomacy interact. The chapter provides the results of an empirical investigation that relates trade performance of 36 countries in the year 2006 to export promotion agencies and embassies and consulates, thus extending the work of Lederman et al. (2006) and Rose (2007).

Part III analyses economic sanctions. Chapter 6 presents an empirical analysis of success and failure of 172 economic sanctions in the second half of the twentieth century. The findings offer empirical support for the theoretical approach developed in Chapter 3. Relevant findings include the structural break in the application and efficacy of economic sanctions that seems to have occurred around 1990 as well as the finding that the target's political system is an important determinant of success and failure of this instrument of economic diplomacy. Noting the lack of a comparable data set for positive instruments of economic diplomacy and building on these findings, Chapter 7 develops an expected utility model of rewards and threats (positive and negative sanctions) in an international context. One key finding regarding the tooling of economic diplomacy is that in the international system, negative sanctions and unconditional rewards are inferior to conditional rewards. The failure of unconditional exchanges focuses attention on the need to design mutually beneficial economic relations that emphasise conditionality, implying that exchanges should be reversible.

Part IV develops a research agenda and draws policy conclusions. Chapter 8 offers some economic reflections on the 'market' for economic diplomacy. In the past the costs and benefits of diplomatic and economic relationships have not been expressed properly to decision makers, so that the actual outcome for diplomatic co-operation and diplomatic hostility has been inefficient. The aim of this book is to provide a better insight in order to reduce this inefficiency. The recent credit crisis, the climate issue and human rights issues have shown that globalization, although inevitable, cannot provide acceptable benefits unless progress is made in global governance of such issues. The efficiency of economic diplomacy is thus key to our future.

NOTES

[1]   See Felipe and Vernengo (2002) on the Methuen Treaty and the theory of comparative advantage and Duguid (2007) on the historical context of the Methuen Treaty and an overview of appreciations by contemporary observers.

[2]   Moreover, due to the treaty, Portugal did not further develop other agricultural products and its manufacturing industry. Consequently, it missed the industrial revolution. However, a clear political benefit was that the Treaty helped to preserve a power base regarding Portugal's most important colony, Brazil.

[3]   It may even have been worse. Sideri (1970) argues that the wrong type of specialization pattern was forced on Portugal.

[4]   See Neary (2004). The Geneva Round started in April 1947 with 23 countries and took 7 months. The Doha Round started in November 2001 with 141 countries and was 101 months underway when this book was finished in March 2009.

[5]   See, for example, Baldwin (2006), Leamer (2007) and McCann and Acz (2008).

[6]   Chang *et al.* (2004) review the literature and endogenize conflict, co-operation and trade with distance as one of the major drivers of political and economic interaction. For 30 countries in the years 1958–67 they find that net conflict does not have a significant independent effect on trade but that trade enhances co-operation. See also Murshed et al. (2008) for an analysis in a bilateral context).

[7]   See, for example, Linders (2006). However, Brun et al. (2005) report a reduced impact of distance. A 10% larger distance was associated in 1962 with a 13.5% lower bilateral trade flow and a 12% lower bilateral trade flow in 1996. The impact of distance on trade thus reduced by 1.5 percentage points (or 11%). As this result occurred over a 35 year period, it is numerically disappointing from the point of view of those that believe in the death of distance hypothesis.

[8]   Other proposed explanations for the distance puzzle comprise Anderson and van Wincoop's (2004) 'distance neutral' technological progress or Frankel's (1997) suggestion that short-distance trade has benefited relatively strong.

[9]   Fratianni and Kang (2006b) recognized the existence of heterogeneity of distance elasticities across countries and country groupings; the point in this section is that the distance effects also change over time.

PART I

Economic Diplomacy and Trade Uncertainty

2. Trade and Conflict (and *Vice Versa*)

Economists often neglect the political dimension when they analyse the economic relations between countries. Their domain pre-eminently is international trade, capital flows, the transfer of technology and the co-ordination of macroeconomic policy, in sum the whole area where co-operation among countries yields higher welfare for all. One wonders whether this abstraction in the analysis is desirable.[1] Relations between countries are just as unlikely to be permanently harmonious as personal relationships. Conflict seems to be a radical characteristic of human activity. Disregard of this dimension may yield deceptive results in the analysis of the international economic system. Still, textbooks on international economics hardly deal with the impact of politics on international trade and investment patterns. Indeed it is difficult to find a textbook that warns the student of international economics that to 'attempt analysis of a specific international issue solely in economic terms is liable to result in some very silly conclusions' (the caveat is from Schiavo-Campo, 1978, pp. 7–8n). Admittedly, this quote is a bit out-dated, but (and this is the point) it is still accurate as is the description of the neglect of politics by mainstream economics (see also Strange, 1998)

This chapter reviews earlier findings on the theoretical and empirical relationships between, on the one hand international trade and investment, and on the other hand international conflict and co-operation. The focus is on the influence exerted by the diplomatic climate on foreign trade, but we will also look into the twin question of the influence of trade on the diplomatic climate. Our knowledge about the trade–conflict relationship essentially derives from five sources.

The first source is the eighteenth and nineteenth century political economy literature in combination with some of the Marxist and development literature that remained outside the realm of mainstream neoclassical trade theory. The second source is the formal theoretical literature on the national defence tariff, that was essentially developed in the 1970s. The third source is the political science approach which deals with the impact of trade on political conflict and co-operation. The fourth source is a number of scattered empirical studies that follow up on Tinbergen's 1962 seminal analysis for the Twentieth Century Fund's study *Shaping the World Economy. Suggestions for an International Economic Policy*. Related to the fourth source is the empirical literature that deals with the impact of politics on international capital flows (lending and investment). Trade and capital are often related phenomena. Hence it may be useful to look into the relationship between, on the one hand international capital flows, and on the other hand co-operation and conflict as a fifth source on the trade-conflict relationship. The final section of the chapter draws some conclusions and identifies a number of white spots in the literature.

1 THE POLITICAL DIMENSION OF INTERNATIONAL TRADE RELATIONS

It is often argued that the theory of international economics on the whole tends to neglect the interactions between economic and political variables in the international sphere. Bailey and Lord (1988, p. 93), for example, state that 'no subject has been more unjustifiably ignored than the relationship of economics to national security.' According to Intrilligator (1987, p. 367), 'It is impossible to separate out and treat economic issues independently of political, military, and other issues. These concepts of global interdependence have yet to be analysed in a fundamental way...' Frey (1984, p. 11) even asserts that 'the theory of international economics has as a whole refused to take into account the fact that political factors influence the international economy', while Spero (1977, p. 2) claims that 'politics and economics have been divorced from each other and isolated in analysis and theory'.

This is probably true for mainstream neoclassical economics. There exists, however, an old tradition of International Political Economy, the study of all conditions that affect the wealth and power of organized societies and the policy options of their governments (Knorr 1975, p. *xi*). It is well beyond the scope of this chapter to discuss the extensive literature on this subject, which has been reviewed by Hirschman ([1945] 1980, esp. pp. 3–12), Kindleberger (1970), Baldwin (1985, esp. pp. 70–95), Rosecrane (1986), Hutchison (1988), Hont (1990), de Wilde (1991) and so on. Neither is it feasible to discuss the reasons for the trade economist's expulsion of the political influence from his theory.[2] Instead some highlights on the topic will be discussed briefly.

For the founding fathers of international free trade theory, political and economic relations were very much interrelated. The domination of political considerations over free trade is already well established by Adam Smith. Smith ([1776] 1976, pp. 484–7) argues for the necessity of trade regulation if national defence requires so: defence is of much more importance than opulence. The influence of political variables on international trade was recognized even by Ricardo, who is sometimes seen as the archetype of the modern neoclassical economist (Collini et al. 1983, pp. 56–7) and who as we saw in Chapter 1 did not explicitly recognize the importance of the Methuen Treaty for the trade between Britain and Portugal and rather put comparative advantage to the fore as an explanation. Ricardo ([1820] 1962, p. 231), however, stressed the importance of political power for the determination of the division of the gains from trade between the motherland and her colonies. Indeed, Ricardo did pay a lot of attention to the exogenous disturbances imposed by both war and peace (Grampp 1987). Such alterations in the state of the international system, Ricardo argued, cause considerable distress to trade as this changes the optimal allocation of capital over sectors. Essentially Ricardo was dealing with reallocation issues. He deemed government intervention a prerequisite for this process since capital would have been allocated in the previous period in directions 'from which (one) is unable to withdraw without the sacrifice of a great part of (one's) capital' (Ricardo ([1820] 1962, p. 177). So Ricardo's *Principles of Political Economy and Taxation* often deals with political power and questions related to peace and war. The same is true for John Stuart Mill. Mill ([1840] 1968, p. 594) believed in contradistinction to Smith (who argued that foreign trade enriches a country and that this helps its defence) that intensified international economic relations would reduce the incentives for conflicts among nations:

> It is commerce which is rendering war obsolete, by strengthening and multiplying the personal interests which are in natural opposition to it.

Here we find a reason why trade economists might not be interested in problems related to war and peace. If commerce can supersede war, specialisation probably pays. So analyse and stimulate free trade as pure economists and secure peace as a by-product. Schumpeter (1954, pp. 766–7) points out that around 1870 many observers implicitly and explicitly 'expected the victory of those principles and practices of foreign policy that are associated with free trade, such as the settlement of disputes by mutual concessions or arbitration, reduction of armaments ... and the like'.[3] See also Friedman and Friedman (1980, pp. 43–4) and Ratnapala (2003) on this connection. A more concrete empirical proposition is that the probability of conflict between countries, as opposed to co-operation, can be reduced by intensifying economic relations (see, for example the discussion on the work of Polachek in section 3 of this chapter). Anyhow, neoclassical theory which dominates mainstream economics, generally speaking, hardly ever reflects on the politics of trade.

The belief – shared by classical and neoclassical economists – that intensified economic ties could be the basis of peaceful relationships between countries at first sight makes economic analysis of co-operation and conflict unnecessary. It is almost as if economists should do their job and focus on ways to secure free trade and full employment.

Not all economists, however, would agree even if these topics have never become an issue in the general economic discourse. Although their example was hardly followed by the profession, individual economists have often been involved in economic analysis of questions related to conflict and co-operation.

Keynes, for example, took substantial risks, both financially and with regard to his career, in publishing his *Economic Consequences of the Peace* ([1919] 1984). He was well aware of the aridity of economic science with respect to his topic. Keynes ([1936] 1986, pp. 380–82) was especially concerned with finding solutions for the war problem in terms of demand management, pointing out the economic causes of war: pressure of population and the competitive struggle for markets.

> But if nations can learn to provide themselves with full employment by their domestic policy (...) , there need be no important economic forces calculated to set the interest of one country against that of its neighbours (... and) there would no longer be a pressing motive why one country need force its wares on another.

Marx introduced a new analytic framework subjecting historical events, such as wars and social institutions, to the explanatory process of economic analysis. Marxism treats these factors not as exogenous variables or data (the usual approach in economics), but as endogenous variables (Schumpeter [1943] 1966, p. 47). Although Marx did not put a meaning to wars-between-states as a phase in the development of capitalism, Marx and Engels ([1848] 1928, p. 14) did recognise that modern industry needed more and larger markets (especially in undeveloped countries) both as an outlet for its production and to supply raw materials. They did not deal with the struggle between nations in their major work, but they were fascinated by military technology and tactics and Marx dealt with the war topic in a lot of newspaper articles (Maclean, 1988). Using Marx's box of tools, others developed the theory of imperialism (*cf.* Went 2003).

The Marxist point of view on international relations has to a large extent been influenced by Hobson's *Imperialism* ([1902] 1988). *Imperialism* seeks to explain war-like tendencies amongst the major capitalist countries around the turn of the century on the basis of the growing economic and political power of large private companies, typically exercised over less developed countries. The discovery of economies of scale caused a top-heavy production apparatus in the industrialized world and led to such a superfluous supply of goods that the domestic market could no longer absorb domestic production. Hence international markets had to be won in order to create the necessary outlet. This meant colonization as a defence against the competition from other capitalist countries that had identical problems at home. The resulting clash of commercial interests would *notwendigerweise* result in a more or less permanent war threat.

Schumpeter heavily criticised the theory of imperialism: 'the more completely capitalist the structure and attitude of a Nation, the more pacifist – and the more prone to count the costs of war – we observe it to be' (Schumpeter [1943] 1966, pp. 128–9). Interestingly, moreover, leading communists also pointed out the possibility that commercial relationships might help establish peaceful political relations among countries. Lenin ([1920] 1967, p. 90) stressed the benefits of attracting foreign direct investments from the West.

> We shall thus gain a lot and make it difficult for capitalist powers that enter into deals with us to take part in military action against us, because war cancels everything, and should one break out we shall get possession of all the buildings, installations and railways.

Bernstein, the father of Revisionism, was an outspoken supporter of free trade (Hyrkkanen, 1987). He argued that the struggle against protectionism should be a socialist principle and that the international exchange of goods and services should be the basis for a network of mutual interests and interdependencies as an antidote against 'aggressive' imperialism.

The end of the Second World War started the era of decolonization. While political colonization visibly ended, some authors contended that formal dependence was replaced by *de facto* economic colonization. The literature on this 'new' imperialism or neo-colonialism is relevant for our discussion because the politics are so obvious in this theory of the world economic system. Explaining the global pattern of specialization is one of the main tasks of this so-called structural approach. In addition economically exploitative relationships are seen to give rise to violence, military take-overs and political repression. As an outgrow of Marxist thinking by amongst others Baran and Sweezy, *dependencia* or centre–periphery theories invaded economic thought via the work of Prebisch, the first Secretary General of UNCTAD (Jolly et al. 2004). The literature is vast; I will be brief and deal with the basic issues only.[4] *Dependencia* theory argues that fundamental structural disadvantages limit the scope for growth in the developing countries. Income elasticities, for example, in the rich 'centre' are low with respect to their export products, so that an increase in export volume will result in terms of trade losses. The upshot is that these structural impediments will continue unless appropriate policy measures are taken. This focuses attention on the international political power structure and on political efforts to change international institutions. *Dependencia* theory inspired the movement toward a New International Economic Order (NIEO) in 1974. The four main issues of that NIEO were renegotiation of debts, market access at favourable trade conditions, reform of the IMF and compliance with UN targets for development assistance. Ironically, neo-Marxists see aid as a means of opening up a developing country so that exploitations by the centre can begin. Radical Marxists contend that aid, like trade, is an instrument for the centre's control and profit only.

Neo-Marxism remained quite peripherical in economics as the neoclassical paradigm prevailed. The lack of attention for political factors, however, has increasingly become a bottleneck for the creation of relevant economic knowledge. Weck-Hannemann and Frey (1992, p. 31) argue that political forces must be taken into account if one moves from the theoretical world of perfect competition and frictionless exchange to reality. This aspect however, has been neglected in the established international trade theory. Interestingly, Bhagwati (1991, p. *xvi*) in the introduction to the fifth volume of his collected writings complains 'Economics and politics are natural bedfellows: How can we possibly explain what happens unless we bring in the political equations into our modelling at the same time?'

Since the early 1990s the scientific community seems to have accepted the challenge with the revival of the international political economy approach and the start of scientific journals like *Economics and Politics* which provides an important outlet (and consequently a major stimulus) for analytic work and scientific progress.

2 NATIONAL DEFENCE TARIFF THEORIES

The national defence argument is often classified as one of the so-called non-economic reasons for government intervention in foreign trade. In general economists accept the validity of such policies on national security grounds. GATT, for example, embodies this exception to the free trade principle in article *XXI* that explicitly allows countries to invoke security considerations to refuse disclosure of sensitive information, and to impose import and export controls. In addition article *XXI* allows GATT contracting parties to take appropriate (trade-related) actions in pursuance of their obligations under the UN Charter for the maintenance of international peace and security.[5] Adam Smith ([1776] 1976, p. 484) has already noted that a case would seem to exist

> in which it will generally be advantageous to lay some burden upon foreign (trade), for the encouragement of domestic industries (namely) when some particular sort of industry is necessary for the defence of the country.

Often trade-related measures are justified by pointing out that trade would improve on the adversary's military capabilities. This justification, however, as it is based on the strategic use of foreign trade, clearly belongs to the domain of negative economic sanctions which will be discussed in Part III. The national defence considerations that will be considered in this section deem the free trade outcome suboptimal because specialization in the 'wrong' kind of good reduces the skills and goods that are considered vital for the nation's defence capability. What is at stake then is the need to secure a minimal level of economic activity in terms of either production in key industries (for example aerospace), consumption of dual-use goods (such as computers) or certain skills. Trade intervention, however, is in these cases clearly a second-best policy. Standard theory shows that it is most efficient to subsidise output, consumption and schooling in order to internalise the national defence externality (Srinivasan 1987). In addition the practical applicability of the national defence argument can be questioned because of the very substantial information requirement for knowing how to cure the market failure, identifying the precise source of the policy problem or to establish the probable length of an embargo (Helpman 1987).

Consequently, theoretical (or formal) interest in political factors shaping trade relations has remained rather limited. An interesting literature, however, developed in the second half of the 1970s. This highly formalized literature deals with policy responses to the threat of market disruption and shows that the classification of the national defence tariff as a non-economic phenomenon is inappropriate since such a tariff can be justified on criteria that are related to economic efficiency. Essentially this new approach argues that the costs of an abrupt change in the production pattern that is forced upon an economy when trade is blocked suddenly, may be so high that it may be a wise policy to limit the international division of labour to some extent. In their seminal 1976 article Bhagwati and Srinivasan examine the optimal policy intervention required in an exporting country when there is a possibility of a market-disruption-induced trade restriction being invoked by the importing country. They use a traditional general equilibrium model in the 2 goods x 2 countries x 2 periods setting. Bhagwati and Srinivasan investigate how first-period (free trade) actions may influence outcomes in the second period that is characterized by trade disruption. Such actions comprise of investment to create second-period production capacity and the first-period allocation of the factors of production over the various sectors if reallocation takes time and/or is costly. They also analyse the possibility of an endogenous probability of trade disruption, for example, if this probability depends on the volume of trade in the first period. Their subject is trade disruption in general so that this kind of endogeneity seems to be a reasonable assumption: so-called Voluntary Export Restraints, for example, are more likely to be imposed when import volumes are considerable. So some self-restraint may be useful in preventing trade disruption in the near future. In the same vein, using duality theory Marrewijk and Bergeijk (1993) show that endogenous trade uncertainty, for example in the context of an increased use of economic sanctions, may actually lead countries to specialize against their comparative advantage.

Mayer (1977) deals with a country's optimal trade policy when embargoes and other trade interruptions are threatening, while individual consumers and producers have imperfect foresight. Actually, Mayer assumes that economic subjects believe that the relative price structure will not change. Given the perceptions of the policy maker an optimal pre-embargo (second-best) tariff and a pre-embargo (first-best) subsidy can be calculated. Unfortunately, Mayer leaves the central question unanswered of why government officials in this setting provide better estimations of the probability of trade disruption *vis-à-vis* their private sector counterparts.

Optimal policy choices, moreover, depend on the behaviour of both individual consumers and individual producers. It seems reasonable to assume that the costs of trade disruptions will be internalized by economic units that trade with foreign economic units. Tolley and Wilman (1977) use a partial equilibrium framework to analyse the impact of an expectation of trade disruption which may be expressed in terms of both an embargo frequency and a probability distribution of embargo length. The expectation of trade disruption should lead to private adjustments to specialize to a lesser extent in accordance with comparative advantage and hence to restrict the potential for foreign trade. An embargo leads to unequal long-run marginal value responses in consumption and production. This is so because embargo losses result from individual behaviour along short-run curves. These short-run curves determine the scope for individual action at a given point in time. The position of the short-run curves, however, depends on the long-run equilibrium quantity. Hence a rationale for government intervention emerges if private decisions do not internalise the potential embargo losses. Unfortunately, the analysis of Tolley and Wilman is restricted to the consequences of decreasing possibilities to import and neglects the effects in the exporting sector of the economy. Moreover, they do not answer the question of whether or not private decision making is superior to collective action. Marrewijk and Bergeijk (1990) show the sub-optimality of private decentralized decision making in a situation characterized by trade uncertainty.

We will return to these issues in the next chapter, but in addition it is noteworthy that several authors have investigated specific policy measures such as strategic stockpiles, which may be a viable option for non-perishable goods if these goods are both difficult to produce and essential for either the economy or the defence sector. The analysis boils down to a trade-off between the certain cost of the stockpile and the uncertain benefits if this stockpile is available during emergencies (Bergström et al. 1985). An additional gain may be that the stockpile counteracts market power or helps to prevent price hikes due to unexpected supply shocks. An example is the case of the strategic oil reserves that OECD-countries hold since the 1973 oil crisis. These strategic reserves proved to be very useful in 1990 in reducing the economic impact of the political supply shock during the Iraq crisis.

3 CONFLICT AND TRADE

In the early 1980s Polachek initiated a new research strategy on the topic of how the volume of bilateral trade and the extent of conflict between nations may be related. His approach starts from a different perspective – unlike the present chapter the title of Polachek's influential 1980 article puts the word 'conflict' first, hence inverting the suggested causality.[6] While the findings of this line of analysis may improve our understanding of the problems at hand, the causality is a matter of ongoing debate (see, for example, Pollins 1989b, Sayrs 1988 and 1990 and Murshed and Mamoon 2010). The main virtue of the new research agenda was its orientation from the start on vigorous empirical investigations.

Polachek's approach especially appealed to political scientists, probably because it fits in a tradition that goes back to Richardson's (1960) well-known analysis of the impact of trade on arms races. Polachek starts from the assumption that a rational utility maximizing government will take the potential impact of its diplomatic and military activities on its international trade and investment flows into account in the decisions that a country has to make about its foreign relations:

> Specifically, if conflict leads to a diminution of trade, then one implicit cost of conflict is the lost welfare gains associated with trade. Ceteris paribus the rational actor would engage in smaller amounts of conflict the greater the associated potential welfare loss. In short, trade enhances co-operation and deters conflict (Polachek and McDonald 1992, p. 273).

Polachek justifies his assertion with a standard neoclassical trade model in which maximizing material welfare is the nation's policy goal. From an economist's point of view the crucial assumption would seem to be that conflict leads to terms of trade losses.[7] At first sight this hypothesis seems reasonable: more conflict makes trade difficult because of retaliatory measures such as tariffs, quotas, embargoes and other prohibitions to trade and investment. Unfortunately, this link between the terms of trade and conflict is an assumption only that so far it has not been tested. Indeed the fact that conflict influences potential trade in an *ex ante* sense may prohibit the proper identification of such a relationship from the actual *ex post* observations. Guided by his formal model, Polachek estimates reduced-form equations in which the dependent variable is the diplomatic climate and the explanatory variables are bilateral trade flows and country attributes such as population, schooling, economic activity and defence expenditures.

The main weakness of this approach lies in the assumption that politicians include in their decisions the implicit (and often invisible) costs and benefits of diplomatic activity in terms of both trade and investment opportunities, whereas these shadow costs of political behaviour appear in the real world to be hardly ever considered. Another weakness is that Polachek wants to consider 'net' conflict, although conflict and co-operation are not simply two sides of the same coin. This particular assumption that conflict and co-operation can be aggregated into one meaningful indicator was first made in Richardson's seminal 1960 study on arms race modelling. It leads Polachek to use an index measure for the overall conflict between any pair of trade partners. This index, the so-called net frequency of conflict, is defined as the frequency of conflictual events minus the frequency of cooperative events. According to Sayrs (1988, p. 5):

> the result of such linear blending has been to discern effects for trade which are based on an underlying false continuity. The net conflict measure (conflict minus co-operation) widely used in this literature not only obscures differences in the effect of trade on co-operation as distinct from conflict, but the measure disregards the actual relationship between conflict and co-operation, i.e., they are not reciprocal behaviors.

These critical remarks, however, should not deny the main result of the conflict and trade approach, namely its consistent finding of a negative relationship between net conflict and trade, both across methodologies and for very different periods and countries. Moreover, the findings of the conflict–trade literature increase our awareness of the problems posed by causality: does trade influence diplomacy; or does the chain of causation run the other way around? Several attempts have been made to redo the Polachek approach deploying other indicators, weighing schemes, and so on. Table 2.1 summarizes the findings of these conflict and trade studies. The table reports the elasticities of net conflict between a pair of nations with respect to their bilateral trade flows. Gasiorowski (1986) points out some methodological flaws in Polachek's empirical analysis, mainly about the definition and measurement of the variables. Polachek uses simple counts of hostile and friendly events for the construction of his net conflict measure and the dollar value of imports and exports for the trade variable. Both measures may introduce a bias in cross-sectional investigations creating a statistical artefact when events in important nations are deemed more newsworthy. This implies that the size of an economy may be positively correlated with both the volume of trade and the number of counted events. Gasiorowski's main point, however, is that theory is ambiguous about the impact of trade on the diplomatic climate.[8] Yes, the gains from trade may provide an important incentive to limit conflict. At the same time, however, trade may create diplomatic problems, for example, between the United States and Japan over Japanese cars or between the EU and the United States over agriculture. Correcting for the methodological problems by using relative instead of absolute values, Gasiorowski finds (1986, p. 36) that 'trade interconnectedness is associated with a decline in conflict only when its costly effects have been controlled for'.

Table 2.1 Percentage reduction in net conflict due to a 1 % increase in trade

Source	Period	N	Conflict elasticity to		
			Trade	Export	Import
Polachek (1980)	1958–67	30		0.19	0.19
	1958–67[a]	30		0.15	0.15
	1958–67[b]	30		0.36	0.31
Gasiorowski (1986)	1960–77	44	0.33[c]		
Lundborg (1988)	1946–81	157	0.30		
Polachek (1992)	1958–67	105		0.19	0.19
	1948–78[a]	105		0.15	0.15
Polachek et al. (1992)	1948–78[b]	105		0.36	0.31
	1973	14	0.47	0.28	0.50
	1973[d]	14		0.12	0.35
Li et al. (2004)	1975–99	112	0.002		

Notes: N is number of countries included in the study
     a. including country attributes
     b. two and three stages least squares
     c. standardised regression co-efficient
     d. manufactured goods only.

Polachek's approach has also found applications outside his methodological framework or related to other measures and manner of conflict. Lundborg (1988) analyses 5,246 roll-casts in the United Nations General Assembly for the years 1946–1981.[9] He finds that the effects of both US and Soviet trade with individual member countries yield significant results. More trade increases the agreement on the issues that are brought to the fore in the General Assembly. Interestingly, the elasticities of trading with the Soviet Union are considerably higher than the corresponding elasticities of trading with the United States. Recently the relationship between transnational terrorism and trade has been investigated empirically in order to test the assumption that globalization facilitates transnational terrorism as the increasing volumes of travel, trade and finance would make detection of illegal activities much more difficult if not impossible. The only study to date that addresses this issue empirically does not support this particular assumption. Li and Schaub (2004) analyze the relationship between transnational terrorism and trade and find a small but significant terrorism-reducing impact of trade. Their sample covers 112 countries and the years 1975–99. They explain their finding partly by the fact that globalizing economies tend to achieve higher levels of economic welfare, which in itself may provide a partial antidote against terrorism (see also Frey and Lüchinger 2003). The Polachek hypothesis may, however, be a relevant explanation as well.

It is also important to note that a more disaggregated approach to the trade–conflict relationship may be appropriate. Recent empirical work by Schneider and Schultze (2003) points out that sectoral and distributional differences are important determinants of observed patterns of trade and conflict as they influence the political economy considerations at the national level. Likewise, Hegre (2003) finds that the development level of a country matters and Mansfield and Pevehouse (2003) highlight the empirical relevance of the institutional context in which foreign commerce is conducted.

The Case of Europe

Clearly the best-known 'policy experiment' that would seem to be relevant for this line of research is the formation of the forerunners of the European Union such as the European Coal and Steel Community (ECSC). The ECSC, founded in 1951, was the first organization to be based on the principles of supranationalism and in addition the Benelux countries brought the former belligerents France, Germany and Italy together. Clearly the ECSC – which later developed into the European Economic Community and subsequently in the European Union – is a success story. It shows that mutual economic benefits and increased trade can reduce conflict. This is not only the case because European supranational institutions unified Western Europe during the Cold War and created the foundation for European democracy in the post-Second World War period. European integration also helped to secure peace and democracy in new member countries. First in Western Europe (Portugal, Spain and Greece are examples) and later in central Europe. However, the ultimate success should not blind us for the risks that were run directly after the fall of the Iron Curtain in 1990, as the following quote from Sinderen and Bergeijk. (1994, pp. 269–70) illustrates:

> Reviving nationalism is found both inside the EC, and within its borders. On its Eastern borders, communism for decades suppressed popular movements. Now that the old rule has ended, an unfortunate by-product appears to be that irresponsible populist leaders increase the heating; the most vivid example is former Yugoslavia. But the same goes (fortunately to a lesser extent, although tension is building) for former Czechoslovakia and the former USSR. Actual disintegration is also found in the EC, for example, in Belgium, while tendencies toward nationalism are evident in Italy and Spain ... This *tour d'horizon* suggests some provoking questions. Will nationalism become a threat to further economic integration? Does market integration stimulate nationalism?

Indeed, under the veil of the EU's success many countries disintegrated increasing the number of countries on the European continent so that an alternative interpretation of this story would point out an underlying negative correlation between political integration (at the national level) and economic integration at the international level.

Equally relevant are cases where bilateral trade is substantially below potential as happens in a number of non-European cases. Here the issue of non-trade relationships of neighbouring countries attract attention. Examples comprise the Middle East (Israel and the Palestinian National Authority; see, for example, Denters and Klijn 1991) and Asia (India and Pakistan; see Murshed and Mamoon 2010). Successful peace processes could increase intra-regional trade to a large extent in such cases and once established mutual benefits of economic integration could be a strong binding political force.

4 EMPIRICAL FINDINGS ON THE TRADE–POLITICS RELATIONSHIP

Empirical research on the impact of international politics on trade made a good and lasting start when Tinbergen (1962) first published the results with a gravity model. Measurement was crude, but using dummy variables for preferential and semi-preferential trade relations, Tinbergen (1962, p. 288) found substantial 'colonial or ex-colonial' trade multipliers. Tinbergen himself appears to have been a bit puzzled by the actual size of the political trade multiplier, that, however, even today is a consistent finding in alternative specifications and data sets. Tinbergen attempted different valuation methods for Gross National Product (GNP) and derived the value of bilateral export flows not only from the trade statistics of the exporting countries, but used the import statistics of the countries of destination as well.

His data set is for 1959 and covers about 70% of world trade. It comprises 42 countries, both developing nations and major OECD countries. Tinbergen starts from a model in which only economic variables play a role. Noting that the correlation co-efficient is not high – about 0.8, which leaves at least 35% of the variance of exports essentially unexplained – Tinbergen sets out to identify deviations between the actual observed pattern of trade and the normal ('ideal' or theoretical) trade pattern that could be expected on the basis of economic variables such as GNP and distance. Tinbergen estimates the trade-increasing effects of adjacency at about 75% of the normal trade volume. The trade-stimulating effect of preferential treatment is estimated to yield 'colonial or ex-colonial' trade multipliers of about ten, indicating that colonial ties give rise to ten times the usual trade volume.

The further development of Tinbergen's research programme is a typical example of the 'overlapping generations approach' in which PhD students become supervisors themselves, so that generations of academics can continue to work on the original problem. Tinbergen's associate and doctoral student Linnemann, for example, whose 1966 publication has become the standard reference on the gravity model in international trade, is the tutor of Bikker who wrote a thesis on the subject in 1982.[10] The latter, incidentally, in a more recent study asserted that the preferences based on colonial ties from the past have become weaker in the course of time (Bikker, 1987, p. 330).

This may or may not have been true, but equally strong political distortions were present in the 1990 world trading system.

The Case of East West Trade and *Détente*

A clear example is the distortion in East West trade where large trade multipliers pointed out that trade was reduced to levels of perhaps only ten percent of its potential. Indeed, in the early 1990s a substantial empirical literature developed on the policy relevant question of the impact of *détente* on the trade potential of Central Europe, giving credence to the assumption that the change of diplomatic climate between East and West would result in substantial improvements in trade orientation and performance in the formerly Centrally Planned Economies. Examples of these studies – that typically deploy gravity-type trade models with dummy variables that mimic political barriers in the bilateral trade flows between East and West – are Bergeijk and Oldersma (1990), Havrylyshyn and Pritchett (1991), Wang and Winters (1991), Döhrn and Milton (1992), Ezran et al. (1992) and Hamilton and Winters (1992). These studies show substantial improvements of the world trade potential and important shifts in global trade patterns. Havrylyshyn and Pritchett (1991), for example, establish that a revolution is also to be expected in the geographic pattern of trade by the mid-European countries. In the past 60–80% of their activities focused on the Comecon partners and only about 20–30% on Northern and Western Europe. According to this World Bank study, however, the natural trading pattern is exactly the reverse. The upshot of such studies is that the conflict-era of the Cold War imposed substantial costs on the economies both in the East and in the West, reducing trade well below 'normal' levels, so that the end of conflict was expected to substantially enhance trade, as it actually did. Actual developments confirmed the correctness of the gravity model predictions as double digit growth rates were characteristic for trade of Central Europe with the OECD area in the early 1990s.

Beyond Binary Measurement of Conflict and Co-operation

The result that political factors are very relevant was also found when the measurement of international relations was refined beyond the stage of crude dummy variables.[11] Here the availability of the events data registered in the Conflict and Peace Data Base (COPDAB, see Azar 1980) was a major stimulus for research. These events are occurrences between nations which are distinct enough from the constant flow of transactions (trade, mail, travel and so on) to stand out against this background as reportable or newsworthy.[12]

Pollins (1989b) is the first to combine COBDAB and trade data in this way. He sets out to test the empirical relevance of incorporating a measure of diplomatic relations into a 25-nation gravity model of international trade for 16 annual cross-sectional estimations for the years 1960–1975.[13] The investigation covers 80% of world trade. In addition to traditional economic variables such as GDP, prices and distances, Pollins includes dummy variables for GATT-membership and for 'intra-trade' by members of regional trade organizations, such as the EC, Comecon and the Latin American Free Trade Association (LAFTA). His major innovation is the inclusion of a diplomatic climate indicator based on political events that have been collected in the COPDAB data set. The theoretical justification for this assumption is meagre. According to Pollins (1989b, p. 741), political factors should be included in the utility function because of 'very traditional security concerns, the desire to reward friends, to punish adversaries, and to minimise risk'. Pollins decides to combine conflict and co-operation into one 'net' indicator, rather than to include these flows of diplomatic exchanges individually, because of strong covariation and since a net indicator represents the general tone or climate that he contends to be of importance for the development and direction of international trade flows. Pollins's weighed co-operation index W_{ij} represents the 'amount' of non-operation sent by county i to country j and is defined as $W_{ij} = C_{ij} \times C_{ij} / (C_{ij} + H_{ij})$, where C is the 'amount' of co-operation and H is the 'amount' of hostility. Pollins's indicator, however, is logically flawed as it is included in a multiplicative way, implying that trade is only possible if some sort of political co-operation takes place. Indeed in his model a positive trade flow formally requires $C > 0$, which may or may not be the case.

Table 2.2 Gravity equations including non-binary indicators of diplomatic and political interaction

Source	Period	N	Elasticity to	Estimate
Pollins (1989a)	1955–78	6	Net conflict	0.01 – 0.06
Pollins (1989b)	1960–75	25	Net conflict	0.04 – 0.37
Summary (1989)	1978–82	66[a]	Arms transfers	0.2
			Foreign agents	0.3
Bergeijk (1989b)	1985–86	25	Co-operation	0.22 – 0.49
	1985–86	25	Hostility	-0.27 – -0.20
Bergeijk (1994a)	1985–86	40	Co-operation	0.11– 0.44
			Hostility	-0.56 – -0.06
Nitsch et al. (2004)	1960–93	200	Terrorism	-0.04
Rose (2007)	2002	20[b]	Embassies	0.08 – 0.11
Nitsch (2007)	1948–2003	3[b]	State visits	0.08 – 0.13
Maurel et al. (2007)	1997–2005	57	Embassies	0.07 – 0.17
Yakop et al. (2007)	2006	63	Embassies	0.06 – 0.13

Notes a. US *versus* 66 trade partners

　　　　 b. 220 export destinations

In his 1989a article, Pollins builds a traditional import demand equation of bilateral trade flows on the basis of a public choice approach. In this model the same summary indicator of international conflict and co-operation is included. The import demand equation is estimated for Egypt, India, the Soviet Union, East and West Germany and the United States *vis-à-vis* 24 trade partners for the years 1955–1978. Most interestingly, the investigation suggests the possibility of differences in the way countries manage their trade relations. The effect of diplomatic co-operation in East Germany and the Soviet Union, for example, is at least twice as large as it is in West Germany and the United States. Unfortunately, Pollins's econometrics are clouded by a desire to produce nation-specific equations that link levels of trade to levels of co-operation. This by-product of a related modelling effort for the GLOBUS world model (Bremer 1987) unnecessarily introduces substantial problems related to heteroscedasticity and autocorrelations that could have easily been prevented if rates of change instead of levels had been used.

Anyhow, in both studies Pollins (1989a, 1989b) finds that the relative co-operation and hostility of bilateral political ties does affect trade flows, that the importance of these ties is as large as economic variables such as prices and that the estimates are robust and warrant inclusion on both statistical and theoretical grounds.

In addition to COPDAB data, trade analysts have developed other non-binary indicators for political and diplomatic interaction that met their specific research needs or could be observed better, more accurately or with less delay. Table 2.2 summarizes a number of such gravity model studies which we will discuss in some detail.

Summary (1989) develops a gravity-type model for the United States *vis-à-vis* 66 trading partners, including 40 developing countries, 15 OECD countries, five oil exporters and six Warsaw Pact countries. Semi-economic and international political factors, such as arms transfers from member countries of the North Atlantic Treaty Organisation and the number of foreign agents registered in the United States, appear significant enhancement factors in export and import equations for the United States in the years 1978 and 1982. The estimated equations explain 80% of US exports and 60% of US imports. The elasticities for the significant semi-political determinants of exports and imports range between 0.2 for US arms transfers and to 0.3 for the number of foreign agents. The number of US civilian government employees in the trade partner's country was significant only in the export equations with an elasticity of about 0.2. The political (or human) rights situation in the trade partner's country did not significantly influence the flow of trade. Although Summary's results are representative only for the United States and do not allow for the separation of semi-economic from political factors, the study shows that 'pure' economic factors are not the only determinants of US trade.

Bergeijk (1992 and 1994a) has used Azar's (1980) coding scheme to classify 'newsworthy' events that have been summarized in *Keesings Historische Archief*. A traditional gravity model is applied to bilateral trade flows of 40 countries in the years 1985 and 1986 and yields separate estimates for hostile diplomacy (ranging from mild verbal dismay via the recall of ambassadors to military conflicts and right-out war) and co-operative diplomacy (which ranges from minor official exchanges and verbal support via the beginning of official diplomatic relations, to the creation of a common market and unification'. The estimated co-efficients are highly significant and imply that about 30% of the variance in bilateral trade can be attributed to the two diplomatic variables (Figure 2.1). The estimated elasticities for co-operative behaviour range from 0.1 to 0.5. This broad spectre contrasts with later empirical research that makes a clearer and more unambiguous link between trade and trade-related activities. The focus is on specific manner of diplomatic exchange such as that exerted by the full infrastructure of embassies and consulate (Rose 2007 and Yakop and Bergeijk 2007), changes in this infrastructure (Maurel and Afman 2007, specifically aimed at Eastern Europe) and official visits (Nitsch 2007). Typically these specific diplomatic activities yield significant estimated elasticities of about 0.1. We will return to these issues in Chapter 5.

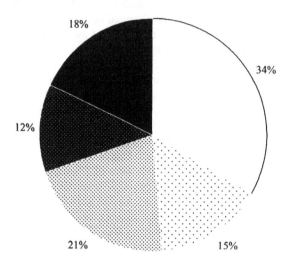

□ Exporting economy □ Importing economy ⊠ Distance ▨ Cooperation ■ Hostility

Figure 2.1 Contribution to the explanation of the variance of bilateral trade of 40 countries in 1985–6

Since '9/11' interest in a particular manner of conflict emerged, namely transnational terrorism, which can be defined as inter-country violence at the non-state level. A number of gravity-type approaches can be discerned. For a sample of about 200 countries and the period 1960–1993, Nitsch and Schumacher (2004) show that trade on average reduces by 4% when terrorist actions double; a result confirmed by Blomberg and Hess (2006) finding for the more recent period 1968–1999 on the basis of a sample of 170 countries that a terrorist incident is associated with a 5% decline in bilateral trade. In addition to trade in goods, trade in services will be influenced as well. Frey et al. (2004) review a number of empirical studies that investigate the negative impact of terrorism on tourist arrivals and tourism revenues in the 1980s and

1990s when national terrorist activities occurred in a number of European countries. Relative strong reductions occurred in Spain, Austria and Greece; continental Europe as a whole lost about 2% in annual tourist revenues. Admittedly, this would seem to be a modest number, but as Blomberg and Hess rightly point out,

> this effect exceeds a number of trading cost components that are traditionally part an parcel of the trade theorist's tool box.

In addition to the gravity approach other techniques have been developed. Roemer (1977), for example, investigates trade patterns using area and sector intensities for 43 sectors of manufactured goods. The investigation focuses on the United States, Japan, the United Kingdom, Germany and Canada *vis-à-vis* 14 areas of the world in the year 1971. A trade intensity relates the share of country *A* in country *B*'s import market to country *B*'s share in the imports of the rest of the world, and reveals, so to say, the relative preference of country *B* for the products of country *A*. Trade intensities are calculated for total (bilateral) trade flows, for manufactured goods only and for specific industries. What emerges from the calculations is a biased sectoral pattern of trade in manufacturing – the five countries typically tend to market their weak sectors disproportionately in their strong areas. Roemer looks into two types of market imperfections that may explain the biased sectoral pattern, namely transportation costs (distance) and sphere of influence causes that reflect historical and political factors (for example, better communication channels, preferential tariffs, tied aid, tastes and the activities of multinational subsidiaries). Roemer finds that trade intensities in the Western world cannot be explained solely by economic factors, but must result in part from causes that are in the narrow sense not economic. Indeed, according to Roemer (1977, p. 327),

> trade intensity may be part of (an) imperial legacy, whereby former colonies remain bound to their mother countries through ties of culture, communication and influences of various sorts. In some cases these ties may be concretely observable in tariff structures or exchange controls (... or tied aid); in other cases the mechanism may be ... more subtle embodied in utility functions.

All in all, sphere of influence effects, also in this study, appear important in explaining trade intensities and in the case of the United Kingdom they are even absolutely more important than transportation costs.

5 CAPITAL, CONFLICT AND CO-OPERATION

Empirical research on the impact of capital flows on conflict is scarce although the liberalization and globalization of international capital markets has been spectacular. According to Schneider et al. (2003, p. 5), 'the impact of foreign direct investment ... on the likelihood of conflict has almost disappeared from the research agenda'.[14]

Stability (both economic and political), however, is often a prerequisite for obtaining private foreign funds. Political factors have long been considered important by bankers and international investors. Bankers are probably most sensitive to political risks.[15] Indeed most banks have large departments that assess the extent of country risk (Cataquet 1985). Two econometric studies support the banks' sensitivity with respect to political factors in particular. Citron and Nickelsburg (1987) find that the number of changes of government, which proxies domestic political instability, significantly influences the probability that a debtor country defaults on its foreign loans. Balkan (1992) shows that the level of democracy reduces the probability of default. As in the case of trade and conflict, causality may be ambiguous with respect to capital flows as Balkan (1992, p. 1004) concludes that 'efforts to support democratic movements in (developing countries) would contribute to stability of the international financial system'.

Foreign direct investment is another area of decision making in internationally operating firms that acknowledges the importance of political factors. Schneider and Frey (1985) give a review of two literatures: the 'much politics, little economics' approach to foreign direct investment and the 'much economics, little politics' school. No clear picture, however, emerges from their review of these early econometric investigations. So Schneider and Frey proceed to assess by means of a politico-economic model what role economic and political factors play for 31 countries in the years 1976, 1979 and 1980. Bilateral aid appears to provide strong political incentives and disincentives to invest. It stimulates the flow of foreign direct investments for Western aid, but the impact is negative if communist countries provide aid to the potential recipient country.

Political instability may also be a significant barrier to Foreign Direct Investment (FDI). Following the seminal study by Schneider and Frey (1985) many studies have investigated the impact of political instability and risk on FDI econometrically. Li's (2006) review of the recent empirical literature provides a mixed picture with a lot of ambiguity essentially because some regionally focussed studies within a relatively short time frame report positive or insignificant correlations between FDI and political instability. Consequently, Li investigates a larger sample for 129 countries and the years 1976–96, finding that the impact of political risk and violence on FDI especially relates to the choice of the host country by the investor and less to the level of investment once that choice has been made. This result mainly reflects the long-term character of investment and the difficulty to opt out and withdraw if political factors deteriorate. More recent empirical studies on foreign direct investment extend the available data sets and delve into these issues at different levels of analysis (that is at the sector or at the firm level) and continue to high light the importance of political factors with respect to decisions about international investment.

Noting that institutional characteristics of the host and neighbouring countries affect the various types of FDI (purely horizontal, export platform, purely vertical, and vertical specialization/fragmentation), van der Ploeg and Poelhekke (2008) include Country Risk indicators on institutional quality (such as the strength of property rights, absence of corruption and so on) into an empirical analysis of the spatial distribution of such investments. They find a consistently significant and positive effect for their sample that relates to the years 1984–98 and covers 75 countries: better institutional quality attracts foreign investment, especially if neighbouring countries provide lower levels of institutionally quality.

Fortanier (2008, pp. 95–124) investigates foreign direct investment in the context of the emergence of bilateral investment treaties. Her regressions cover the period 1990–2002 and deal with 156 home countries and 162 host countries. She runs separate regressions that relate FDI to indicators for institutional quality (that is several indicators for governance, political risk, political constraints and the legal system). She often finds that indicators for institutional quality exert a positive impact on the inflow of foreign direct investment. More importantly she notes a strong and significant correlation with bilateral investment treaties and in general the strength (and signs) of the effects appear to depend on GDP size and skill endowments. So the instrument of bilateral economic diplomacy in the field of international investment is especially strong for nations that have weak domestic institutions. Interestingly Fortanier concludes that the announcement effects of a proposed treaty are significant (rather than the effects of signing and implementing the treaty). Indeed, according to Fortanier (2008, p. 123),

> Countries that do not have the institutions to credibly commit themselves to agreements with investors, can use [bilateral investment treaties] and the international dispute settlement procedures associated with them to show investors their commitment to protect their property rights, and to lock in policy changes so that sudden regime changes will not negatively affect investors.

All in all private capital flows appear to be to a large extent correlated with international and domestic political variables. Interestingly, foreign direct investment may become an instrument of economic diplomacy especially if non-state actors get involved as we discussed in Chapter 1. This is not a really new insight of course. For example, Olson (1979) already argued that manipulation of capital flows and aid may be more effective than trade sanctions. Not much is known empirically and according to Polachek and Seiglie (2007, p. 1058) 'FDI's effects on international relations is still at its infancy', but they are able to report estimates for 1990–2000 including a significant elasticity of 0.3 implying that a 1% increase in FDI increases co-operation by 0.3% on average. Moreover, the elasticity of FDI with respect to co-operation is estimated to be 1.04 (Polachek and Seiglie 2007, pp. 1058–60, especially Table 5).

Of course the influence of political factors on capital flows extends beyond private lending and investment. The activities of the multilateral institutions appear to be governed by political considerations as well. Frey and Schneider (1986) test four competing models for the World Bank's lending behaviour. The models are informal and heuristic: they mainly describe assumptions about the relevance and assumed influence of subsets of possible explanatory variables. Their first model assumes that World Bank lending aims at those countries in greatest need of official foreign finance. This 'needs' model links World Bank credits to indicators for poverty, scarcity of real resources and the strain of demand on foreign resources. Their second model assumes that World Bank credits go to countries with large potential for development. This 'deserts' model takes creditworthiness into account and focuses on indicators of economically and financially responsible behaviour.[16] Their next model (called the benevolence model) starts from the official World Bank charter which states that the World Bank is a multilateral non-political organization. Hence the variables of the pure neoclassical model appear in the quasi-reduced form equations in combination with a dummy variable that captures the organization's hypothesised preference for a capitalistic climate.

The fourth model is 'politico-economic' and deals with both internal and external political motives. With this model Frey and Schneider study the role of bureaucratic, possibly game-theoretic, motives. Next to these political considerations of top officials in the World Bank the model looks at variables that in a technical sense determine capital requirements and lending capacity. Frey and Schneider use the four models to explain the patterns of World Bank loans and International Development Assistance with combined cross sections/time series for 60 developing countries in the period 1972–81. Although some important partial derivatives (for example, with respect to external debt) may convey mistaken information, the politico-economic model performs best in the econometric tests. The results suggest that decision making in the World Bank is often informally influenced by political donor–recipient relationships, such as former colonial ties, economic dependence and trade linkage. The conclusion is that students of international capital flows will have to take international political variables into account if they want to produce a useful description of their topic.

6 WHITE SPOTS

Perhaps the reader will be impressed by the amount of empirical and theoretical evidence that was presented for the existence of a relationship between international economics and international politics. In particular the rich literatures of the 'old' international political economy, the studies on the economic national defence tariff and the conflict and trade approach seem to provide an important underpinning for the empirical investigations that were discussed.

More probably, however, the reader will be amazed that it is indeed necessary to present such arguments to the scientific economic community. It is common-sense that economics and politics are inseparable in the real world. Reading one's newspaper or listening to international bankers, businessmen and investors would seem to provide ample evidence as well and probably in less time and in a more accessible way.

Modesty, however, is more appropriate. First, most research is clearly on-going. Many questions remain unanswered, while at the same time discontinuity is an important characteristic of this subject, as research efforts appear to be rather scattered with respect to both time and place. Second, the theoretical underpinning of the trade–conflict relationship is not completely convincing (at least not to economists, especially if they are trained in the neoclassical tradition). Third, the relevance of the empirical findings may be questioned as most research is dated, deals with regularities that relate to the 1960s to 1980s (or if the research relates to more recent years, it often only deals with isolated years or specific regions). A similar criticism concerns the focus on a limited subset of (especially large) countries. Fourth, behavioural differences between countries and different types of transactions need further investigation.

For these reasons it is important that the existing knowledge is refreshed and where possible extended. In particular it is important to investigate how the emergence of new players and new rules may impact on the efficacy and effectiveness of economic diplomacy.

NOTES

[1] Indeed in contrast to international economics, the macroeconomic analysis typically considers political factors to be important. See, for example, Drazen (2000).

[2] See, however, Reuveny, 2000, pp. 38–9 who suggests that this may be due to the long-term orientation of trade theory or the fact that that economic theory is micro oriented thus neglecting the 'macro' effect of inter state political activity.

[3] See also Kennedy (1989, p. 158) on this particular view on the world economic and political systems.

[4] The reader may wish to consult Griffin and Gurley (1985) for a more critical review.

[5] A rigorous discussion of the national security exceptions in GATT appears in Carter (1988, pp. 95–8 and 131–40).

[6] See, for example, Erickson (1975) for an early study on the possible simultaneity of trade and diplomacy.

[7] See, however, Sayrs (1990) for a political scientist's perspective. She signals three assumptions that may be crucial as well. These assumptions are that the state is a unitary actor, that domestic policies can be treated as a constant and that conflict and co-operation can be derived from the same utility calculus.

[8] Compare Keohane and Nye (1977).

[9] See Richardson (1978) for an early study on the impact of dependence on UN voting behaviour.

[10] And Hans was a member of my PhD supervisory committee.

[11] Empirical political science research on the trade–conflict relationship has been further developed on the basis of gravity models that include militarized interstate dispute, and different forms of institutional settings and alliances (good examples are Morrow et al. 1998 and Keshk et al. 2004 which also contain reviews of relevant literature). However, this fits more into the crude Tinbergen approach since these influences are mainly investigated by means of dummy variables.

[12] See, for a recent discussion on the measurement of conflict and co-operation, Pevehouse (2003) and Reuveny (2003).

[13] The order of publication would seem to contradict the order of origination. In this discussion I follow the order in which Pollins appears to have written the articles, rather than the order in which he got his research output published.

[14] According to Weede (2004, p. 169) 'the conceivable pacifying impact of FDI still lacks sufficient empirical investigation'.

[15] See, however, for a very instructive view on actual banking practices – and other forms of human ostrich attitudes: Guttentag and Herring (1986).

[16] A comparable 'deserts' model for private bank lending is Lensink and Bergeijk (1991).

3. Trade Uncertainty and Trade Disruption

Uncertainty is a fact of life in international economic relations. Volatility of exchange rates, of (relative) prices and of trade flows in general influences the decisions of private firms and consumers and, consequently, determines (the possibilities for) foreign trade (see, for example, Ruffin 1974, Pomery 1984 and Kofman et al. 1990). Most of the literature considers uncertainty as an exogenous phenomenon, at least as unrelated to the levels of consumption, production, trade and so on. As we discussed in the previous chapter, Bhagwati and Srinivasan (1976), however, have argued that the possibility of quantitative trade restrictions (import quota, voluntary export restrictions, boycotts, and embargoes) may also be affected by the volume of one's exports. This is relevant, because the importance of economic sanctions appears to be increasing at this point in history (see Figure 1.1 in Chapter 1). In addition, economic sanctions are increasingly being considered as a means to enforce international environmental protection conventions (Subramanian 1992), while strategic trade policy considerations may increase the demand for foreign trade sanctions too (Carter 1988).

This chapter deals with the impact of uncertainty on the pattern of specialization and on the concomitant decisions about consumption and production. The analysis in the present chapter, however, does not restrict itself to the impact of politically inspired trade restrictions because it also covers economically motivated government intervention such as quantitative ('voluntary') export restrictions, like those studied in the seminal paper by Bhagwati and Srinivasan (1976), as well as uncertainty that results from strategic behaviour by private competitors. In the case of economically inspired trade uncertainty it seems reasonable to assume that the more you trade the higher the probability of trade disruption (fuelled by lobby groups abroad; see, for example, Bhagwati 1992). So we will pay attention to both exogenous and endogenous trade uncertainty in this chapter.

First the settings and the model will be introduced. The model is simple and relates to a small country, but it has the merits that it enables a transparent analysis of exogenous trade uncertainty, allowing for both risk neutrality and risk aversion.[1] The small trading economy cannot influence its terms of trade so that the international price level is given for the small economy. This assumption answers the critique by Helpman and Razin (1978) concerning the difference between *ex ante* and *ex post* trading decisions. They pointed out the shortcoming of the traditional *ex ante* analysis, which assumes that trading decisions are made before the resolution of uncertainty. This inconsistency is avoided in the present model because the economy *a priori* decides on the pattern of specialization (that is production of the two goods *x* and *y* that the economy is assumed to produce and consume). However, as will become clear, an actual export an/or import commitment will only be made once the uncertainty concerning the trading possibilities is resolved. The first section deals with the cases of autarky, free trade and unexpected isolation in order to analyze the relationship between exogenous uncertainty, the specialization pattern and the resulting volume of trade. Section 2 then goes on to discuss a number of aspect regarding the simple basic model in order to include into the analysis such topics as the manner of decision making (centralized versus decentralized) as well as dynamic considerations (including anticipation) and political economy aspects. The final section discusses policy implications with a keen eye on role, costs and benefits of economic and commercial diplomacy in the context of this particular model.

1 THE BASIC MODEL

Figure 3.1 depicts production, consumption and trade. Vertically we read the volumes of consumption, production and trade of good *y*. On the horizontal axis we can read for the same categories the respective quantities for good *x*. Production is represented by the production possibilities curve (or transformation curve) *I* which shows the maximum attainable combinations of goods *x* and *y* that can be produced by the economy given the available endowments and technology The function is convex and its shape reflects decreasing returns (that is moving to the left increasing amounts of *x* have to be given up to increase the production of *y* with one unit). Points within *I* such as *Z* can of course be produced but these points are inefficient as the economy can be reorganized so as to get a higher level of *y* for the observed level of *x*.

Consumer preferences are depicted by a selection of four concave indifference curves C_1, C_2, C_3 and C_4 that each represent combinations of *x* and *y* that yield a constant level of utility. The further the transformation curve and the indifference curve lie from the origin, the higher is the level of production *c.q.* the utility that these curves represent.

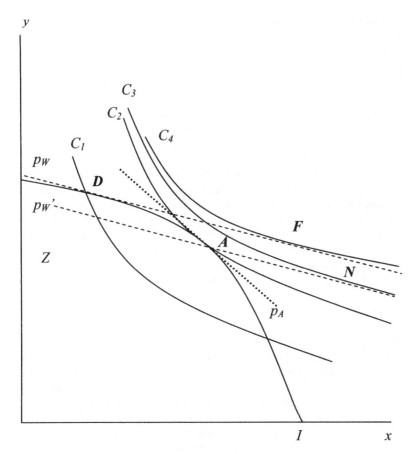

Figure 3.1 Production, consumption and specialization at different stages of international trade

Finally the figure contains two price ratios: the ratio p_A that results in autarky (that is if the economy does not intend to trade), and the price ratio p_W which is the world price (this price is to be considered as a given price for the small economy that is studied in this chapter).[2] Note that four points of special interest (A, D, F and N) have been marked in Figure 3.1.

The first point to note is A, the 'autarky point'. This is the point that reflects production and consumption in the hypothetical case that no other country exists with which our economy trades or wants to trade. Specialization is absent because no trade is possible in this case. Hence the market outcome in autarky is determined by the endowments, the production function (that is the transformation curve) and consumer preferences. Markets are in equilibrium balancing demand by consumers and supply by producers for the two goods: in point A the rate of transformation (the tangent to the transformation curve) equals the marginal rate of substitution (the tangent of the indifference curve) and in A obviously x and y are exchanged against the price ratio p_A.[3] The other points, that will be discussed next, reflect that international trade allows the economy to exchange its products and to consume outside the boundaries of the production possibilities curve I.

The second point to note is F, the free trade point, which features prominently in the standard textbook treatment of international trade. F is the consumption point (at a superior utility level of C_4); the concomitant production point is D and export of y and import of x can be easily read as the difference between D and F on the horizontal and vertical axes, respectively. Since D is to the left of A the economy has a comparative advantage in y: it specializes in the production of y and exports of y are traded against imports of x at the international price ratio p_W. The utility level of free trade C_4 exceeds the utility level of autarky C_2.

An alternative interpretation for the third point of interest D exists in the case of uncertain trade. International specialization conform comparative advantage does not always yield a utility outcome that improves on welfare in the case of autarky. Whether this happens or not depends on the particular trade regime that occurs. In the free trade situation the economy consumes in point F and achieves utility C_4. But if the no-trade situation emerges while the economy is fully specialized, consumption drops to D, the production combination that is actually being produced. Since this production combination is the result of decisions that assume that international trade is possible, the resulting consumption combination logically cannot be optimal if trade is impossible. Indeed, in the no-trade situation it is the allocation of the factors of production that determines utility.

Impact of Trade Uncertainty on Specialization

It seems quite reasonable to assume that economic subjects will take into account that the possibility of trade disruption exists when they must make their decisions about the extent of their specialization. In general, economic subjects will consider the expected utility of their production decisions and thus will prefer a pattern of specialization that is associated with a point in between the autarky production point A and the free trade production point F, that is they are willing to give up some of the benefits from full specialization in order to reduce the welfare loss when the no-trade situation occurs. In order to model the decision process we will draw up two functions that have as an argument the specialization point (identified by the amount of x; y

follows directly from x as it lies on the production possibilities frontier $y = I(x)$). This specialization point is related to the utility that is realized in the case of free trade $f(x)$ and no-trade $g(x)$, respectively. Remember that a small economy is investigated so that the international price ratio is given and by assumption certain.

The economy decides on the pattern of domestic specialization before it is known which state of the world will occur (that is whether the free trade or no-trade situation occurs). Once the decision about the optimal pattern of domestic specialization has been taken, the allocation of the factors of production cannot be changed. Hence the model essentially is formulated within a two-period framework and deals with the short-term consequences of *ex ante* trade uncertainty. If the planning horizon is to be increased (as will be done later in this chapter) the costs of reallocation would have to be taken into consideration (or alternatively, the time needed to make adjustments, which also is an important cost component, of course). For the moment, reallocation costs are implicitly assumed to be infinite which in the short term is a reasonable and workable assumption.

This economy is confronted with uncertain trade possibilities, that is, with a stochastic volume of trade. In order to keep the analysis as transparent as possible, two extreme trade regimes will be discerned. This abstraction can, however, be interpreted as describing the economy's actual view on the future in terms of an average of these extreme states of the world. First, in the free trade regime the economy can in principle trade any quantity at the prevailing international relative price (because it is 'small' and thus a price taker on the world market). The indirect utility free trade function $f(x)$ relates to this world. We know that $f(x)$ has a global maximum represented by C_4 in point F in Figure 3.1. Second, in the no-trade situation the economy is isolated and international trade comes to a virtual halt. The direct and indirect no-trade utility functions $g(x)$ coincide, because no trade takes place in this state of the world. Note that the no-trade production combination only equals the traditional autarky production point (where the indifference curve is tangent to the production possibilities curve) if individual producers and consumers believe that the no-trade regime will prevail in the second period, and themselves opt for a production combination that does not enable free trade. The autarky production point is the global maximum for $g(x)$, because all other points on the production possibilities curve I describe a situation that is not optimal if the no-trade regime occurs. Figure 3.2 illustrates these functions. The option to trade in the free trade regime implies that $f(x)$ always exceeds $g(x)$ with the exception of the traditional autarky point where firms and consumers independently decide not to trade.

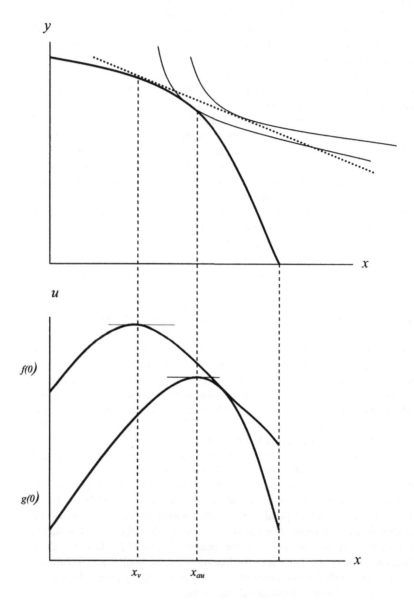

Figure 3.2 The free trade and no-trade utility functions

Now let π be the subjective probability that the free trade regime occurs. This subjective probability can be influenced by economic diplomacy. Obviously, long lasting trade relationships will be influenced by other factors as well. One can easily think of factors that explain the existence, quantity and direction of trade flows, such as uncertainty that results from price fluctuations, technological developments, changing consumer preferences, bad harvests, exchange rate variability and transfer problems. So, evidently, in general many more factors may play a role, but since this book deals with economic diplomacy such factors are not explicitly considered in order to keep the analysis as transparent as possible. We may thus think about π as a function of economic diplomacy E so that $\pi = \pi(E)$ and an increase in E leading to higher π, so that $\pi' > 0$. The choice set now can be summarized in Table 3.1.

Table 3.1 Choice set

Produce x, I(x)		
Trade regime	Free trade	No trade
Probability	π	$1-\pi$
Ex post utility	$f(x)$	$g(x)$

First we investigate this problem for a unitary actor economy, for example, by assuming an omniscient social planner that takes consumer and producer interests simultaneously into account when maximizing von Neumann-Morgenstern ([1944]1980) expected utility.[4] Of course this perfect bureaucrat does not exist in the real world, but the solution for the model is most transparent if we make this assumption and we will confront our analytical results later on with results that follow from the assumption of decentralized decision making (for example when coordination takes place through the market process). The decision problem may now be formalized as a maximization of expected utility with x (read: the pattern of specialization) as the instrument variable.

$$\max_{x} \pi f(x) + (1-\pi)g(x) \tag{3.1}$$

The first order condition of this problem is $\pi f_x(x) + (1-\pi)g_x(x) = 0$. This problem has a unique solution for the production combination (x, y). The boundaries of the area of possible solutions are the autarky product combination x_{au} and the free trade product combination x_v as illustrated in Figure 3.2. If $\pi = 0$, then x_{au} is the solution since $\pi = 0$ by equation 3.1 implies that $g_x(x_{au}) = 0$. Likewise if $\pi = 1$, then the solution to problem 3.1 is $f_x(x_v)$.

So the no-trade function $g(x)$ has a global maximum for x_{au} and the free trade function $f(x)$ is at its global maximum in x_v. Both functions are under the usual assumptions strictly concave, increasing to the left of x_v and decreasing to the right of x_{au}. Consequently, the expected utility of the chosen product combination $(x, I(x))$ that is a weighted average of these functions (with the subjective probabilities as weights) must have a global maximum between x_{au} and x_v.[5] For a country with a comparative advantage in the production in good y (implying that $x_v < x_{au}$) the total differential of the first order condition of problem 3.1 becomes:

$$\{\pi f_{xx} + (1-\pi)g_{xx}\}\,dx = \{g_x - f_x\}\,d\pi \qquad (3.2)$$

As the first order condition of problem 3.1 implies that $f_x = (\pi-1)g_x/\pi$, we may rewrite equation 3.2 as

$$dx/d\pi = g_x/\ \pi\{\pi f_{xx} + (1-\pi)g_{xx}\} < 0 \qquad (3.3)$$

So more (less) trade uncertainty implies less (more) x which in this case amounts to less (more) specialization. In this collective decision making process we thus have a strict one-to-one correspondence between the subjective probability π that the free trade regime prevails and the extent of specialization. A reduction of trade uncertainty induces a shift of the production point in the direction of the free trade production point.

Hence international specialization according to comparative advantage increases and so does the *potential* trade flow. If trade actually takes place (so when the free trade regime prevails) then one may observe that trade flows increase. Likewise an increase in (perceived) trade uncertainty will reduce specialization and thus the observed trade flow (if the free trade regime occurs) is lower. In the no-trade situation of course no trade flows are observed, but the specialization point is observable as in principle is the reduction in welfare (the reduction in consumption). The policy conclusion is that reducing trade uncertainty by increasing political trust (for example through economic diplomacy) is an important instrument with a potentially high pay-off in terms of efficiency and welfare.

2 EXTENSIONS

The model that was developed in the previous section has been extended along several lines. Since its conception in the early 1990s the theory of uncertain trade has been made more general in the sense that:

- the theory now covers other institutional settings for decision making;
- an arbitrary number of goods and services can be included in the model (without altering the conclusions);[6]
- trade uncertainty has been endogenized on the volume of trade; and
- the dynamical consequences including anticipation and learning (with respect to the probabilities) are now part and parcel of the theory.

This section discusses the main theoretical developments and the main results for institutional setting, endogeneity of uncertainty, dynamics and anticipation, while trying to prevent the argument being swamped by the mathematical abstraction that is often unavoidable if one wants to prove one's point formally. (The reader will be referred to the original contributions for the mathematically rigorous proofs for the main results.)

Decentralized Decision Making

Will a decentralized market economy produce at the optimal point of production as well? This is a relevant question since producers and consumers face given prices if markets are characterized by perfect competition. If we ignore the limiting cases where either free trade or autarky is certain, then a private decentralized economy will not produce in the point that would be optimal given the concomitant probabilities.

Figure 3.3 illustrates the decisions facing households and firms. Both producers and consumers incorporate the possibility of a no-trade and a free trade regime into their decisions. If the free trade regime prevails, consumers maximize utility in point F where the price ratio equals the international terms of trade p_W. In the no-trade regime, however, the consumption combination D results, which given the indifference curves, will yield the domestic price ratio p_d. Rational risk-averse utility maximizing households will prefer a price ratio between p_W and p_d; that is a production combination between point D and point G (where the transformation curve is tangent to the no-trade domestic price ratio). Producers on markets that are characterized by free competition face the choice between point G which would maximize their profits if the domestic no-trade price ratio equals p_d and point D which maximizes their profits in the free trade regime. So like consumers in this decentralized economy, expected profit-maximizing firms will choose a production combination between D and G.

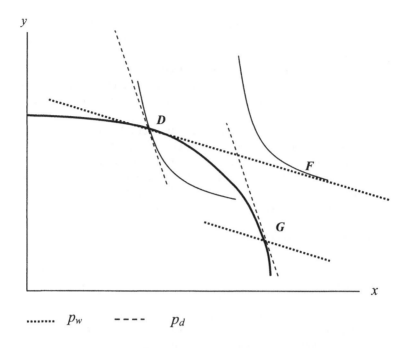

Figure 3.3 Prices and quantities that play a role in the consumers' and producers' decisions

There is, however, no *a priori* reason why consumers and producers for given and identical subjective probabilities would hold identical preferences about the optimal point of production.[7] Producers solve the following problem:

$$\max_{x} \pi(x+p_w I(x)) + (1-\pi)(x+p_d I(x)) \qquad (3.4)$$

The first order condition is $\{\pi p_w+(1-\pi p_d)I_x\}+1=0$. However, if the no-trade regime occurs, domestic prices will have to adjust (they are no longer exogenous) such that consumers want to consume at the chosen production point $(x, I(x))$, requiring $p_d=U''((x,I(x))/U'(x)=p_d(x)$.

We can derive the partial derivative of the first order condition in analogy of equation 3.3 for the case of decentralized decision making:

$$dx/d\pi = I_x(p_d-p_w)/[I_{xx}\{\pi p_w+(1-\pi p_d)\} + (1-\pi)p_d]< 0 \qquad (3.5)$$

This again gives a strict one-to-one relationship between an increase in trade uncertainty and a reduction in the extent of specialization over the relevant interval between the autarky production combination and the free trade production combination.

Centralized and decentralized decision making will, however, not yield the same quantitative reaction to uncertainty (although in both cases the economy will specialize to a lesser extent in accordance with comparative advantage if uncertainty increases). This is obvious from the comparison of the partial derivatives in equation 3.3 and equation 3.5, respectively. Indeed, it can be shown that the risk-averse decentralized economy trades at more than the optimal quantity (which given some level of uncertainty follows directly from equation 3.1).

The intuition behind this result is as follows. Under certainty the standard neo-classical model formally optimizes production and consumption in two steps. That is to say, production is first chosen so as to maximize national income for given technologies and given world prices. Next, consumption is determined given domestic production, world prices and consumer preferences. Once uncertainty is introduced, the optimality of this procedure may break down, as production decisions need no longer to be consistent with consumption decisions.[8] The implication is that decentralized economies will trade too much in relation to the existing trade uncertainty and will thus have a larger drop in welfare than the centralized decision making economy if the no-trade regime occurs.

Accordingly, our model indicates that trade disruption in a centralized regime would be expected to be less harmful. This implication yields a testable proposition that can be investigated (and confirmed) for economic sanctions as we will see in Chapter 6: autocratic regimes do *ceteris paribus* not trade 'too much' and will thus be less vulnerable to politically inspired trade disruption.

Endogenous Uncertainty

So far uncertainty was assumed to be exogenous. Indeed, most of the literature considers uncertainty as an exogenous phenomenon, at least as unrelated to the levels of consumption, production, trade and so on. The introduction to this chapter, however, has already pointed out the possibility that quantitative restrictions (import restrictions, voluntary export restrictions, boycotts, and embargoes) are affected by the volume of exports. It is illustrative that, as was already discussed in Chapter 1, the use of economic sanctions appears to have been increasing since the early 1990s while the sanction cases (as will become clear in Chapter 6) are characterised by higher levels of pre-sanction trade linkage than in the past. Trade uncertainty, however, is not only related to politically inspired trade restrictions because it also covers economically motivated government intervention such as quantitative ('voluntary') export restrictions, as well as uncertainty that results from strategic behaviour by private competitors. Endogenous trade disruption is thus a relevant possibility worthy of further investigation.

Marrewijk and Bergeijk (1993) show that endogenous trade uncertainty may force an economy to specialize in the production of the 'wrong' good (that is the good with comparative disadvantage), although this reversal in the pattern of incomplete specialization in production is not reflected in the trade pattern. The probability of trade may be influenced through a country's level of exports although this country does not have monopoly power so that it cannot influence the terms of trade.[9] The relationship between the volume of trade and its uncertainty can be expressed as an elasticity (the so-called 'responsiveness of trade' parameter), which is positive by assumption (if it were zero the model would reduce to the case of exogenous trade uncertainty). Changes in this 'trade inclination' parameter reflect shifts in exogenous uncertainty induced by such factors as political instability, unbalanced capital flows, the diplomatic relations between trade partners or an active 'voluntary' export restraint policy that all have an impact on the trust in free trade.

As illustrated in Figure 3.4 an increase in the trade inclination parameter initially decreases the probability of trade and reduces the extent of specialization. If the elasticity becomes too large, the probability of trade becomes negligible and the optimal production point will be at autarky. For intermittent values of the trade inclination parameter specialization may be against comparative advantage. Indeed it may be shown that an economy may increase the probability of the free trade regime by specializing against comparative advantage. Moreover, if the probability of trade is endogenous and its level is comparable to that in the exogenous case we should expect a lower optimal point of trade in the endogenous case. The more the economy trades the more likely trade distortion becomes.

Note that gains from trade do still exist if the endogeneity of trade disruption forces an economy to specialize against its comparative advantage, even though the gains of trade will be substantially below the level that is reached in a deterministic setting. Moreover even when such a perverse pattern of specialization occurs in the production pattern, exports will continue to be of the comparative advantage type. Hence the model of endogenous trade uncertainty does not affect the analytical use that one can make of comparative advantage to explain the direction of trade flows. Endogenous trade uncertainty, however, makes the traditional tool of comparative advantage less able to explain the existence of international trade.

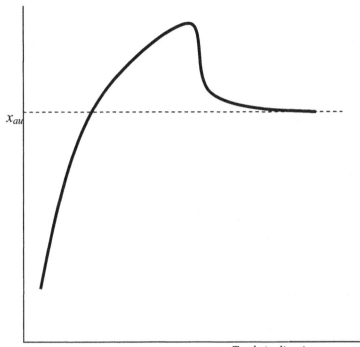

Trade inclination parameter

Source: Marrewijk and Bergeijk (1993, Figure 3, p. 692)

Figure 3.4 Optimal specialization and trade inclination parameter

The upshot is that comparative advantage *per se* is not sufficient to explain international trade. In other words, trade uncertainty destroys potential international exchanges that would be mutual advantageous for the countries concerned.

Dynamics

The comparative static analysis allowed us to uncover the gains from trade and the *ex ante* extent of specialization that is optimal given the existing extent of uncertainty about the trade regime. In a dynamic analysis the model acknowledges that international trade can take place while changing the pattern of specialization over time.

The economy can at time T remain in the autarky production point but will still achieve a superior level of utility in point N *in* Figure 3.1 (note that this is why in Figure 3.2 $f(x_{au}){>}g(x_{au})$). The free trade point can only be attained, however, when the economy *moves* from A to F in Figure 3.1 (the production point *moves* from A to D) and increasingly trades internationally until finally the maximum trade volume is reached. Such movements are costly and take time as the factors of production have to be reallocated between sectors. The resulting dynamic adjustment path is illustrated in Figure 3.5, where utility levels u_A, u_N and u_F refer to the indifference curves C_2, C_3 and C_4, respectively (see Figure 3.1 for the derivation of the latter).

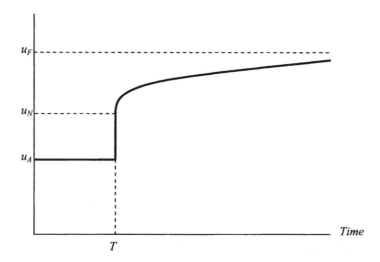

Figure 3.5 Time path of utility (economy moves from autarky to free trade)

The occurrence of trade disruption is not the mirror image of the movement from autarky to free trade, essentially because an internationally trading economy will be specialized to some extent. A complete disruption of trade implies that a fully specialized economy will fall back to D in Figure 3.1 (where consumption is on the indifference curve C_1 with utility u_D well below the autarky point). With the passages of time the economy again adjusts and utility increases. Ultimately the economy reaches the autarky utility level u_A as illustrated in Figure 3.6.

This particular time path is documented in both *ex ante* and *ex post* empirical analyses of individual cases of trade disruption. Firstly, in the short term a substantial drop in output can be expected that may actually exceed the original reduction of trade significantly. Khan (1988, p. 136), for example, uses a Social Accounting Matrix for South Africa to calculate that a decline in exports by $1 million leads to a reduction of output by $3 million. So a drop of utility in a trading economy to a level below the utility that can be reached in autarky is by no means a theoretical mirage. Secondly, the time path that is illustrated in Figure 3.6 suggests that after the first-period cool down, import substitution takes off and may actually lead to higher annual rates of output growth than experienced before the trade disruption occurred. The UK-led sanctions against former Rhodesia in 1966 may have been a case in point, as the Rhodesian growth rate reached almost 6%, thus illustrating that the so-called infant-industry argument may be relevant in the context of international sanctions (see Bornstein 1968; Hermele and Odén 1988). Of course, it is by no means certain that such textbook developments will actually occur in real world cases, but the examples at least merit further consideration of their implications in a policy context.

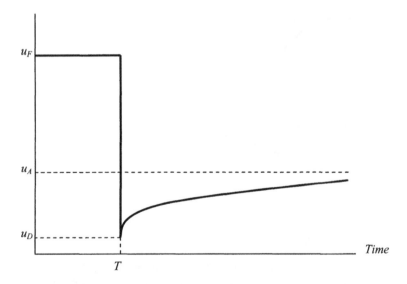

Figure 3.6 Time path of utility (economy disrupted from free trade to autarky)

Anticipation

Another potentially relevant issue is that the government of this economy may anticipate the occurrence of future trade disruption and react by stockpiling or by other policies aimed at reducing its vulnerability to foreign pressure.

Typically, the intention to apply economic sanctions is announced before these measures are implemented. This may happen explicitly, but the threat may also be implicit as it is communicated through the motions in international organizations that establish – in an international diplomatic framework – the threat to or breach of peace that constitutes the legal basis for boycotts and embargoes. Thus typically anticipation is possible so that the extent of specialization may be an instrument for the target economy to reduce its vulnerability, a case that is portrayed in Figure 3.7.

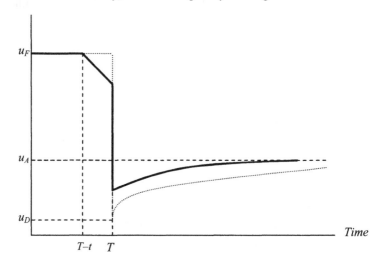

Figure 3.7 Anticipation of trade disruption

At time $T-t$ the economy anticipates trade disruption and starts to adjust at the expense of a lower level of utility until time T. However, giving up some of the benefits of free trade appears to be quite rational since the drop in utility at time T is substantially less than the reduction in welfare illustrated in Figure 3.6 and the economy also returns quicker in the autarky equilibrium point (another alternative may be to specialize against comparative advantage as discussed earlier).

The main message of Figure 3.7 is that the threat of potential trade disruption will probably lead to a lesser extent of specialization in accordance with comparative advantage

Political Economy

It is by no means accidental that the previous sections derived practical examples from the application of negative economic sanctions. Trade disruption does not occur often. (Incidentally, opening up to trade is also a relatively unique phenomenon and the debate on its economic impact still rages as we will see in Chapter 4 and so few testing grounds exist for the time path that is described in Figure 3.5). Typically, trade is halted only in rather extreme situations, for example, during macroeconomic breakdowns or currency crises, or when international exchange might spread acute problems to other countries (such as contagious diseases, dangerous materials and terrorist activities) or when large political disputes occur (for example, when a war is threatening). In this spectrum of possible situations that may disrupt trade, negative economic sanctions occur with a relative high frequency. It thus pays to consider sanctions as a source for learning more about both the impact and the management of trade disruption. Indeed, cases of 'inverted trade liberalization' may give a lot of information about the gains from trade that emerge when an economy opens up to international trade.

From this perspective understanding the time path of utility is important. Figure 3.6, for example, showed a substantial decrease in utility, but once 'the bottom has been hit' at time T, only positive growth rates occur and this may provide the population of this economy with a positive connotation even though the end value of utility in this case is and remains well below that of the free trade equilibrium. Figure 3.7 showed a smaller drop at T so that the perception of the population will be that the economy was less hard hit (even though clearly upfront costs were incurred between $T–t$ and T) and as in Figure 3.6 we see positive growth rates afterwards.

The policy implications are that the imposition of economic sanctions should be quick and unexpected and that the passage of time reduces the chance that a sanction will succeed. Indeed, in this regard Dekker's (1973, p. 396) observation is relevant that the welfare loss of a negative sanction should be sudden and unexpected in order to prevent the target population from becoming, as it were, conditioned to make ever-increasing sacrifices.

3 CONCLUSIONS: HOW TO REDUCE TRADE UNCERTAINTY

Introducing uncertainty with respect to the trade volume in a traditional neoclassical trade model for a small open economy yields less specialization in accordance with (and perhaps even against) comparative advantage and hence to a reduction of international trading opportunities and global welfare.

This result is independent of both the number of goods that are considered in the analysis, the extent to which economic decision making has been centralized or decentralized or the question of whether this uncertainty is exogenous (that is 'systemic') or endogenous ('trade volume-related').

From the present analysis several general conclusions emerge with respect to economic diplomacy, trade and commercial policy. A first conclusion is that in the decentralized private market economy government intervention *could* improve on welfare by co-ordinating economic decisions whenever uncertainty exists with respect to the future trading climate. Trade uncertainty is a market distortion and public intervention is thus legitimate provided that the benefits of co-ordination (that is removing this distortion) exceed the costs of public actions and instruments. It is important to note that a general argument based on endogenous trade uncertainty and the deployment of the incentives such as quantity controls, border taxes or subsidies can in practice hardly be distinguished empirically from trade interventionism which is guided by the 'new trade theory' proposed by Krugman, Helpman and Razin, and so on.[10] This is especially the case when endogenous trade uncertainty is a consequence of commercial activities by foreign competitors on the world market and addressed in a bilateral framework. The upshot is, firstly, that measures to reduce the externalities of trade uncertainty may often be perceived as protectionist measures; secondly, that proposed measures should be analysed empirically in order to establish that they actually work and; thirdly that a cost-benefit analysis is appropriate to establish that the cost of solving the market failure do not exceed the benefits of reduced trade uncertainty.

So the second conclusion from this chapter is that first-best government action therefore should be aimed at reducing uncertainty *per se*, possibly through WTO membership, strict adherence to conflict settlement procedures or other instruments of economic diplomacy that aim at increasing trust in free trade. Indeed, such policies tackle the source of the problem from which the uncertainty externality arose in the first place. It may be especially relevant for small countries as the WTO seeks to protect their interests in open and multilateral trade against the (market) power of the large economies. Indeed, if international politics were to resort to economic warfare and economic surveillance more often, this would impose substantial costs on the world economic system.

The point to take home from this chapter thus is that trade uncertainty is an additional argument to strive for greater security for trade and so this chapter supports efforts to arrive at an open multilateral trading system, guided by WTO rules as a clear commitment to free trade.

NOTES

[1] The models in this chapter reflect earlier contributions to the literature and are based on Bhagwati and Srinivasan (1976, 1982), Arad and Hillman (1979), Marrewijk and Bergeijk (1990) and Bergeijk and Marrewijk (1995).

[2] I reserve 'autarky' for a country that *freely* chooses not to engage in free trade.

[3] Outside A the market mechanism pushes production and consumption toward the autarky point. Take, for example, point D, where the rate of transformation is p_w, which is unequal to the marginal rate of substitution: consumers are willing to exchange y for x. Hence the price of x in this economy increases. The production patter will adjust and more x will be produced until prices settle at p_A in A.

[4] One may imagine a centrally planned economy or a market economy in which some sort of institution, for example by means of taxes and/or subsidies, provides the incentives to market participants that induce the optimal production and consumption pattern. Obviously, this implies an enormous information requirement for the unitary actor and it may not be reasonable to assume that the information is available at he detailed level and speed that is required by the model. We do not dwell on this problem, but simply assume that the information requirements are being met, not so much because these are realistic assumptions, but simply because it does not really matter since our goal is rather modest. We will sketch two extreme situations in order to clarify the mechanism by which different institutional settings (or manners of economic policy making) are responsible for empirically observed differences in trade–conflict patterns

[5] Actually, all one needs is strict concavity of the (indirect) utility functions, since both the free trade and the no-trade equilibrium points are globally stable.

[6] See the Appendix to Marrewijk and Bergeijk (1990).

[7] Note that the assumption of identical subjective probabilities for households and firms can easily be relaxed. This assumption is used here, in order to show that differences in outcomes are due to differences in the decision process and not to heterogeneity with regard to the attitudes towards risk in the sectors of the economy.

[8] Marrewijk (1992) shows that this sub-optimality is neither caused by a lack of stock market (as suggested by Diamond 1967 and Helpman and Razin 1978) nor by different attitudes towards risk of firms and consumers. This sub-optimality results directly from the choice of the numéraire; a small 'two-step' market economy that maximizes expected revenue over-produces the non-numéraire good.

[9] Consider, for example, an embargo. Such sanctions will generally speaking not be effective as we will see in Chapter 6 unless the target's foreign trade exceeds a certain threshold level so that low levels of trade will be associated with low probabilities of trade disruption (see, however, Helpman 1987 for a contrary opinion).

[10] See Bergeijk and Kabel (1993) on the strategic trade literature and Dixit (1990) for a critical evaluation of proposed government interventions when private firms fail to deal with trade uncertainty (for example due to unobservability of individual actions, outcomes and characteristics). Indeed according to Dixit (1990, p. 18) trade taxes and subsidies are justified 'only if a transaction were to affect π by its inherent cross-border nature'.

PART II

Economic Diplomacy and Commercial Policy

4. Commercial Policy and Economic Diplomacy: Why?

It is worthwhile to always be critical about the role of the government when international economic relations are concerned. A long history of misguided stimuli, preferential treatments of exports and protectionism warrant an attitude in which disbelieve and anti-dogmatic thinking are key competences. The roots of many export promoting ideas and policies lay in the Mercantilist approach of which Law (1705) and Cantillon (1755) are well known early examples. In a nutshell Mercantilism can be seen as a set of beliefs and policy prescriptions that maximize the surplus on the balance of trade in order to earn the means that are deemed necessary for warfare (Schumpeter 1954, pp. 364–7). A key element of this theory is the vision on trade as a zero sum game which implies that surpluses on one's trade balance are to the detriment of other countries and thus reduce their capacity to arm themselves and wage war and *vice versa*. A key exponent is the French interventionist set of policies called Colbertism. Around the middle of the seventeenth century Colbert repeatedly argued that trade is the income source *par excellence* for the government that wants to wage a war. Colbert saw the power of England and the Netherlands around 1670 as fully dependent on their commercial success. Thus he was willing to meet his opponents on the international markets – with state companies and all available interventionist instruments – which led to commercial clashed. Indeed, trade wars had a strong military component in those years.[1] Modern theories such as 'strategic trade theories' are often rather neo-mercantilist in nature. Setting aside, however, the geopolitical and power considerations, export promotion is and remains an important issue even for modern policy makers that (in the words of Greenaway and Kneller, 2004, p. 359):

> see promoting export as a good thing. They connect it with exploiting comparative advantage (probably unconsciously) and link it to export-led growth (almost certainly consciously). But what is the evidence for this?

Indeed, also when discussing the impact of commercial policy on trade and investment flows one has to be on guard. As we learned in Chapter 1 from the discussion of the Methuen Treaty, the issue was not whether bilateral trade between Portugal and England increased, but that it did so at the detriment of trade with other countries. The point here is not that the removal of a distortion changes the pattern of trade and that some trade partners will win and some others will lose. Rather the argument is that efficient producers should not be replaced by inefficient producers. Thus it is elementary that the analysis considers the issue of whether commercial policy and economic diplomacy create trade (in which case total welfare at the global level increases as does the volume of world trade) or that trade is mainly diverted (and possibly in the wrong direction). If trade is diverted then the trade economist should be on the alert. Basically an activity that diverts trade can be counteracted by the same sort of activity of another country. Such a race of instruments constitutes a threat to efficiency and may resemble international lobbying thus constituting an example of what Bhagwati and Srinivasan (1982) have coined directly unproductive profit seeking (DUP) activities. DUP activities dupe: they generate shifts in income and profit at the expense of productive inputs at the world scale.

Indeed, *a priori* firms can be expected to enter foreign markets on their own account and if they have to be aided by governments – then, perhaps their products are just not good enough. If so the tax payer's money that ultimately finances commercial policy and economic diplomacy is wasted, just as in the case of a traditional export subsidy. When the government offers an export subsidy, shippers will export the good up to the point where the domestic price exceeds the foreign price by the amount of the subsidy. In the exporting country, consumers are hurt, producers gain and the government loses because it must spend money on the subsidy. However, there is an additional terms of trade loss because the price in the importing country falls, while the price in the exporting country increases. Also from this perspective it is quite understandable that economists are very suspicious about commercial policy and economic diplomacy, which after all imply a transfer (for example a free service) from the public sector to commercial activities while it is *a priori* unclear if the private benefits exceed the cost of providing the public service. Still economic diplomacy and commercial policy remain relevant real world phenomena. Is this because the economic recipe is wrong, or is this just an other case of economists that are right but are unable to get it right?

Anyhow, with these caveats in mind we can take a closer look at the economic arguments that have been put to the fore for economic diplomacy and commercial policy from a welfare theoretic point of view. First we will take a look at the perceived benefits of stronger international economic relations as these must be the motivating forces for any kind of commercial policy and economic diplomacy. These benefits may arise at the macro-economic level, that is through trade's impact on GDP and/or its growth rate, but the effects should also exist at the microeconomic level. The second section then investigates whether a rationale exists that justifies government involvement. We will be concerned with the major market failures, in particular with those market failures that generate border effects (that is that make domestic markets and foreign markets different) and that cannot be fixed by simply relying on market dynamics. Also we will see what policies have been used to overcome border effects and to repair market failures. Here it will be important that one type of 'bad' (market failure) is not replaced by another 'bad' (government failure). Next we move to the empirical literature on three instruments of commercial policies and bilateral economic diplomacy (the foreign service, state visits and export promotion) in order to provide some background for our econometric investigation in the next chapter.

1 BENEFITS OF TRADE

The argument for more international trade is compelling. International specialization increases welfare. International competition increases efficiency and dynamism of the economy. It is true that due to an increase in international trade some will lose, but losing sectors and factors of production can be compensated as the overall welfare gains on balance are positive. Empirical research overwhelmingly shows that the benefits of trade are significant and substantial.[2]

Macroeconomic Benefits

In the 1990s studies by Frankel and Romer (1996) and Sachs and Warner (1995) uncovered a substantial impact of trade openness on GDP. Frankel and Romer (1996) estimated a 2% increase in the level of GDP. Sachs and Warner (1995) even found a significant impact in growth regressions for the years 1970–89 in the order of magnitude of 2% *per annum* (see also Dollar 1992 for comparable findings for a group of 95 developing countries in the years 1976–85) These results were criticized by Rodriguez and Rodrik (2000) amongst others because free trade and other 'good policies' tend to correlate so that it is difficult to find out the exact contribution of international trade.[3] Indeed, the findings of Sachs and Warner appear to have been a bit of an overestimate of the effect of openness on growth since recent studies find a more modest impact.

Table 4.1 lists a number of relevant findings. Of particular relevance is the review of the empirical literature on the trade–growth nexus by Lewer and van den Berg (2003). Lewer and van den Berg analyse 246 cross-section regressions and 596 time series regressions that were reported in 83 econometric studies that were published in scientific journals over the years 1960–2002. The studies deploy many theoretical models and econometric techniques, but despite these differences the studies *grosso modo* agree that the relationship between growth and trade is positive: deploying a 95% confidence interval this happens in 85% of the 848 regressions. On the basis of the point estimates the studies on average yield a consensus view that a 1 percentage point increase in multilateral trade linkage (that is exports and imports in per cent of GDP) on average increases annual long-run growth by 0.2 percentage points. The exception to this consensus are the 19 studies that find almost double this effect in a category of models that follow the framework developed by Feder (1982) who takes into account that the export sector is more productive and that trade generates externalities.

Table 4.1 Impact of a 1 percentage point increase in multilateral trade linkage on annual long-run GDP growth

Study	Period	N	Effect
Italianer (1994)	1961–92	EU-6	0.2%
Wacziarg et al. (2003)	1970–99	141	0.1%
Lewer et al. (2003)	1960–2002	83	0.2%

One may doubt the validity of the implicit argument that openness will continue to increase growth. Assume a world consisting of two countries. Unite these two countries by way of experiment. Is a permanent increase in the rate of growth logical (there is now perfect openness)? Or is a decrease of economic growth the logical consequence (note that international trade now becomes zero)? It would indeed seem reasonable to assume that the impact of openness is on the level of GDP, rather than on the growth rate of GDP. For one thing diminishing returns would seem logical.

An interesting feature of the literature is that the effect of further trade liberalization (as distinct from the effects of further increases in trade and investment) seems to wane off and disappear from the data – at least it is increasingly difficult to distil evidence from the data. Wacziarg and Horn-Welch (2003) investigated and updated the earlier findings of Sachs and Warner and found that their results break down completely for the period 1990–98, although the within-country growth regressions continue to yield significant positive effects of trade on long-run growth, as shown in Table 4.1. Wacziarg and Horn-Welch explain their findings by pointing out that a simple dichotomous indicator of openness will no longer be able to discriminate in a cross-country setting because policy openness differs through time and between countries and thus more nuance is needed, for example, measurement by a continuous variable of openness would be more appropriate.[4] This finding is echoed in other studies as well.[5] Generally speaking non-trade instruments appear to have become more relevant for changes in the levels of export and import. An example is Nicoletti et al. (2003) who find for the OECD in the years 1980–2000 that national regulations are more important than bilateral tariffs and FDI restrictions (Figure 4.1).[6] Indeed, the combined impact of regulation in the domestic market and in partner countries would seem to exceed that of the combined effects of the barriers to trade and invest that traditionally used to be the focal point of trade negotiations.

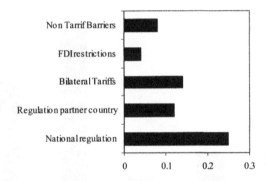

Source: Based on Nicoletti et al. 2003

Figure 4.1 Elasticity of trade with respect to a decrease of policy variables

The strength of other non-traditional determinants of competitiveness and trade volumes could be the logical consequence of the progress that has been made through the World Trade Organisation and its predecessor the General Agreement on Tariffs and Trade in reducing those formal trade barriers. Tariffs for selected GATT/WTO members, for example, have been reduced by a third in each of the multilateral trade negotiations between 1968 and 1999 (World Trade Organisation 2007, p. 207). The shift in weight between the well-known formal trade barriers and the less visible and less well defined non traditional trade resistance factors may, however, also have been induced by the fact that the (relative) importance of other trade hindering factors (possibly including cultural distance or political frictions) has increased – as argued in Chapter 1 (compare Table 1.4). Anyhow, whatever instrument is needed to achieve stronger multilateral trade linkage, the benefits from trade are important at the macro-economic level and may increase growth rates over the medium term by some 10 to 20 basis points.

Microeconomic Benefits

Also at the microeconomic level the benefits from trade may motivate public interest in trade and foreign investment as recent micro-data studies into the heterogeneity of firms uncover for many countries a positive correlation between productivity at the firm level and the extent of internationalization of the company. Firms that export, import, invest or have a head office in an other country are more productive, larger, do more research and development, have a higher survival rate and pay better wages than firms that are only connected to local markets.

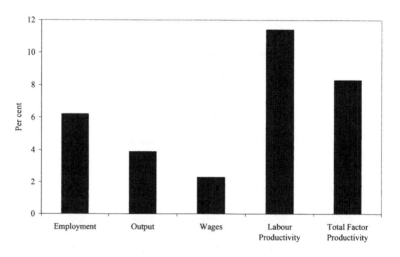

Source: Greenaway and Kneller 2004, p. 360, Table 1, column 3

Figure 4.2 Export premium in per cent (United Kingdom)

Figure 4.2 shows representative findings for the export premium by Greenaway and Kneller (2004) for the UK. The reported components of the export premium show how much better exporters perform than non-exporters. The findings are statistically significant at the 95% confidence level and better, notably also after corrections for determinants other that the exporting decision (such as time effects, capital intensity, industry and/or structure effects and scale) so that the comparison is more accurate than comparisons of simple means of the respective sub-populations of firms.

Since productivity is the key driver for welfare, the case for government stimulation of trade and direct investment would seem to be obvious and straight-forward, but whereas the correlation between openness and performance is robust, the mechanism and especially the causality are not yet well understood at the microeconomic level. Do firms learn as they export and invest abroad and do they become more productive due to this learning? Or do firms need to be more productive before they can take the risk and make the investment in knowledge and networks that is required to enter foreign markets? – a question first asked at the micro level by Bernard and Jensen (1999). If the latter is the case – and although the jury is still out, the empirical micro-study evidence appears to be tilting in that direction[7] – we will observe that firms self-select and all policies aimed at stimulating firms to internationalize could be a waste of taxpayer money. Greenaway and Kneller (2007, p.430) suggest that this result should be conditioned on the actual scope for learning: 'For example, the entry effect might be smaller if exposure to trade is already high, or the gap to the technology frontier is small.'[8] Another post-entry effect, that relatively recently has been investigated for the first time by Aw et al. (2008) pertains to increases in R&D and profitability. Still the main conclusion from the micro-data remains valid: firms that do not self-select probably are not sufficiently productive to pass the hurdle of sunk costs that need to be made to enter foreign markets.

The policy conclusion that follows from the observed firm heterogeneity, however, clearly is not that internationalization does not pay off. The message of the new literature on firm heterogeneity is that a one-size-fits-all approach is probably not productive and that selection criteria based on economic performance and a realistic assessment of potential success should be applied before firms are allowed to enter costly export promotion activities. Moreover, the question would seem to arise where the macroeconomic welfare derives from if firms do not become more productive while they internationalize their commercial activities. This micro–macro paradox of international economics can be reconciled when we consider the effects of industry restructuring, that is that more productive firms drive out less productive firms. This adjustment process to globalization and its impact on Total Factor Productivity (TFP) plays an important role in recent theoretical models (Melitz 2003, and for a more elaborate analysis that in addition shows that the effects are stronger in sectors with comparative advantages: Bernard et al. 2008), but the empirical evidence is in a preliminary state and to date best characterized as 'mixed'. For example, whereas Baldwin and Gu (2004) report that a fifth of TFP growth in Canada is related to industry restructuring that is induced by international trade and Bernard and Jensen (2004a) for the US arrive at an estimate of 40% for TFP growth that is induced by globalization-related restructuring, Marinov et al. (2008), do not find any empirical support in France for the key hypotheses and conclude that the model needs further refining.

Still this may be a very powerful mechanism as illustrated by Figure 4.3 that by way of illustration provides a picture of a decade of restructuring in the Netherlands: since 1995 employment and productivity have consistently grown in the international sector weeding out other firms that after the year 2000 employ less people even though their productivity has continued to increase too – although at a lower rate of growth. (Note that an alternative explanation could be that the most productive firms were targeted by foreign direct investment.)

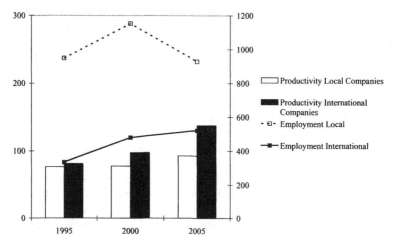

Source: CBS Statistics Netherlands

Figure 4.3 Development of employment (right axis) and labour productivity
(left axis) for Dutch locally operating firms and international
firms in the Netherlands (1995–2005)

These findings have two important implications for policy. Firstly, since structural change and adjustment are the key mechanisms for generating productivity growth, flexibility of institutions and the economy are elementary while at the same time credibility of policies and stability of the macroeconomic environment are very important (Bergeijk and Haffner 1996). Thus policy should ensure that labour, product and capital markets function well, that relative prices (including the wages) reflect opportunities and scarcity, that budget constraints are hard, that the population is well educated and that schooling continues so as to provide the skills and flexibility to move within and across industries. These would seem to be necessary policy requirements. It is worth noting that whereas traditional trade theory focussed on mobility across industries, the new literature finds larger within sector dynamism and mobility (especially in the sectors with comparative advantage). Thus the perspective on labour mobility has to change. Typically, policy makers were thinking about re-education and regional economic policies to address problems of decaying industries. The key insight of the new theories is that people will be working for larger numbers of different firms in the course of their working life and if so problems related to the housing market and portability of pensions become more relevant. Indeed such 'new barriers to mobility' have to be given more attention in order to be able to increase labour productivity.

Secondly, government might want to facilitate the process of restructuring by encouraging internationalization of commercial activities. If so it is noteworthy that the benefits of more trade cannot – at least not to the full – be reaped unless the necessary pre-conditions are met. Indeed, Hoekman et al. (2004, p. 3) are right when they argue that many policies that could be implemented to facilitate the business sector's adjustment

> are [of] second order relative to ensuring a stable macroeconomic environment and an institutional infrastructure that supports the functioning of modern markets in general.

With this caveat in mind, let's turn to the things that make international trade such a relative rare activity in the population of firms.

2 BORDER EFFECTS AND MARKET FAILURES

One of the main reasons to think harder about economic diplomacy and the distance puzzle that features in applied trade analyses is the continued existence of huge border effects. A key study is McCallum (1995) who found that a national border (between the US and Canada) reduced trade flows by a factor 22. This finding stimulated an enormous amount of research. Part of the border puzzle has been solved, in particular after the seminal study by Anderson and van Wincoop (2003). Head and Mayer (2007), for example, show for the US and for Europe that measurement errors regarding distances increase the estimated border effects by 50 to 100%. Likewise Straathof (2008) solves a mathematical problem surrounding the linearized approximation in Anderson and van Wincoop (2003). The key messages from such corrections are, however, that these border effects remain significant and relevant even when distances are measured with appropriate exactness.

This leaves us with one obvious potential explanation, namely that unconventional barriers may exist, for example insufficient knowledge about foreign markets and/or ways to get access to those markets. Krautheim (2007) provides an interesting model that analyses how the fixed upfront costs of exporting can be reduced through the creation of informational networks. The number of internationally trading firms is endogenous and depends on the variable trade costs and is, moreover, related to the available knowledge about foreign markets. One merit of the model is that it suggests a solution to the distance puzzle since in this set-up the fixed costs of exporting are endogenously increasing in trade.

Another issue that is highlighted is that improvement and enlargement of networks over time reduce border effects. In this model the government could reduce costs of exporting by stimulation the number of exporters (the so-called extensive margin), although the effect may be a relative concentration of the geographic trade pattern on nearby markets (*cf* our discussion in section 3 of Chapter 1, especially Figure 1.2 and Table 1.5). It would perhaps be sensible to do so, because Krautheim's model highlights that the sunk cost investment in knowledge about foreign markets may have some characteristics of a public good with external effects that are not reaped by individual firms and for that reason, investment in such knowledge may be sub-optimal.

It is important to see that the decision to export is quite exceptional: most firms do not export even when their productivity level would in principle be high enough to be able to meet the international markets and may thus reflect extreme risk aversion (driven by financial tightness, low quality management or product attributes). One key issue is that generally speaking we do not know much about these issues, as stressed by Bernard and Wagner (2001, p. 122) when they point out that

> ... an important area for future research is the measurement of the various components of sunk costs of export entry and the extent to which they take on the characteristics of public goods.

Given the present state of our empirical knowledge, caution is warranted. Before government intervention is to be invoked we should be sure that public sector involvement is both justified and cost efficient. The justification for government intervention ultimately is the existence of a market failure, that is a situation where the free market does not generate an efficient allocation of goods and services. Typically market failures arise due to market power, the occurrence of externalities and situations that are characterized by transaction costs, agency problems, information asymmetries and ill-defined or difficult to enforce property rights.

Incidentally, it is noteworthy that international trade can be a strong antidote against market failures based on (the abuse of) market power – the so-called competition effect. This is relevant if domestic demand is characterized by (near) monopsony so that external demand can reduce buyer power or if domestic supply is characterized by (near) monopoly in which case import competition can reduce distortions. These co-benefits of free trade are generally speaking not considered in the debate about market failures and commercial policy and economic diplomacy since it is not the considered government intervention that solves the problem of malfunctioning domestic markets, but rather the firms in other countries. Moreover, more direct means are available to policy makers, such as vigorous competition policy.[9]

The existence of a market failure is, however, a necessary but never a sufficient condition, as noted by Hoekman et al. (2004, p. 3):

> Pro-active support policies of whatever stripe should be subject to cost-benefit analysis and be informed by answers to the following types of questions: where is the market failure? What is the objective of a policy? How is the performance and cost effectiveness going to be monitored? It should also be recognized that such interventions are frequently associated with the risk of misdiagnosing the problem and the possibility of capture by rent seekers.

The government intervention should in addition generate more benefits than costs (including the distortions introduced by taxation). Indeed, mostly an imperfect market outcome is to be preferred to government failures. Moreover, markets may generate positive and negative market failures. In the case of international trade it may thus be relevant to consider the negative externality for the environment resulting from transportation and the positive externality of more efficiency which could result in a better and more eco-friendly use of scarce resources (Bergeijk 1991). These caveats should always be kept in mind when one has to consider actual proposals for policy intervention.

Now, how do these market failures explain border effects and to what extent do they appear to justify commercial diplomacy and/or economic diplomacy? A great many potential market failures have been considered in the context of international trade and investment (overviews are provided by Harris and Robertson, 2001, Harris and Li, 2005, and Alexander and Warwick, 2007). Let's consider the most relevant of these market failures and the possible policy responses in some more detail.

Information Barriers, Network Effects and Externalities

An exporter needs a lot of information about foreign markets before he can successfully attempt to export to a country. Sometimes this information is acquired experimentally by trying to enter the country, but often consultants and business trips as well as information from export promotion agencies or colleagues will be tapped. [10]

The relevant topics about which firms typically need information include:

- local consumer preferences and their ability to adapt to new products *c.q.* the need to adapt products and their marketing to local needs (including language, technical and meteorological, religious and cultural aspects);
- the reliability of local trading partners, that is the opportunities to establish long-term relationships which may include customs as well as laws and legal procedures;
- the distribution networks that exist or can be developed (which typically also involve the availability of modern communication networks, harbour facilities and so on);
- quality standards and legal, environmental and institutional requirements;
- prospects for markets, in particular the niches and products where profit opportunities exists; and
- the local negotiating and contracting procedures as well as the extent to which contracts are actually enforced.

Each of these elements makes international trade different from domestic trade and may thus constitute a border effect. Indeed this is probably why cultural and institutional barriers are increasingly found to be significant trade resistant factors as we discussed in Chapter 1.

As a general rule, the necessary information requires substantial investment (even when acquired on a trial and error basis) and will be imperfect in nature. Often such manner of information has an asymmetric character; because the firms in the importing country have a substantial advantage in both acquiring and developing such country-specific knowledge and in assessing the reliability of such information. Typically, this manner of knowledge is built in networks of foreign firms (because proximity and existing business and personal networks are often a pre-condition), but such networks may also act as a barrier to entrée. Moreover, investing in better knowledge does not take place in the private sector because of externalities (such as demonstration effects that can be followed suit by competitors), free rider problems or due to the public good character of certain manner of information, which according to Harris and Li (2005, p. 74) include:

> unique, reliable and impartial access to information, such as through the global embassy network and other government channels and contacts, which become available through the government's very long-term, and non-commercial attachment to overseas markets.

The relevant rationale for government intervention, that is an active role in the generation of knowledge or the allocation of subsidies to investments in such knowledge, rests on the fact that the production of knowledge about foreign markets will be sub-optimal and that access to such knowledge in some cases actually requires involvement of government officials. Indeed, if such learning externalities do exist then the market does not supply the optimal investment of firms in international activities basically because expropriability problems exist. Therefore financial and non-financial incentives can help to extend international development of markets and risk taking (Hoekman et al. 2004, p.16).

Governments moreover have an other role to play, for example, in signalling the quality of its exporters. Generally speaking they can clarify that their firms have to meet high standards in terms of product quality, environmental standards, corporate responsibility and, moreover, they may be able to communicate that their economy is a reliable partner in international trade. Such promotional information may be seen as an investment in the exporting nation's trademark or 'trade capital' and as such has a public good character.

Financial Barriers

Financial markets may fail because a situation exists in which the exporter's bank is unable to assess the risk of an export project to countries where it has no foreign branches. Alternatively, banks in the importing country may be unwilling to lend to this exporter because the collateral is in the exporting country, or such banks may simply not exist or be cash-constrained. In these cases markets appear to be missing and the government may want to step in to solve this failure so that profitable exchanges can take place. This is, however, not a clear case of economic diplomacy solving a market failure since the problems typically are relevant for small and medium enterprises on the domestic market as well and general policies aimed at their problems in raising capital will be more appropriate. Moreover, this problem arises from the specifics of the banking market and other government instruments (for example competition policy) may be more appropriate and no role would seem to exist for bilateral economic diplomacy.

The case of capital market imperfections is, however, not that clear cut. It is, for example, important to consider that capital market distortions may arise from several causes. The political risk of the country where the trading partner is located may be very high and this will represent an important hidden transaction cost. This is relevant because the private sector is unable to cover all risks related to exporting. In particular the so-called country risk, that is a default by the whole country, will not be covered due to the inherent political nature of debt repudiation. A system of publicly guaranteed export credits will reduce this kind of friction that significantly impedes international trade (Moser et al., 2006). Clearly such export credits help to tilt the export decision of firms and are especially relevant for export destinations in newly emerging economies and the developing countries. The funds that are available for officially insured credits may thus especially benefit these countries. Differentiation with regard to countries or sectors appears to be difficult. The use of insurance schemes as some sort of hidden export subsidies (through *premia* that do not cover the losses in the long run) has become virtually impossible since 1995 when the WTO Agreement on Subsidies and Countervailing Measures came into force; this *inter alia* is also an outcome for economic diplomacy (Dewit 2001). Export credit would thus not seem to be an instrument of economic diplomacy since it does not allow for the selection of a specific country. The point, however, is that an export credit scheme may be a necessary condition for bilateral economic diplomacy and commercial policy because market entrée may be impossible in countries in early phases of development without this instrument. Economic diplomacy, moreover, may be important to reduce this barrier as well, for example by engineering investment protection agreements or by increasing mutual trust.

Do Governments Have a Role?

Some of these market failures may at least partially explain the existence of observed border effects, but do not seem to belong to the domain of bilateral economic diplomacy proper. Rather the policy recipe would seem to be to directly address the market failures that hinder firms when they want to export, import or invest in international markets (*cf.* Alexander and Warwick, 2007, p. 180).

Still market failures appear to exist that may justify at least some extent of government intervention. This is particular the case whenever the generation of knowledge is involved. Here the obvious analogy is the case of innovation and research and development. In addition, the government may have a role to play when first mover advantages appear to be relevant in newly emerging markets where the public sector is still dominant. Indeed, here strategic trade policy considerations may be relevant: to enable market access in an early phase of a high risk but fast growing market government may have to bear the risk and take and support initiatives (see, for example, Krugman 1996). In this particular case the game may be of a zero sum nature, but it would not be purely predatory since the world economic system obviously would benefit from early established commercial relationships with new entrants.

3 NETWORKING ABROAD: EMPIRICAL FINDINGS

The previous section stressed the importance of networks and the initiating role of the public sector with respect to the new players in the world economy. Typically the state interacts with other states through a network of embassies and consulates (which provide so to say the infrastructure for exchange) and through state and other official visits and this is the topic on which we will focus in this chapter.

International interaction also takes place at the level of civilians (tourism, migration) and entrepreneurs (who may also set up affiliates and travel), but these atomistic activities are not the focus of this book although they are important numerically. Neither are we concerned with digital exchange, that is the Internet. Attempts have been made to digitalize such interactions and virtual missions have at least been (alas: unsuccessfully) tried between a number of OECD countries. Several studies show that interaction has to be personal and direct at least in the crucial stage of setting up a business or developing a plan. Leamer (2007) convincingly makes this point: presumably 'I love you' works better in person than digitalized. Anyhow, the remainder of this chapter will review empirical analyses of concrete networks of bilateral economic diplomacy. The next chapter will investigate empirically whether such networks exert a measurable and significant influence on bilateral trade flows and thus will provide the 'proof of the pudding'.

Embassies and Consulates

Embassies and consulates may be of interest for two distinct reasons. Firstly, good political relations reduce the risk of future distortions and trade disruptions. Secondly, embassies and consulates help to generate knowledge about (future) opportunities for trade and investment and thus may add to the stock of knowledge of foreign markets which – if shared with (potential) exporters – reduces the costs that have to be incurred for exporting to and investing in these markets. Summary (1989) was the first to show a correlation between diplomats and trade for the US exports, but Rose (2007) provides the first empirical investigation for a large number of countries into the question whether exports are in fact systematically associated with the number of diplomatic representations abroad.[11] Rose uses a gravity model for the year 2002 for 22 exporting countries and 220 export destinations and asks the question whether there is 'any room left over in the residual for the presence and number of foreign missions'.[12] The first data column of Table 4.2 reports the estimated co-efficients of this gravity equation with a significant value of 0.10 for the co-efficient of interest (that is of the number of embassies and consulates).

*Table 4.2 Results of gravity equations that include the number of embassies
and consulates amongst the explanatory variables*

Study	Rose (2007)	Yakop and Bergeijk (2007)		
		Replication	Restricted	Unrestricted
Number of exporters	22	22	63	63
Number of destinations	220	63	63	63
Number of observations	4123	1356	3730	3730
Year of observation	2002	2006	2006	2006
Embassies and consulates	$0.10^\$$	$0.06^\$$	n.a.	$0.09^\$$
	(0.02)	(0.01)		(0.02)
Distance	$-0.69^\$$	$-0.79^\$$	$-0.76^\$$	$-0.74^\$$
	(0.04)	(0.04)	(0.04)	(0.04)
Exporter GDP pc	$0.86^\$$	$0.86^\$$	$1.25^\$$	$1.23^\$$
	(0.03)	(0.04)	(0.02)	(0.02)
Importer GDP pc	$0.83^\$$	$0.89^\$$	$1.03^\$$	$0.99^\$$
	(0.02)	(0.02)	(0.02)	(0.02)
Population exporter	$0.96^\$$	$0.98^\$$	$1.30^\$$	$1.28^\$$
	(0.03)	(0.03)	(0.03)	(0.03)
Population importer	$1.01^\$$	$1.00^\$$	$1.22^\$$	$1.18^\$$
	(0.02)	(0.02)	(0.03)	(0.03)
RTA	$0.86^\$$	$0.29^\$$	$0.38^\$$	$0.37^\$$
	(0.08)	(0.07)	(0.06)	(0.06)
Currency union	-0.27	-0.10	-0.32^*	-0.34^*
	(0.18)	(0.15)	(0.18)	(0.18)
Product area	$-0.15^\$$	$-0.14^\$$	$-0.19^\$$	$-0.20^\$$
	(0.01)	(0.02)	(0.02)	(0.02)
Common language	$0.57^\$$	$0.34^\$$	$0.75^\$$	$0.71^\$$
	(0.07)	(0.10)	(0.09)	(0.10)
Land border	$1.06^\$$	$0.37^\#$	$1.03^\$$	$0.90^\$$
	(0.16)	(0.16)	(0.17)	(0.17)
Landlocked country	$-0.75^\$$	$-0.31^\$$	$-0.23^\$$	$-0.23^\$$
	(0.05)	(0.09)	(0.08)	(0.08)
Island	$-0.27^\$$	-0.05	-0.09	-0.07
	(0.05)	(0.06)	(0.06)	(0.06)
Colony	$3.25^\$$	0.14	0.11	0.04
	(0.38)	(0.15)	(0.18)	(0.18)
R^2	0.77	0.77	0.67	0.67

Notes: $ significant at 99% , # significant at 95% , * significant at 90%
            n.a. not applicable
            (Standard errors reported in parentheses)

The framework set out by Rose has been used and further developed in a number of studies. A straight forward extension is Gil-Pareja et al. (2007) who focus on tourism flows that originate in the G7 countries (156 destinations) and find a co-efficient of 0.17–0.35. Segura-Cayela and Vilarrubia (2008) investigate a data set for 1999 that describes bilateral trade relations between 21 exporting countries and 163 importing countries at the level of 62 sectors and find that a foreign service office increases the probability of trade by 11 to 18% although they find no clear impact on trade volumes. Maurel and Afman (2007) use the gravity analysis in the context of East West trade (56 countries) for 1997–2004 and estimate that the effect of a foreign service office is the equivalent of a 2–8% *ad valorem* tariff reduction.

Yakop and Bergeijk (2007) replicate Rose for the year 2006 while extending the data set to a matrix of 63 x 63 countries (63 exporters and 63 importers; the data set is symmetrical in this respect), because they want to check whether Rose's results hold on a larger scale and for a larger sample of exporting countries (Rose mainly considers the exports of high income countries). Their replication takes place in three steps. First they re-estimate the Rose equation for the same set of exporting countries but their limited set of 63 importing countries. The findings for the key variables of the gravity equation (distance, GDP, population) are comparable and more importantly the elasticity of the number of embassies and consulates is significant although it is marginally smaller. Second they estimate for their full sample of 63 exporting and importing countries a restricted model in which embassies and consulates are not included in the regression. Third they estimate an unrestricted model where they find a comparable result with a co-efficient of 0.09, thus offering an indication for the robustness of Rose's (2007) econometric findings.[13]

Table 4.3 Co-efficient for embassies and consulates in gravity equations for sub-samples distinguished by income level

		To importing countries	
		Lower (Middle) Income	Upper Middle and Higher Income
From exporting countries	Lower (Middle) Income	$0.52^{\$}$ (0.18)	$0.29^{\$}$ (0.06)
	Upper Middle and Higher Income	$0.37^{\$}$ (0.07)	0.03 (0.02)

Notes: $ significant at 99%
(Standard errors reported in parentheses)
Source: Yakop (2009)

Yakop (2009) further investigates how the level of economic development interacts with the impact of embassies and consulates on trade (Table 4.3). He shows that this effect between or within the group of higher income countries is not significant. Probably information about these markets and their institutions is sufficiently well established so that public intervention is not necessary.

All in all the empirical evidence suggests that Rose's finding, at least for the 1990s and although it needs further elaboration, is genuine and robust since in essence the same manner of results are found with different methods, countries and sets of dependant variables.

State Visits

State visits are important and very visible instruments to establish or improve relations between countries. As we noted in Chapter 1 (Figure 1.1), state visits have shown very strong growth figures in the second half of the twentieth century. This may be because such bilateral diplomatic events are clearly defined. Indeed, a state visit is a good moment to conclude agreements on economic co-operation and in the slipstream one often encounters delegations of firms that try to establish commercial relationships. Such public sector visits are distinct from missions that consist of the private sector only and which have a function that is distinct from missions with public sector involvement. Typically such private sector missions (that may exist of a great many firms or business organisations) are focussed on networking and hands-on experience and knowledge of particular foreign markets.[14] There is thus also no *a priori* reason to especially conduct such activities in the context of official visits.

State visits can be organized at different levels that extend beyond the formal definition of a visit by the Head of State (the king, the president or the prime minister). Indeed at the slightly lower levels (Ministers, parliamentary delegations and high ranking government officials) such visits can be expected to be more effective from the point of view of bilateral economic diplomacy and commercial policy because these visits can be better focussed, are much more flexible in timing and can be repeated more often.[15] Finally, many more visits take place at even lower levels of representation. Such visits do hardly stand out against the background of usual visits by business persons or tourists, are – thus – generally speaking not newsworthy and it is therefore (perhaps erroneously) expected these 'non-events' should not be expected to have a significant measurable effect. In the long run the cumulative effect may be substantial and in particular instance such 'silent' economic diplomacy may be crucial. Anyhow, typically the public sector's involvement may be necessary for three reasons.

- The type of product requires public sector involvement either on the demand side (for example large infrastructural works) or on the supply side (military or dual use goods).
- The type of importing country requires public sector involvement at the side of the exporter, for cultural reasons or because the public sector is dominant and/or (former) state enterprises are involved (typically this is relevant for the relatively new entrants to the world economic system such as China and Russia).
- High ranking government officials are needed to signal the importance that a country pays to the commercial relationships that will be discussed thus offering an implicit guarantee that these relationships will be free from political disturbances.

All three arguments boil down to the fact that public sector involvement is a necessary condition for market access and thus an instrument to reduce or eliminate cultural non-tariff barriers to trade and investment or because the diplomatic representations provide for superior knowledge (see on these issues, for example, Kostecki and Naray 2007).

Earlier empirical studies (Bergeijk 1992, 1994a, especially pp. 154–62) that included such visits as an explanatory variable in gravity models for international trade (as well as the agreements that were concluded and the nature and intensity of the official statements that were made during such visits) found elasticities of 0.3 to 0.5 suggesting that a doubling of such friendly international activities would increase bilateral trade by some 15 to 25%. Export and import equations that were estimated at the level of individual exporting and importing nations for the years 1985 showed a significant co-efficient for co-operative diplomatic exchange in the export and import equations for 9 out of 40 equations at the 95% confidence level and better. Interestingly, political indicators were not significant in the trade flow equations of Germany and Japan, whereas for the other G8 countries significant influences were found. Anyhow, the use of a comprehensive variable for bilateral diplomatic co-operation was rather rough and later studies improved upon these first attempts to distil the 'weight of diplomacy' by means of a more precise and narrow focus on state visits over a long time period.

Nitsch (2007), to date, offers in my view the most comprehensive analysis of the economic impact of such visits. Nitsch investigates the State Visits of the United States, (West) Germany and France *vis-à-vis* 220 export destinations over the years 1948–2003 by means of a gravity-type model (incidentally these three countries represent about a quarter of world trade). The estimated elasticities are in the order of magnitude of 0.08–0.13. Nitsch extensively tests for robustness and also includes official visits at the sub-

Head-of-State-level of 'working visits' for which he finds significant elasticities of 0.10–0.15. Focussing on rates of export growth, Nitsch shows that the impact of visits decays over time (typically significant effects are no longer found three years after the visit) and, moreover, he uncovers that it may require frequent (that is repeated) visits to a country in order to have a measurable impact on trade.

Head and Ries (2006) investigate the impact of Canadian State Visits using a gravity model for 160 countries over the years 1994–2002 and make a distinction between trade missions headed by the Prime Minister and the Minister of Trade, respectively. Trade missions are found to significantly influence bilateral trade (by as much as up to 300%). This result remains valid even when controlling for average excess trade with mission target countries (that is for the fact that all countries tend to trade more with the countries that were visited by Canada) and exporter fixed effects and time varying fixed effects for importer countries are included. Such effects control for unobserved trade intensities and year effects. In these estimates missions headed by the Prime Minister are associated with a stronger positive effect (almost double the effect of the other missions; the estimated co-efficients range from 0.1 to 1.2). This effect, however, vanishes in the equation that is preferred by Head and Ries (2006) and which corrects for country-pair fixed effects. Thus the proposition of increased trade is not supported in this specification. In the first difference version of the gravity equation (that deals with rates of growth) post-trade mission periods are associated with lower growth rates of trade. These findings may reflect a lack of experience (as the trade mission programme was initiated in 1994) or the fact that hardly any frequent visits appear to have occurred (only 5 out of 44 missions were a repeated visit).

It is noteworthy that both Nitsch (2007) and Head and Ries (2006) independently report that their regressions show that trade missions *c.q.* official visits are targeted to countries that show increased levels of trade with all *other* countries. If this reflects common practice then one expects that many visits by many countries occur with respect to these potential markets. This has two potentially relevant implications for policy. Firstly, trade missions and official visits may be purely motivated by defensive arguments (as in the case of a zero sum game). Secondly, if everybody is doing the same (that is if we see herding behaviour) then it will be very difficult to empirically establish the contribution of the specific action that is being studied. (Incidentally, this identification problem may be even worse: if countries especially visit markets that are 'difficult' and thus require focussed economic diplomacy then lower levels and growth rates may determine actual policy choices to visit such a country.) Keeping these sceptic remarks in mind, it is really hopeful that especially the impact of trade missions and official visits in the *import* equations appears to be amongst the most significant and empirically relevant findings of all gravity approaches that were discussed in this section. If anything this suggests that the motivation of state visits may be Mercantilist, but that their impact is not. State visits stimulate exports ... of the visited countries.

As a final note, it is worth to point out that the effects reported in the studies imply that economic and commercial policy may generate huge welfare gains. This is illustrated by a cost-benefit study that aims at estimating the net present discounted value of economic missions at the Head of State and Ministerial levels for the Netherlands (van den Berg et al., 2008). This analysis is based on very conservative estimates that, amongst others, assume that the Netherlands is only able to reap one tenth of the effects that are reported by Nitsch (2007), use a relatively short time horizon and include the cost of taxation (that is the distorting effect). Still the study arrives at a net present discounted value of some €100–200 million.[16]

Export Promotion Activities

Apart from the involvement of politicians and high ranking diplomats, many activities take place to promote exports, such as trade shows, trade fairs, commercial missions (consisting only of business persons and their organizations, so with no involvement of politicians or high level social servants) and objective market information programmes (including computer-generated trade leads). This is quite a different species and the public provision and/or involvement of the government is rather dubious. Indeed, in some countries this function is supplied by the private sector. It has not been easy to find a positive effect of such activities on trade. Wilkinson and Brouthers (2000), for example, for 47 US-states in the year 1990, actually report a significant negative correlation between commercial trade missions and exports. Trade shows have a positive impact while the result of objective market information appears to depend on the type of goods (it is positive for knowledge intensive goods) but this result may be driven by the fact that data for six states are lacking in the high-tech export regression. Bernard and Jensen (2004b) using a panel of 13,350 US manufacturing plants for the years 1984–1992 find positive, but very small and insignificant co-efficients for export promotion subsidies. However, since the sample especially relates to large plants, the data set may not pick up the effects of state export promotion activities, which typically target small and medium firms. Another reason why the effect of export promotion in these studies is not significant may relate to the fact that the US is a high income country with little or no need to actually help its exporters. Indeed the effectiveness of commercial diplomacy may to a large extent depend on the level of economic development of the exporter.

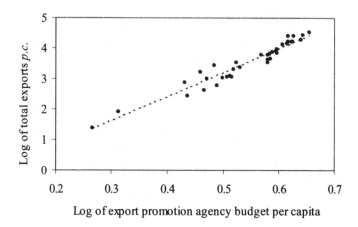

Source: calculated on the basis of Lederman et al. (2006); selection of 36 countries as motivated in Chapter 5

Figure 4.4 Exports per capita *and export promotion* per capita *(2005)*

Recently, Lederman et al. (2006) took up the issue of the effectiveness of export promotion in a group of 104 countries and the year 2005. The data set is based on a rich survey answered by 83 agencies, covering questions about their institutional structures, responsibilities, objectives and strategies, resources and expenditures, and activities and client orientation. Lederman et al. thus are able to give a good description of export promotion practices around the world. This study, however, is especially quoted for having found a correlation between *per capita* export promotion and per capita exports (the multiplier for the median export promotion agency is 40 as is also suggested by Figure 4.4). The elasticity at the mean of the sample explains about 8% of the median country's export, which is more or less of the same order of magnitude as found in the empirical studies on the impact of embassies and consulates that we discussed in the previous section. However, these results are driven by the developing countries suggesting substantial heterogeneity across levels of development (indeed for OECD countries the relationship is insignificant; that is the effect is zero). Moreover, Lederman et al. do not take into account the geographic dimension of trade or the potential impact of other instruments so that attribution of exports to export promotion may possibly be due to the fact that relevant variables have been omitted from their research.

Further Research

On the basis of our discussion commercial diplomacy actually seems to reduce or mitigate border effects by addressing some of the relevant market failures. The available studies, however, are not yet sufficient to provide a guide for policy and need further strengthening. One issue is that the instruments of economic diplomacy have so far only been investigated separately. This implies that complementarities and substitution between these instruments has not yet been considered. In addition (and importantly), our knowledge about export promotion basically relates to partial correlates between the national (or state) budgets for export promotion and trade flows that do not take into account that other factors such as distance, transportation costs or GDP are important drivers of such flows. We will study these and related questions in the next chapter.

NOTES

[1] See Heckscher ([1931] 1955, part II, especially p. 17), Hutchison (1988, p. 88) and Kennedy (1989, p. 103) on these issues. Modern versions of mercantilism have been labelled the 'Realist Approach' in foreign policy, see for examples and a discussion of the literature, Schneider et al. (2003). A relevant discussion of this literature and its implication for trade policy is to be found in WTO (2007) as well.

[2] This does not mean that free trade is always found to be the best recipe for a country. See, for example, Yanikkaya (2002).

[3] Rodriguez and Rodrik are especially concerned with the way openness is measured and their scepticism is well-grounded. This methodological point has, however, been largely answered by Edwards (1998) who uses a set of nine different indicators for openness in regressions that explain total factor productivity for a set of 93 countries and the years 1960–90. Edwards almost always (there is one insignificant exception in 18 reported equations) finds that openness is associated with higher total factor productivity growth.

[4] This may also explain why Rose (2004) does not find an impact for GATT/WTO membership which by its very nature is dichotomous (yes/no) as well.

[5] A noteworthy exception is Estevadeordal and Taylor (2008) who use a treatment-and-control empirical analysis of pre-1990 versus post-1990 performance of liberalizing and non-liberalizing economies and find that liberalizing tariffs leads to a one percentage point increase in annual GDP growth.

[6] This finding regarding flexibility of the economy is in line with empirical findings at the macroeconomic level reported by Brakman et al. (1988) for Germany, France, the Netherlands, and Belgium/Luxembourg and at the meso-economic level as reported, for example, by Porter (1990) for 100 industries in Denmark, Germany, Italy, South Korea, Singapore, Sweden, Switzerland, the UK and the US.

[7]   Without even suggesting to be comprehensive (as to even be complete) on this subject, I refer the reader to recently reported findings for Belgium (Pisu 2008), Germany (Fryges and Wagner, 2007), the Netherlands (Kox 2008), Spain (Delgado et al. 2002), Sub-Sahara Africa (Biesebroeck 2005), United Kingdom (Greenaway and Kneller 2004) and United States (Bernard and Jensen 2004a). Useful introductions into and reviews of the literature include International Study Group on Productivity (2007), Ottaviano and Mayer (2007) and Wagner (2007).

[8]   See on the latter mechanism Griffith et al. (2008).

[9]   Note, however, that often a double deficit exists with respect to national and international competition and that cartels often seek protection from foreign competition for example by petitioning for anti dumping measures (see, for example, Lloyd et al. 2001 and Johnston 2006).

[10]   A rich business economics literature exists on the importance of the business person's relationships for internationalization strategies. It is beyond the scope of this book, but the reader is referred to Harris and Wheeler (2005) for a succinct introduction into these issues.

[11]   Incidentally, Rose chose this research topic because it offered him the opportunity to do an instrument variable analysis in which the decision to have an embassy would depend on the climate (that is the weather conditions) and to argue that the major source for diplomats is the travel guide.

[12]   Rose includes the number of embassies and consulates that each exporting nation has in each importing country and relates these quantities of diplomatic representation to bilateral export flows.

[13]   The F test for accepting the unrestricted model is 19.

[14]   Incidentally, it is more difficult to find evidence that the latter type of mission actually adds value at the firm level (see, for example, Wilkinson et al. 2000).

[15]   Rules and traditions surrounding state visits may, for example, stipulate that a country can only be visited once in a reigning period or the *mores* may stipulate that such visits may have to be timed to celebrate a jubilee of diplomatic or international economic relations.

[16]   Moreover, this study uses rather high time preferences (a discount rate of 5.5%) and includes substantial costs of taxation (25%). Also on this account the reported net welfare gain is highly likely to be a significant underestimate.

5. The Weight of Bilateral Economic Diplomacy and Commercial Policy Revisited

This chapter investigates the relationship between trade and bilateral economic and commercial diplomacy econometrically, not to discover the obvious, but to see whether an empirical basis exists to either confirm or refute common sense: does economic and commercial diplomacy matter and does it have a measurable impact on bilateral trade flows? The economic rationale is that border effects exist and may be related to insufficient private investment in knowledge about foreign markets and the way to sell products abroad. Here the government may step in to solve a market failure and provide its knowledge as a public good. Two sorts of public sector knowledge centres appear relevant. First, the Foreign Service (that is the embassies and consulates abroad) may have superior knowledge about local market opportunities and unique experience in doing business in the specific cultural, institutional and political context of a country. Second, the export promotion agency may be an important source for businesses that consider an international strategy as it has knowledge about doing international business in general and about markets abroad. Typically the role of an export promotion agency would seem to be more linked to trade in general (so irrespective of destination) whereas embassies and consulates would be more directly linked to specific bilateral trade relations. Export promotion would thus seem to reduce to some extent the hurdle of the sunk costs involved in the export decision (that is have an impact on all export markets), whereas the activities of an embassy or consulate could be expected to reduce border effects only with respect to the country where they are located.

Unfortunately, no research exists that investigates these functions simultaneously. Indeed, the empirical studies that we discussed in the previous chapter generally speaking showed that the economic and commercial functions of diplomacy matter, but it did not become clear from these investigations how much each of these functions separately contributes to international trade. Raising this empirical question is timely at this point in time, because an increase in export promotion agencies is evident especially since the turn of the millennium (Figure 5.1).

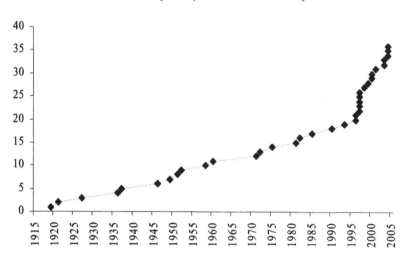

Source: Based on Lederman et al. (2006).

Figure 5.1 Development of the number of export promotion agencies in the sample (1915–2005)

One issue at stake is whether the different instruments interact positively (so that there is synergy) or that the instruments are substitutes (crowding out'). Another question relates to the possibility that the impact of these instruments may differ with regard to the target markets – an issue that has so far not been investigated for bilateral trade flows. In the end this manner of research questions is important for the choice of both the combination and the intensity of instruments. It is important to analyse these issues in relation to geographic patterns that evidently also exists with respect to the location of embassies and consulates as is illustrated in Figure 5.2 that relates the number of embassies and consulates to the distance from the 'mother country'. Interestingly, the strongest diplomatic networks appear to be maintained with countries that are nearby.

The goal of the present chapter is to make a contribution to our empirical knowledge about these issues by simultaneously investigating the impact of export promotion agencies, embassies and consulates and the interaction between these two instruments and by considering if and how these relationships change when different markets are distinguished on the basis of their level of sophistication (income per head of the population will be used as a proxy).

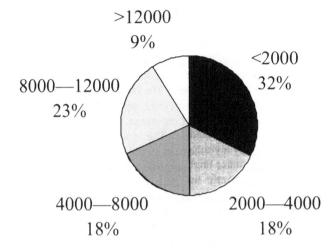

Source: Calculations based on Yakop and Bergeijk (2007)

Figure 5.2 Diplomatic network (share of embassies and consulates in relation to bilateral distance in kilometres, 2006)

The first section introduces the basics of the gravity analysis which gives a useful empirical short-hand description of the geographical pattern of world trade. The section provides a bird's eye view of the history of this applied trade model (many findings have already been discussed in previous chapters) and a short description of recent theoretical advances. Moreover some data and estimation issues are discussed. The second section presents the empirical results of a cross-section gravity equation that deals with the bilateral trade flows of 36 countries in the year 2006. These 36 countries are a subset of two recent investigations that deal with export promotion agencies (Lederman et al. 2006) and embassies and consulates (Yakop 2009) which measure the explanatory variables in years prior to 2006 so that reverse causation and the possible problem of simultaneity can be expected to be reduced. The investigation shows that whereas the Foreign Service significantly contributes to bilateral trade flows, export promotion agencies do not on average. The latter result, however, is largely driven by developed economies, as is shown in the third section that analyses the trade – diplomacy nexus distinguishing markets by level of income *per capita*. Clearly, as discussed in the final section, these findings do not only have implications for the choice of instruments, but also for the theories that currently underpin economic diplomacy and commercial policy.

1 THE GRAVITY MODEL AND THE DATA

A lot of models have been used to describe international trade flows. Models do not only differ with respect to the degree of detail, but also with respect to the specific theoretical interest of the investigator. For the present study I use probably the most simple empirical model. The basic idea of this model was first set out by Isard (1954). Tinbergen (1962, pp. 262–93) developed the gravity model as it is known today. Linnemann (1966) is the traditional reference on the early gravity model.[1] The gravity model became the empirical workhorse for many investigations in economic trade and has a rich history in the regional economics literature where it was also used to analyse issues like migration. Importantly the gravity model was widely used in policy institutions although the traditional formulation of the gravity equation was not cogently derived on the basis of economic theory. This changed in the mid-1980s when Bergstrand (1985) for the first time related the gravity equation to its microeconomic foundations and gave a formal derivation (Bergstrand 1989) of the gravity equation within the context of a general equilibrium model of world trade with imperfect competition and product differentiation.

Around this time, in the early and mid-1990s the model was very fashionable in policy institutions especially for analysing the big changes in the world system when *détente* finally set in and the Iron Curtain fell (see the discussion in Chapter 2, Section 4). The gravity predictions were right on the spot and trade analysts had a great influence in the European policy debate on Eastern Europe's capital requirements as they were able to show that trade would increase sufficiently to finance the transformation from Marx to market (Bergeijk and Lensink 1993). The academic popularity of the gravity analysis, however, appeared to wane again, especially since the gravity equation could be derived from almost any trade theoretic model thus offering no scope to test scientific hypotheses (Hummels and Levinson 1995). Indeed, it is ironic that 'gravity' went from having too little micro-economic underpinning to having far too many theoretical and mutually non-exclusive justifications: Deardorff (1995), Feenstra et al. (2001) and Evenett and Keller (2002) are examples of contributions that showed that the model could be derived from Heckscher-Ohlin, increasing returns to scale, Ricardian models, and so on.

Incidentally, this was offering great confidence to policy makers since advice based on the gravity analysis did not seem to depend on a particular vision on the economic process, that is the gravity equation was robust with respect to economic theories. In a sense the lack of uniqueness of the underlying theory is trivial and unimportant. This is basically so, because the underlying processes are inherently too complex (as happens in other subfields of economics as well – endogenous growth directly comes to mind as an appropriate analogy). What matters is the strong empirical regularity and especially its key message, namely that distance matters and will continue to matter.

Anyhow, then came the turn of the century and gravity became popular in academia again thanks to the very influential article by Anderson and van Wincoop (2003). Policy barriers, information and enforcement costs and diverging rules and legal frameworks were shown to exercise the same impact as an *ad valorem* tariff equivalent of 44% (that is twice the impact of transportation). Indeed, it is this cost component that definitely produces negative externalities and therefore it should be the target for policy makers that want to minimize the cost of distance. This focussed attention on the one key 'gravity' factor: distance, a break through which helped the gravity model recover lost grounds. More importantly empirical research uncovered distance's truly multidimensional (economic, cultural, political and so on) nature (see Linders et al. 2004 for a review of the literature) and also these new dimensions proved to be very stimulating. It is true that a great many puzzles remain to be solved but the scientific discourse is intensive and clearly the model now belongs for the second time in its existence again to the main-stream international economics.

Some Cons and Many Pros of the Gravity Approach

In assessing the potential utility of the gravity approach for the present empirical investigation one has to consider both the strengths and the weaknesses of the method. On the one hand, the critics of the model are right in many respects. For example, the analysis is essentially of a comparative static nature. Only one equation is used to explain the value of total exports to another country. So basically we have a turnover relation in which prices are not specified. Moreover, substitution between trade flows is absent (that is the issue of trade diversion is not really covered; see Bikker, 2007). On the other hand the model's simplicity constitutes its strength, because the model deploys only a limited number of variables and this facilitates computation, keeps the data problems manageable and the results better traceable. Noteworthy is the gravity equation's ability to incorporate 'empirical regularities' such as intra-industry trade, the impact of transport costs and the influence of differences in *per capita* income on trade flows. According to Isard (1988, p. 311), the appeal of the gravity approach is that it lays bare the two key system variables in operation (mass and resistance to movement) without confusion with the many microeconomic forces at play.

More important, however, is the observation that the problem that is to be addressed in this chapter concerns the question of increased explanation when we include certain instruments of economic and commercial policy in a traditional trade model. As this investigation deals with the actual impact of instruments of economic and commercial diplomacy on the level and pattern of bilateral trade flows, the choice of the gravity model is almost unavoidable because the gravity model provides and empirical explanation for the geography and level of bilateral trade flows. In addition, robustness and general acceptance of the method are essential for the analysis in this chapter. Therefore it is relevant that the gravity model presently is accepted both in academic and in policy circles.

So although the gravity model could still be extended and improved upon, for the present study it suffices. This is especially true because the empirical results obtained by the gravity model have always been judged to be very good (see, for example, Deardorff 1984, pp. 503–4.)

The Gravity Approach

In the basic model three explanatory variables appear: *(i)* the exporting country's Gross Domestic Product, *(ii)* the importing country's GDP and *(iii)* the distance D_{ij} between the two countries. The basic model is known in international trade theory as the gravity equation, because of its similarity to the Newtonian law of gravity: the bilateral trade flow is assumed to be a function of the economic masses of the two trade partners and the inverted distance between the two countries. The intuition behind this formula is appealing even to laymen. First, the supply of goods depends positively on the exporting country's economic size and production capacity which is represented by its GDP. Second, the demand for these exports depends positively on the importing country's market which is also represented by its GDP. Third, transportation costs, transportation time and the 'economic horizon' of the exporter (all assumed to correspond roughly with the geographic distance between the exporting and importing country) have a negative impact on trade. Formulated in this intuitive way the gravity equation appears to be the reduced form solution to a not explicitly formulated supply and demand system. Actually Leamer and Stern (1970) did put forward the rationale for the gravity formula.[2] Hence we have the following equation for the gravity model in its simplest form.

$$E_{ij} = Y_i^{\alpha} \, Y_j^{\beta} \, D_{ij}^{\gamma} \qquad (5.1)$$

Here $\alpha > 0$, $\beta > 0$ and $\gamma < 0$, while E_{ij} are the exports from country I to country j, Y_i is the GDP of country i and D_{ij} is the geographic distance between country i and country j. Usually the populations N_i and N_j of the trade partners are added to this equation as are a number of other (often binary or dummy) variables that represent trade enhancing and trade resistance factors that are typically relevant in bilateral exchanges. Examples of such factors comprise, among others, a common border, a common language, a common currency, or an (ex) colonial relationship but may also relate to individual trade enhancing factors such as being an island economy or the area of the economy. The gravity model that is estimated in this chapter includes population but lets the other variables out, because including too many variables makes the procedures unnecessary complicated and the results opaque.[3]

The trade flow equation is estimated cross-country for 36 countries for the year 2006. So we have 36 x 35 = 1260 possible observations. In order to estimate the co-efficients of the model with the Ordinary Least Squares (OLS) method, the gravity equation (see equation 5.1) is rewritten in log-linear form and includes populations and indicators for embassies and consulates EC_{ij} and staff of the exporter's export promotion agency EPA_i and an interaction term $(EC_{ij} \times EPA_i)$ that captures synergy (+) and/or crowding out (−) of instruments. In order to make our results comparable to other gravity equations in the field, we use per capita GDP Y/N as the explanatory variable. The equation to be estimated is

$$\ln E_{ij} = c + \alpha \ln Y_i /N_i + \beta \ln Y_j /N_j + \gamma \ln D_{ij} + \delta \ln N_i + \zeta \ln N_j + \eta EC_{ij} + \theta EPA_i + \lambda (EC_{ij} \times EPA_i) \qquad (5.2)$$

Here c is the constant term and the *a priori* expected signs are $\eta > 0$, $\theta > 0$, while the sign of λ depends on whether substitution effects or rather complementarity occurs between EC_{ij} and EPA_i.

Some Data and Estimation Issues

Before proceeding with the econometric investigation it is worthwhile to consider the economic data in general and the use of the data on commercial and economic diplomacy in particular. Also the selection of countries is a relevant topic.

Economic data　　Data for exports, GDP and population have been taken from well-known sources, such as the World Bank's *World Development Indicators* and the IMF's *Direction of Trade Statistics* and need not much discussion here.

It is, however, relevant to note that the problem of zero trade flows that is often relevant for analyzes with an gravity equation hardly matters for the present investigation since only for 18 of the 1260 trade flows (1.4%) no strictly positive observations are available.

How distance is measured   Distance has been measured as the crow flies and this, admittedly, is not a very accurate measure of the way that goods have to travel between exporter and importer.[4] This measurement issue, however, empirically does not matter a great deal. It is true that as transportation routes have been approximated by the pure geographic distance (the length of a straight line) between the trade partners' capitals. Differences in the use of the modes of transportation have not been taken into account, although transportation costs certainly depend on the choice of mode of transportation and the different natural barriers to trade and travel that they encounter. Obviously, this choice of geographic rather than economic distance is a simplification of the routes that the goods actually have to follow and the distances over which they have to be transported. Geographic distances do not take into account the fact that natural (physical) trade barriers, such as mountains, sea currents and so on, often dictate the course of trade. The approximation, however, seems reasonable since geographic distances are good representations for flying distances and may thus measure the 'mental' distance of the representative exporter well enough.

Export promotion   Data on staff and budget of export promotion agencies have been derived from Lederman et al. (2006) which, incidentally, was made available conditional on keeping the confidential nature of their inquiry so that individual country effects cannot be reported. Since the budgets for embassies and consulates are not available in an internationally comparative manner it is preferable to include as the explanatory variable for export promotion a simple count of the staff. This research approach is also sensible in light of the fact that this figure seems more reliable and transparent than budgets which are often considered of strategic importance and thus secret or at least fuzzy. The budget data in Lederman et al. (2006) have, however been used to check the robustness of the findings (Veenstra 2009).

Embassies and consulates   Without delving into the history of diplomacy and international relations, one can point out international formal agreements between nation states in the last few decades which stipulate exactly how states can choose to represent themselves in other countries. The two most important documents are *The Vienna Convention on Diplomatic Relations* which was signed as a treaty in 1961 and *The Vienna Convention on Consular Relations* (also a treaty) signed in 1963. The first treaty is the international legal framework for embassies defining diplomatic terms such as 'head of missions' or 'head of states' and their functions, codes of conduct, working conditions, legal aspects and immunities and privileges. The second treaty is the international legal framework for consulates and defines different types of foreign representations as well as the matters mentioned earlier (terms, functions, legal aspects and so on).

The obvious source is to visit the Embassy Pages website (www.embassypages.com), but after comparing and checking this data against individual websites of the ministries of foreign affairs it appeared that the information of www.embassypages.com was often rather outdated. Therefore for each of the countries in the sample the website of its ministry of foreign affairs was consulted. This was not always an easy process and in particular cumbersome for some countries, where the websites were not available in English.[5]

Selection of countries   Countries and their *per capita* GDPs are listed in Table 5.1 which also puts the present data set and its exporting country coverage into the perspective of other relevant data sets.

All 36 countries are part of the Yakop and Bergeijk (2007) data set which itself consists of 63 countries. The country coverage *vis-à-vis* the Lederman et al. (2006) data set is 33 out of 83 agencies, but in addition observations for staff and budget regarding another 3 countries have been included (United States, Netherlands and Belgium) for which no data were in the data set that was provided. Finally in comparison to Rose's (2007) data set 13 out of his 22 countries are covered but and additional 23 exporting countries are in the present data set. Note, however, that Rose studies 220 export destinations (importing countries), whereas the present data set contains 36 export destinations only. All in all the data sets describe different samples so that results may differ on the basis of countries that were included in one particular investigation, but not in another one.

Obviously, the choice of countries is partially dictated by the availability of data sets and thus the consequence of both the research design of other students of the econometrics of commercial and economic diplomacy and the response rates of questionnaires that they send out. It is, however, noteworthy that the present data set covered about halve the volume of world trade in 2006 (in particular 46% of exports and 52% of imports), 24% of world population and 62% of world production in 2006 (in terms of gross domestic product).

Table 5.1 Countries included in the empirical investigation, GDP per capita level and relation to the other data sets on export promotion and embassies and consulates

Country	GDP *p.c.* ($1000)	Lederman et al (2006)	Rose (2007)
Algeria	3.4	*	
Australia	37.7	*	*
Austria	38.9	*	
Bangladesh	0.4	*	
Belgium	37.4		*
Brazil	5.6	*	*
Chile	8.9	*	
Czech Republic	13.9	*	
Denmark	50.7	*	
Dominican Republic	3.3	*	
Ecuador	3.1	*	
Egypt	1.4	*	
Finland	40.0	*	
France	36.7	*	*
Germany	35.2	*	*
Hungary	11.2	*	
Ireland	51.6	*	
Israel	19.9	*	
Malaysia	5.8	*	
Mexico	8.1	*	*
Morocco	2.1	*	
Netherlands	40.5		*
Norway	71.9	*	
Portugal	18.4	*	
South Africa	5.4	*	
Spain	27.8	*	*
Sweden	42.3	*	*
Switzerland	50.8	*	*
Thailand	3.3	*	
Tunisia	3.0	*	
Turkey	5.5	*	*
Uganda	0.3	*	
United Kingdom	39.3	*	*
United States	44.0		*
Uruguay	5.8	*	
Venezuela	6.7	*	

The sample, moreover, covers all continents, former communist countries, as well as democratic market economies, all analytical income groups (that is with respect to the analytical World Bank categories), the world's main exporters of industry goods, of raw materials and of food as well as some of the important oil producing countries. Moreover, the sample includes both small, medium and large countries.

So also from these perspectives the sample appears to be sufficiently representative (basically the weakest spot in the present data set is the absence of China and of three of the G8 countries: Canada, Japan and Russia). With these caveats in mind we can now turn to the econometric findings.

2 EMPIRICAL RESULTS

Table 5.2 summarizes the empirical results for four estimated equations. The first column gives for purpose of reference the standard gravity equation with the trade partners GDPs, populations and their geographic distance. The equation explains about three quarters of the variance of bilateral exports in 2006 and the co-efficients are highly significant (at the 99% confidence level) and conform to *a priori* expectations.

The second column presents the results for an equation that in addition contains the exporter's embassies and consulates in the export destination (that is the importing country). The positive co-efficient for EC_{ij} is also highly significant, conforms to *a priori* expectations (bilateral trade is positively associated with an embassy or consulate) and of the same order of magnitude as Rose (2007) and Yakop and Bergeijk (2007); see Table 4.2 in the previous chapter.

The third column shows an equation that includes the number of staff of the export promotion agency (in the exporting country). The sign of its estimated co-efficient, contrary to expectations, is negative. Although the co-efficient is relatively small (in comparison to the co-efficient of embassies and consulates) and less significant than those of the other variables that are reported in the table, the confidence level of 95% is still sufficient to take this unexpected result seriously. The upshot thus appears to be that export promotion agencies are a drag on trade.

The fourth equation in the penultimate column, however, appears to explain this anomaly, when we include both embassies and consulates in the importing country, the export promotion agency staff in the exporting country and the interaction between these terms (actually, this is equation 5.2). In column (4) the co-efficient of export promotion agency staff is zero and the earlier finding appears to be partially caused by negative interaction ('crowding out') between the two investigated instruments of bilateral economic and commercial diplomacy. These findings do not change when fixed effects for exporting and importing countries are included in the regressions (see Veenstra 2009).

Table 5.2 Empirical results of the OLS estimation of the gravity equation for 36 countries in 2006 (N=1242)

Equation	(1)	(2)	(3)	(4)
Exporter's GDP pc (ln Y_i/N_i)	$1.20^{\$}$	$1.18^{\$}$	$1.24^{\$}$	$1.22^{\$}$
	(36.5)	(35.9)	(31.7)	(31.0)
Importer's GDP pc (ln Y_j/N_j)	$1.07^{\$}$	$1.04^{\$}$	$1.07^{\$}$	$1.04^{\$}$
	(32.7)	(30.0)	(32.8)	(30.2)
Geographic distance (ln D_{ij})	$-0.88^{\$}$	$-0.86^{\$}$	$-0.87^{\$}$	$-0.86^{\$}$
	(20.2)	(19.6)	(20.0)	(19.5)
Exporter's population (ln N_i)	$0.99^{\$}$	$0.97^{\$}$	$1.04^{\$}$	$1.01^{\$}$
	(26.1)	(25.2)	(23.3)	(22.6)
Importer's population (N_j)	$1.03^{\$}$	$0.98^{\$}$	$1.03^{\$}$	$0.99^{\$}$
	(27.3)	(23.2)	(27.3)	(23.4)
Exporter's embassies and consulates in export destination (EC_{ij})	n.a.	$0.07^{\$}$ (2.8)	n.a.	$0.11^{\$}$ (3.8)
Exporter's export promotion agency staff (EPA_i)	n.a.	n.a.	$-0.02^{\#}$ (−2.1)	0.00 (0.13)
Interaction term between the economic diplomacy functions ($EC_{ij} \times EPA_i$)	n.a.	n.a.	n.a.	$-0.01^{\$}$ (2.5)
Constant term (c)	$-28.79^{\$}$	$-27.38^{\$}$	$-30.04^{\$}$	$-28.62^{\$}$
	(23.8)	(27.4)	(22.4)	(28.6)
R^2	0.76	0.76	0.76	0.76
Adjusted R^2	0.76	0.76	0.76	0.76
F–test	$771^{\$}$	$648^{\$}$	$645^{\$}$	$491^{\$}$
SSR	2580	2562	2570	2540

Notes: $ significant at 99%
       # significant at 95%
       n.a. not applicable
       (Standard errors reported in parentheses)

The F-ratio that is used to test the restricted model of column (1) against the unrestricted model of column (4) is 10, well above the critical value.[6] Hence it may be safely concluded that the added variables contribute significantly to the explanation of the dependent variable, and the unrestricted model (column 4) should be chosen on statistical grounds.

The findings that are reported in Table 5.2 thus appear to support earlier findings on the importance of embassies and consulates by Rose (2007), and Maurel and Afman (2007), and Yakop and Bergeijk (2007), but at the same time contradict the positive multiplier reported by Lederman et al. (2006) with respect to the trade enhancing impact of export promotion agencies. Note that the reported results in the table concern the staff rather than the budget that is central to the multiplier of Lederman et al. The findings when the budget is used as an explanatory variable in the present investigation imply, however, an even stronger rejection of his findings as the co–efficient for the export promotion agency's budget is negative although insignificant at the usual confidence levels.

3 THE IMPACT OF THE DEVELOPMENT LEVEL

The findings by Lederman et al 2006 regarding the export multiplier of the budgets of the export promotion agencies indicated that the effectiveness of this instrument of commercial policy might be positive at lower levels of economic development (that is in the earlier phases of a country's inter-nationalization strategy). Likewise, Yakop (2009) reports that the impact that is exerted by embassies and consulates on bilateral trade flows depends on the *per capita* incomes of the trade partners (see Table 4.3 in the previous chapter).

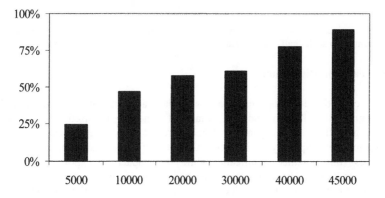

Figure 5.3 Percentage of data set covered below a level of per capita *GDP*

In order to investigate if and how income per head may influence the estimated co-efficients the penultimate equation in Table 5.2 is re–estimated several times. The procedure starts with countries at a *per capita* GDP of less than $5000 and in successive rounds data are added to the sample when higher income countries are considered in the analysis as well, as illustrated in Figure 5.3

Next, Figure 5.4 reports how the estimated co-efficients develop during this procedure and in addition gives information about the significance of the findings by plotting a confidence interval (the dotted lines represent lower and upper bounds of the co–efficient minus or plus two standard errors). The top panel (Figure 5.4a) shows the development of the co-efficient for embassies and consulates, which is significant over the whole range and in the full sample although its numerical value decreases at a *per capita* income level in the range of about $35,000 to about $40,000 (over this range typically the high income OECD countries are added to the sample, in particular Germany, France, Belgium, Australia, Austria and the United Kingdom). In the bottom panel (Figure 5.4b) the co-efficient of the export promotion agency staff consistently decreases when higher income country observations are added to the sample and eventually over about the same range of *per capita* income levels turns insignificant (actually the co-efficient becomes negative at that point).

The implication of these findings is that the Lederman et al. (2006) findings can be salvaged at least to some extent. Indeed, in general commercial and economic diplomacy through embassies, consulates and export promotion agencies would seem to be relevant instruments that can stimulate exports in countries with a relatively modest level of income per head, but not in the medium to high income OECD countries. Another explanation is that the marginal contribution of increasing an already much extended network of embassies and consulates may be relative low. Indeed it is no surprise that Lederman et al. (2006, p. 17) note that:

> the estimated elasticities of about 0.1 suggest that there are strong diminishing returns to scale [and] large expansions of EPAs budgets may not be desirable.

Caveats and Discussion

It is clear that the empirical analysis of the trade–diplomacy nexus should recognize that hidden under a surface of generally reported full sample, average effects heterogeneous forces are at play that warrant closer examination. Typically the impact of the network of embassies and consulates halves (but remains significant) while the impact of export promotion agencies completely disappears when *per capita* income increases over the relevant range. This may be due to the fact that demand in these countries is more sophisticated and homogeneous and that exporting therefore is easier, but other explanations can also be relevant.

Figure 5.4a Embassies and consulates

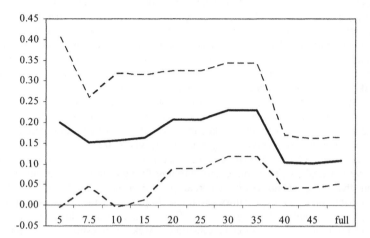

Figure 5.4b Export promotion agency staff (100s)

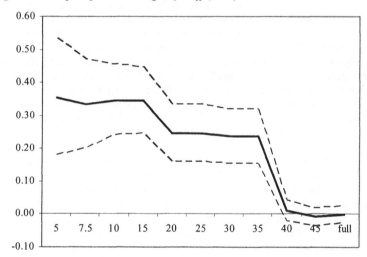

Note: On the horizontal axis: exporter GDP *per capita* in $1000 considered in the sample whereby 'full' denotes full sample

Figure 5.4   Estimated co-efficients and two standard errors confidence intervals for (sub) samples by per capita *GDP (in 1000 US$)*

In particular the *per capita* GDP level may also be an identifier for other characteristics of these countries that have not been included in the regression analysis (omitted variables). OECD economies typically are market-oriented economies that have a long history of trade liberalization and reductions of trade distortions. As such the impact of economic and commercial diplomacy might be limited in these developed liberal market economies. Related to this point is that the findings may reflect the Linder (1961) hypothesis that trade takes place between countries with similar levels of development.

Importantly, the present analysis only covers a narrow subset of diplomatic communication. This is relevant in two respects. First, exchange goes beyond what happens in the embassies and consulates and more stimuli exist than export promotion agencies (state visits are a clear example, but much more relevant exchange takes place between countries). Secondly, we have not dealt with incoming and outgoing foreign direct investment so also on that account no really accurate picture already exists of the 'true' contribution of the explanatory variables.[7] In particular the effect of economic and commercial diplomacy may be different since foreign direct investments and trade are to a large extent substitutes. Making investment more certain, will thus potentially reduce the flow of bilateral trade. By implication we do not measure the benefits of other diplomatic activities aimed at co-operation. These activities may not show up directly on the balance of trade or the current account although they eventually will do so. The findings in this chapter thus provide an underestimate of the impact of economic and commercial diplomacy on international economic relations.

Figure 5.5 illustrates the empirical relevance of commercial policy and diplomatic relationships in another way as it looks at the standardized co-efficients (the so-called β co-efficients). These co-efficients that are obtained if all variables are expressed in terms of their estimated standard deviation (Pindyck and Rubinfeld 1991, p. 85) indicate the relative contribution that the explanatory variable in question makes to the explanation of the dependant variable.

Note that Figure 5.5 compares models that have been estimated for different periods and relate to different quasi-reduced form equations (in particular the definition of the economic mass is different). The broad indicator model uses GDP and an index for all co-operative diplomatic exchange whereas the narrow indicator uses *per capita* GDP and looks at the network of embassies and consulates and its interaction with export promotion agencies. The distance effects are, however, quite comparable for the two models and provide a useful benchmark that indicates that the comparison between the co-efficient for the co-operation index and the co-efficient for the network of embassies and consulates is valid and informative.

The co-efficient in the broad indicator model is roughly twice as large as in the narrow indicator model implying that the model in this chapter underestimates the impact of diplomatic activities by perhaps as much as

50%. In order to get a better picture, future research will have to consider these other diplomatic activities in more detail.

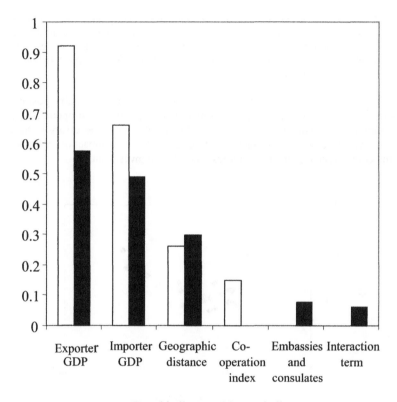

□ Broad indicator■ Narrow indicator

Sources: Broad indicator model: Bergeijk 1994a, p. 157
          Narrow indicator model: based on Table 5.2

*Figure 5.5 Relative importance of the explanatory variables in two gravity
          models (absolute values β co-efficients of the estimated
          parameters)*

A final potentially relevant omission is the focus of the present investigation on the purely positive co–operative interaction between nations and its impact on the reduction on border effects. Pen (1994, p. *xiii*) warns that an almost exclusive focus on international harmony in the analysis of international economic relationships carries the cost, that a substantial facet of reality could become a lost domain for economic theory:

> (T)rade policy, in which harmony and conflict are subtly intertwined, is often reduced in textbooks to a mere description of traditions, procedures and international organizations. The even more circumspect struggle for power, with its negotiations and – often veiled – threats remains outside the scope of traditional economic analysis.

Indeed the diplomatic network is not only used to make or enable positive exchanges, as illustrated in Figure 5.6 that plots hostility and co-operation for a sample of 40 countries in the year 1986. It will thus be necessary to take negative exchanges into account in future research on the impact of economic and commercial diplomatic activities on trade and investment.

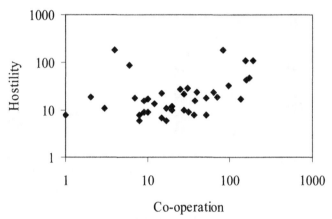

Source: Bergeijk 1994a, Table 7.1, p. 152.

Figure 5.6 Indexes of aggregate hostility and co-operation for 40 countries in the mid-1980s

4 CONCLUSIONS

All in all the calculations show that embassies and consulates are important and relevant determinants of trade, especially when considering non-OECD export destinations. The international diplomatic network thus adds value and it makes empirically sense to include this network in analyses of trade and probably (although this has not been substantiated in this chapter) the same conclusion is valid regarding inward and outward flows of foreign direct investment.[8] The empirical evidence uncovered in this chapter puts several question marks by the results of recent investigations and qualifies the conclusions that can be drawn from that earlier research. In particular we have seen that effects appear not to be homogeneous across countries and to a large extent may depend on *per capita* income levels. These findings will have to be reflected in future research and in the policy choices regarding the question of the mix of instruments used in foreign markets.

It is however, noteworthy that the available evidence offers more direct and unambiguous support for the fact that government policy can reduce border–effects in the sense that it may help to reduce cultural and institutional distances between countries, whereas the evidence for the existence for national network effects (that could be addressed through the activities of export promotion agencies) is mixed. The implication is that theories concerning network effects and market failures leading to too low levels of investment in knowledge about foreign markets may be less relevant for the industrialized countries.

On a final note, it is worth considering that the present chapter has only dealt with diplomatic and commercial activities that may be expected to exert a positive influence on trade and investment. Chapter 2 (especially Table 2.2) discussed a great many studies that have found that positive exchange is only one side of the coin and that conflict behaviour is an equally important driver (but, alas, a negative one) of international trade. Typically, diplomacy may impose substantial costs on the economy. However, only in exceptional cases will the costs of diplomatic incidents and structural political differences be manifested directly (punitive – or 'negative' – economic sanctions that will be studied in the next chapter are an exception to this rule). Hence it is almost impossible to weigh the political gain of gestures of protest, an angry fist or strong verbal dismay against the loss that such political 'actions' will mean for trade in the long run. Also with respect to this issue future research is needed, because the empirical evidence with respect to the conflict and trade nexus by and large relates to the pre-1990 world trading system.

NOTES

[1]   Isard's (1954) contribution is neglected by most students of the gravity method. This one of many examples that primogeneity does not always result in scientific recognition. Ethier *et al.* (1993, p. 14 fn. 6) have labelled this phenomenon – which seems to be a particular nuisance in international economics – 'Gresham's Law of Names'.

[2]   Another rationale put forward by Leamer and Stern (1970) is that bilateral trade is the expected value of two trade partners meeting each other on the world market.

[3]   Extensive checks were, however, performed on regional differences, preferences and other relevant factors (see Veenstra 2009 for details). Although the areas of the trade partners and dummy variables for shared official languages, landlocked and island economies were significant this hardly changed the results while the overall performance of the model was not significantly improved.

[4]   Distances are calculated from the degrees of longitude and latitude of the capitals of the trade partners. Assume the Earth to be a perfect sphere with a circumference of 40,000 kilometers. The coordinates of a point on the unit sphere are $x = \sin\theta \times \cos\varphi$, $y = \sin\theta \times \sin\varphi$ and $z = \cos\theta$, where θ is the normalized latitude $0 \le \theta \le \pi$ and φ is the normalized longitude $0 \le \varphi \le 2\pi$. The angle α between the vectors $a = [x, y, z]$ and $a' = [x', y', z']$ can be obtained from $\cos\alpha = a \times a'$ and $\alpha < \pi$. The shortest distance between the two points over the surface of the globe is $20,000\alpha/\pi$.

[5]   Yakop (2009) remarks that due to the different problems encountered when collecting all the various diplomatic representations, it eventually took him two months to collect the necessary data.

[6]   The test statistic that is used here is (see, for example Pindyck and Rubinfeld 1991, pp. 117–9): $F = (N-8)(SSR_{model\ (1)} - SSR_{model\ (4)})/2\ SSR_{model(1)}$.

[7]   Note that foreign direct investment and export can in some cases be substitutes so that a factor that increases trade may at the same time reduce investment and *vice versa*.

[8]   Charlton and Davis (2007), for example, survey investment promotion agencies in 28 OECD countries in the years 1990–2001 and find a significant increase in the volume of targeted foreign direct investment.

PART III

Economic Statecraft: The Case of Sanctions

6. Failures and ... Successes of Economic Sanctions

The study of economic sanctions essentially requires an introduction to what has been called the 'donkey psychology' of economic diplomacy. Just like a donkey, it is assumed that countries can be induced to move in the right direction by means of both a stick and a carrot, that is to say, by negative and positive economic sanctions. The donkey psychology, however, also points out that sanctions can be counterproductive: if the donkey beater pulls a donkey by the tail, it will run away in an opposite direction. Continuing the donkey metaphor would be boring and cumbersome. So in this discussion the country or group of countries that imposes or threatens to impose the economic sanction is called the sender. The country (or group of countries) on which the sanction is imposed is called the target. Negative sanctions are the most visible economic instruments of foreign policy. A negative sanction is a punishment or a disincentive. Three kinds of negative economic sanctions can be distinguished: boycotts, embargoes and capital sanctions.[1]

- A boycott restricts the demand for certain products from the target country. A boycott can be administered by governments and international organizations, but some notable consumer boycotts have been effective as well. The 1991 oil boycott against Iraq and the consumer boycott of South African agricultural products in the 1980s are examples of both types.
- An embargo restricts the exports of certain products to the target economy. Embargoes are enforced by a system of export licenses and controls of destination, transit and transport. The UN non-proliferation sanctions against North Korea in 2006 are an example.
- Capital (or financial) sanctions restrict or suspend lending (loans, credits, grants and so on) to, and investment in, the target economy and often impose additional restrictions on international payments in order to hinder sanction-busting and trade diversion. In addition foreign assets of the target economy may be frozen. The sanctions by the United States against Iran in the wake of the 1979 hostage crisis are an example.

This strict classification, however, may be blurred in actual sanction cases. Obviously, the combination of these three types may even be advisable in many cases. It is also not necessary that sanctions are complete in the sense that all trade and investment is blocked. An embargo, for example, may be partial; that is, it may cover certain specific products and technologies only.

Positive sanctions are less spectacular, because these rewards or incentives to a large extent, although not exclusively, belong to the domain of silent diplomacy. Many kinds of positive sanctions, such as aid and technological and military co-operation, belong to day-to-day-practice and are hardly ever distinct enough from the constant flows of international interactions to stand out against this background as 'reportable'. Consequently, much less is known about characteristics of positive economic sanctions (Mastanduno 2003). This is the reason to focus in this empirically oriented chapter on negative economic sanctions, but we will encounter positive sanctions in the next chapter.

The debate on the effectiveness of negative economic sanctions runs since the early applications of sanctions by the League of Nations (see Daoudi and Dajani, 1983, for a review of this debate and Baldwin, 2000, Wallensteen, 2000, and Brzoska, 2008, for reassessments of the internally conflicting, ambiguous state of our knowledge at the end of the second millennium). This chapter tries to shed some light on the issue by means of an empirical analysis of post-Second World War cases. The first section deals with some methodological questions related to the definition of the success of economic sanctions, distinguishing between effectiveness and success. Effective sanctions may fail although the economic hardship that they impose on the target is substantial. Likewise, the threat of a sanction may be successful even when no economic damage is done. Indeed, this is why we analyse the question of what we mean by success and how this is related to effectiveness in the delivery of (potential) damage. Section 2 then discusses some promising economic theories of sanctions, related to (potential) impact assessment, political economy and public choice considerations and game theoretic aspects, respectively. Methodology and relevant explanatory variables are discussed in Section 3 thus setting the stage for an econometric evaluation of the variables that economists deem to be most relevant for the success and failure of economic sanctions in Section 4. The final section concludes and suggests further avenues for research.

1 EFFECTIVENESS VERSUS SUCCESS

The most striking characteristic of negative economic sanctions is the combination of their relative lack of success and the economic profession's disbelief in the possible utility of boycotts and embargoes as instruments of foreign policy making. According to *Economic Sanctions Reconsidered* (Hufbauer et al. 2008, the standard reference on this topic) on average only about one out of three sanction cases since the Second World War succeeded in achieving their stated political goals (compare Table 6.1). Moreover, only a rather limited number of cases appear to have induced substantial damage on the target economy. According to Hufbauer et al. (2008), sanction damage was less than 0.1% of the target's GDP in about a third of the 181 cases over the period 1946–2000; only in 14% of the cases did sanction damage exceeded the threshold of 5% of the target's GDP.[2]

Table 6.1 The success rate of economic sanctions (1946–2000)

Period	Sanctions (1)	Successes (2)	Success rate (2)/(1)
1946 – 1955	14	2	14%
1956 – 1965	26	12	46%
1966 – 1975	21	6	29%
1976 – 1985	41	13	32%
1986 – 1995	62	21	34%
1996 – 2000	17	6	35%
1946 – 2000	181	60	33%

Source: Calculations based on Hufbauer et al. (2008)

Given this seeming ineffectiveness, it is not surprising that both popular and scientific interest in boycotts and embargoes as an instrument of foreign policy waned in the 1980s – that is after a period for which (with hindsight) can be observed that the success rate was comparatively speaking low and decreasing. Quite generally the usefulness of negative economic sanctions was considered to be rather low. Adler-Karlsson (1982, pp. 166–7) argued that it would hardly be possible to create the necessary political unity for forceful boycotts or embargoes and (if established at all) sanctions would be easy to circumvent. Lindsay (1986, p. 160), moreover, questioned the plausibility of a change in behaviour as a consequence of punitive economic damage: sanctions being public measures, compliance might damage the target's leadership's world prestige or diminish its domestic support. He considered economic sanctions to be merely symbolic gestures. Seeler (1982, p. 616) pointed out that the lapse of time between the decision to use economic sanctions and their actual bureaucratic implementation offers the target country the possibility to adjust its economy, thus reducing the potential damage of the sanction. And some even, as for example Reekie

(1987) in the case of South Africa, went so far as to deny that sanctions could ever work. Indeed, according to Baldwin (1985, pp. 55–7), the tendency to denigrate the utility of economic sanctions was a salient characteristic of the literature on economic statecraft at that time. Leitzel (1987, p. 286) accordingly observed that 'the gulf between policy significance and theoretical and empirical development is probably wider in the area of economic sanctions than in any other region at the confluence of economic and political streams of thought'.

In sum, according to mainstream international economists in the 1980s five reasons pointed to the ineffectiveness of economic sanctions as an instrument of foreign policy. First, failure was considered to be evident in some widely publicized and discussed cases (for example, South Africa, Israel). Second, the urge for free trade was considered to be too strong, implying that sanction-busting, smuggling and trade diversion were the most probable outcomes of economic sanctions. Third, the assumption that behaviour could be changed by means of economic damage was doubted on both political and psychological grounds. Fourth, a long-lasting complete embargo appeared hardly possible, either on economic grounds (for example, cartel theory) or on the basis of political arguments. Finally, the empirical evidence showed a rather low success rate.

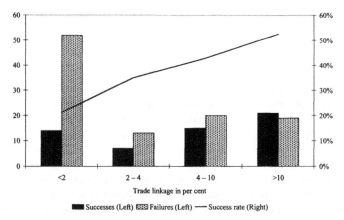

Trade linkage in per cent

■ Successes (Left) ▦ Failures (Left) —— Success rate (Right)

Notes: Proportional trade linkage is the bilateral trade flow between sender and target as a percentage of the target's GDP in the year prior to the sanction. Figure 6.1 is based on fewer observations (161) than Table 6.1 (181) because data on bilateral trade flows or national products in the year prior to the sanctions are not always available.
Sources: See the Data Appendix.

Figure 6.1 Success rate and proportional trade linkage (1946–2000)

The numerical predominance of failures *per se*, however, hardly provides evidence for the ineffectiveness of the diplomatic use of international commercial relations. More specifically, a sanction should fail if the – theoretical – conditions for a success are not being met.

This caveat would seem to be fairly obvious. A sanction simply cannot be expected to succeed if, for example, economic linkages are too low so that no or hardly any damage can ever be done. To illustrate this point, Figure 6.1 relates the success rate of sanctions to the proportional trade linkage *ex ante*. As expected a clear positive relationship between the success rate and proportional trade linkage emerges: sanctions fail if trade linkage is not sufficient. This point, however, was generally overlooked in the analysis.

Consequently, it is clear that not every failure is evidence for the inefficiency of the economic instruments of modern diplomacy. Sanctions should be expected to fail if the necessary organizational conditions for a successful sanction are not being met (Frey 1984, pp. 106–7). Only from the comparison of sanction outcomes and the values of potential determinants of failure and success can we possibly draw some valid conclusions about the potential utility of economic sanctions.[3]

A first step toward such an evaluation is to distinguish between sanction success – that is the achieved change in political behaviour – and sanction effectiveness – that is the (potential) economic damage of an economic sanction (Losman 1972).[4] The effectiveness of economic sanctions is probably the first natural line of approach for economists and this is the question with which we will be involved in the first part of the next section.

2 THE ECONOMICS OF SANCTIONS

The theoretical foundations for the use of a sanction as an instrument of foreign policy appear rather strong. The two basic premises belong to the core of economic science. First, boycotts and embargoes deprive the sanctioned economy from (some of) the gains from international trade and investment, and consequently sanctions reduce welfare. Second, the idea that (the mere threat of) this disutility influences the victim's behaviour can also be traced to the tenets of economic catechism.

The back bone of the economic analysis of sanctions is the traditional neoclassical trade model that we discussed in Chapter 3. Trade liberalisation and the associated gains from trade are useful concepts because complete embargoes and boycotts are the mirror images of the movement from the no-trade situation of autarky to a state of the world in which free trade prevails and all countries benefit from international specialisation according to their respective comparative advantage. Leaving the political aspects aside, this is the economist's realm *par excellence*, as Pen (1967, p. 37) once remarked: the comparative advantage of economists lies in analysing comparative advantage. At intermediate levels – where economic isolation is not (expected to be) complete – political trade distortions can be modelled by taking the sender's market power into consideration for example through the analysis of residual demand (Bayard et al. 1983) or by considering imperfect competition and the number of relevant competitors in a market (Schultz 1989).

From the 'inverted trade liberalisation model' of economic sanctions (Kemp 1964, pp. 208–17, Frey 1984, pp. 103–21 and Carbaugh 1989, pp. 144–7) follows that a sanction will produce more hardship on the target economy, the larger the pre-sanction target's dependence on trade with the sender and the more inflexible the target's consumption preferences and production structures.[5] Since both demand and supply rigidities are basically short-term phenomena, it follows that the passage of time reduces the effectiveness of sanctions. This yields the testable proposition that sanctions have a better chance to succeed, the larger trade linkage and the shorter the duration of the sanctions.

Effectiveness, however, is not a sufficient condition for success. Consider, for example, the UN sanctions against the Iraqi occupation of Kuwait that were very effective in delivering economic damage to Iraq and showed that the achievement of the international political unity that is considered to be a necessary condition for a forceful – and difficult to circumvent – embargo can be a matter of days (Smeets 1990). Indeed this is a unique case since the international community was able to impose severe and almost watertight sanction measures (Switzerland participated for the first time in history) and this was done within an extremely short period of four days.[6] At the same time, however, these very promising sanctions did not succeed and eventually by necessity were followed by the military intervention of 'Desert Storm' (see Aspin 1991 and Baldwin 2000, pp. 103–5). This suggests that the political economy aspects are also a crucial determinant for sanction success.

Political Economy and Public Choice Aspects

For long, the economic approach to the sanction phenomenon has merely asserted that damage (or potential damage) influences the target's behaviour, assuming that the target's population is homogeneous, that decision making is rational and fully informed and so on. In reality, however, different (interest) groups of the target's population will be hit differently – both in a relative and in an absolute sense. These topics are dealt with in the public choice approach to economic sanctions, pioneered by Kaempfer and Lowenberg (1986, 1988, 1992 and 2007). The public choice approach would *a priori* seem to be viable for both the sender and the target: an embargo will create vested interests in the continuation of a sanction in the target country as competition from abroad is limited in the target's import competing industries. Likewise, a boycott may protect import competing industries in the sender economy generating the excess profits that provide a strong incentive for lobby-groups. Decisions about sanctions or policy changes in the target could thus require the simultaneous analysis of the public choice context of both actors. Empirical research, however, suggests that the applicability of the public choice approach is especially relevant for the target economy. Regarding the impact of different bargaining strategies on the duration of the sanction cases in the Hufbauer et al. 1990 data set, Dorussen and Mo (2001, p. 418) conclude:

> Rent-seeking is particularly important for the target, whereas it is nearly insignificant for the sender. With respect to audience costs, we can only find evidence that support matters as a commitment strategy, and the substantive effect of this strategy is also much stronger for the target.[7]

How do pressures by interest groups work through the target's political system to yield some public goods or bads? Consider Figure 6.2 which describes the political market that determines the level of misconduct *M*.

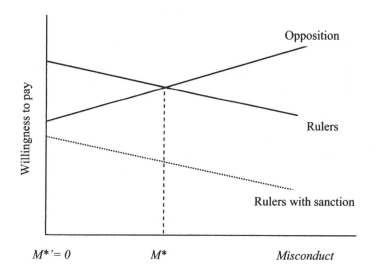

Figure 6.2 The political market for misconduct

We have two interest groups for which the demand schedule for misconduct is derived by aggregating the maximum willingness to pay to achieve more (less) utility-enhancing (decreasing) misconduct through the political market. The opposition suffers from misconduct and is willing to pay or to make sacrifices in order to achieve lower levels of misconduct. Its schedule is upward-sloping because a rational opposition will use instruments that entail larger costs (for example, the risk of execution) at higher levels of misconduct

The rulers derive positive but decreasing marginal utility from misconduct and their demand schedule slopes downward showing that their willingness to pay is larger at lower levels of misconduct. Note that this interpretation that the ruling interest group benefits from misconduct follows logically from the fact that economic sanctions would not be necessary if the decision makers oppose misconduct. Figure 6.2 illustrates that the processes on the political market yield a positive equilibrium level of misconduct M^*. The primary channel, through which a sanction works, is through its potential impact on the demand schedule of the rulers that shifts downwards reducing the equilibrium level of misconduct.[8] The outcome in the illustrated case in Figure 6.2 is an intersection of the demand schedules for the opposition and the rulers *cum* sanction to the left of the y-axis (so the sanction is a full success: $M^{*\prime} = 0$).

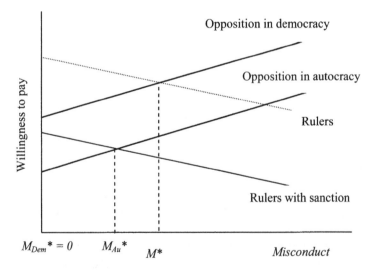

Figure 6.3 Democratic and autocratic institutions and success of sanctions

Next consider Figure 6.3 which illustrates the impact of the strength of democratic and autocratic institutions on the success of sanctions.[9] The stronger autocratic institutions *vis-à-vis* democratic institutions, the lower the opposition's political effectiveness, as pointed out by Kaempfer and Lowenberg (1988, p. 790):

> If a group is constitutionally excluded from the nominal policy-making process, the only option open to members of such a group are costly ones like insurrection or civil disobedience, which reduces their revealed willingness to pay for lower levels of [misconduct].

So the opposition's demand curve will *ceteris paribus* be lower if institutions are less democratic and less open. Figure 6.3 illustrates that a sanction that is a full success in a democracy $M_{Dem}* = 0$ will be less successful in an autocracy $M_{Au}* > 0$ even though the sanction is still successful in reducing the level of misconduct from its original level $M*$ (see also Kaempfer et al. 2004 for a detailed application of the dictatorship model to sanctions). This yields the testable proposition that sanctions against democracies have a larger chance to succeed than sanctions against autocracies.

The Sanction Game

Game theory has contributed the insight that not only the implementation of economic sanctions, but also the mere threat to use them can be an adequate policy instrument. The sender utters a strategic threat consisting of the announcement that economic sanction measures will be applied. If behaviour is altered the game ends and the sender attains its objective in the most efficient way, as it does not have to bear the costs of the sanction. If, however, a threat is not sufficiently credible to change behaviour, punitive action has to be carried out. This is painful and costly for both the sender and the target since both parties will be unable to reap the full benefits of free and undisturbed trade. Consequently, a sanction might be too costly to be carried out and the threat may appear false. Against this background two stylized facts of sanctions are peculiar (see Table 6.2).

Firstly, the implementation of a sanction today does not necessarily imply that this sanction will be implemented in the next period as well. Indeed, slightly less than one out of five unsuccessful economic sanctions lasted one year or less. As the target of the sanction did not change its behaviour, the reason for implementing the sanction in the first place continued in these cases. Evidently then, continuation of a sanction is uncertain. Secondly, the majority of the successful foreign policy sanctions took longer than one year to succeed. If the intentions of the imposing countries and the perceptions of the target country are known with certainty, the sanctions should either work directly or never at all. Many successful sanctions appear to take some time to work. Indeed, about two thirds of the successful sanctions require two years or more to achieve compliance, that is the desired change of behaviour.

Table 6.2 Distribution of duration of post-1945 sanctions

Duration	Failures (%)	Successes (%)
Less than and up to 1 year	17	41
2 years	6	14
3 years	15	9
4 years	11	12
5 or more years	51	25
	100	100

Note: Totals may not add up to 100% due to rounding

Source: Calculations based on Hufbauer et al. (2008)

The history of the economic sanction instrument thus contains cases of sanctions that work directly, of sanctions that work only after some time and of sanctions that never seem to work. This finding is essentially why any theory of economic sanctions should not start from a deterministic setting. Theory has to deal with the stochastic outcome of situations in which economic sanctions have been applied. Moreover, theory has to acknowledge the impact of (subjective) expectations and probabilities in the decision making process. From this perspective the passage of time may also become a positive determinant of success, for example, if targets learn and understand the extent to which sanctions will (continue to be) applied in the next period (Bergeijk and Marrewijk 1994, 1995) If so, actual implementation of sanction measures increases the expected value of the threat as even partial implementation increases the probability of (possibly full) application in the next period.

Game theorists have also argued that it may be wrong to apply decision theory instead of game theory when more than one rational actor is involved, an error coined the 'Robinson Crusoe Fallacy' by Tsebelis (1989), who also develops a model (Tsebelis 1990) in which these interactions are modelled explicitly. He shows that the target's equilibrium strategy only depends on the sender's payoff matrix. His model ably explains three stylized facts of the application of sanctions as an instrument of foreign policy: small countries are not inclined to use economic sanctions, few sanctions succeed and policy advice on the selection and application of sanctions is poor. Tsebelis's model, however, requires a number of unrealistic assumptions. The payoff matrices of the players have to be known and are assumed to be independent (the latter is simply wrong in international economics), much information is required about the valuation of uncertain outcomes and the sanction game is to be repeated a great many times. Tsebelis's model predicts that an increase in potential sanction damage does not influence the success rate, a proposition that will be tested empirically in the next section.

3 WHAT DRIVES SUCCESS?

Our short discussion of international trade economics, public choice and game theory suggests a number of hypotheses (potential determinants of success and failure) that can be tested econometrically. We will use 172 post-1945 cases that have been published in the 2008 volume and on the website of the Peterson Institute for International Economics (see www.iie.com/). The appendix to this chapter discusses these data (and the sources for the explanatory variables) in detail. In the econometric investigation the binary variable y_i serves as the dependent variable.

$y_i = 1$, if the i-th sanction is a success
$y_i = 0$, if not

The relation between the dependent and the explanatory variables will be estimated with LOGIT. LOGIT-analysis makes it possible to calculate the probability π that a specified sanction case ends successfully. If this probability exceeds 0.5, a success is 'predicted'; if not, a failure. We may write:

$$\pi\,[y_i = 1] = 1/1 + e^{-\theta_{i,j}}, \text{ where } \theta_{i,j} = \alpha_{0,j} + \Sigma^N_{k=1}\alpha_{i,j,k} \cdot x_{i,k} \qquad (6.1)$$

That is: we write the probability of success π for observation i and specification j as a function of the observed inputs (explanatory variables) x and the estimated co-efficients α.[10]

A sanction is successful if behaviour satisfactorily changes and the sanction significantly contributes to this outcome.[11] As a general rule, the outcome of a sanction case as given in the Hufbauer et al. 2008 study is adopted as the final decision about the value of y_i. As each outcome is the result of an evaluation of the literature on a specific case, it seems probable that differences of opinion exist about the value of the dependent variable in certain cases (Pape 1997). Hufbauer et al. (1990, 2008), for example, code the British sanctions against Argentina in 1982 as relatively successful in removing Argentinean forces from the Falklands, whereas the Royal Marines would seem more deserving of the credit. We will not be concerned with their judgements about the outcome of sanctions in individual cases and simply accept their findings (however, in cases that have been split in order to reflect that multiple goals existed the dataset that is used in this chapter only takes the most difficult into account; that is the lowest value of the success score). A second important difference is that the data set in this chapter (unlike the calculations by Hufbauer et al. 2008) does contain the identified threat cases (that is cases that never went beyond the stage of a threat and were not actually implemented). These special cases are included for three reasons. First, we know from game theory that these are potentially the most cost-effective cases. Second, in line with Morgan and Schwebach (1995) the inclusion of such cases reduces the risk and extent of biasing the research. Thirdly, the argument for non-inclusion, namely that in these cases no damage can be assessed (Hufbauer et al. 2008, pp. 106–7 and 182), is not valid: the costs *ex post* are after all known to be zero by definition.

This brings us to the choice of explanatory variables that measure the impact of the sanction. First of all it is, however, important that we recognize the necessity to be parsimonious. We will only have 172 observations available for our logit analysis. Aldrich and Nelson (1984, p. 81) argue that about 50 cases per explanatory variable should be available if the dependent variable is a dichotomous variable and this reasonable rule of thumb leaves us with three to four explanatory variables at most. Our strategy will thus be to construct a small quasi-reduced form equation that reflects the determinants that are *a priori* expected to be of most importance for the potential economic impact and the political setting, respectively. Next different versions or specifications of this equation (with different sets of variables) will be tested, so as to check for the robustness of the findings.

Impact Variables: Trade Linkage and Time

Hufbauer et al. (2008, p. 50) see costs as the main determinant of success:

> Stripped to the bare bones, the formula for a successful sanction's effort is simple: The cost of defiance borne by the target must be greater than the perceived costs of compliance.

The *ex post* damage that appears as the costs of the imposition of sanctions in the Hufbauer et al. 2008 study may not be the most appropriate explanatory variable. It is not the actual *ex post* damage done but rather the *ex ante* threat of disutility that influences behaviour. The most efficient sanction immediately changes behaviour, implying that punishment is not necessary. As a consequence no externally imposed economic costs for the target economy might be measured.[12] It is also less appropriate to include the costs of the sanction together with other variables that are supposed to explain the extent of the sanction damage, as multicollinearity can be expected. This motivates our choice to use trade linkage as a proxy for potential damage of the sanctions.

Wolf (1983) distinguishes absolute trade linkage and proportional trade linkage (incidentally both measures are shares). Absolute trade linkage relates the bilateral trade flow between sender and target to the target's total trade flow. High absolute trade linkage indicates dominance of the sender in the external economic relations of the target. The target's valuation of the potential sanction loss, however, depends on the importance of the bilateral trade flow in relation to other (domestic) economic activities. Low absolute trade linkage may imply a bigger loss for an open economy than high absolute trade linkage may imply for a closed, almost autarkic economy and this is the reason to consider proportional trade linkage as well.[13]

Let $X_{s,t}$ be the sender's exports to the target. Our notation is that $X_{s,t} = M_{t,s}$ which stands for the target's import from the sender.[14] Likewise $X_{t,s}$ is the target's export to the sender and $X_{t,s} = M_{s,t}$. Further Y_t is the target's national income, X_t is the target's total exports to all destinations including the sender and likewise M_t is the target's total import. Measurement always takes place in the year prior to the sanctions.[15] So we have:

$$Absolute\ trade\ linkage = (X_{t,s} + M_{t,s}) / (X_t + M_t) \qquad (6.2)$$

$$Proportional\ trade\ linkage = (X_{t,s} + M_{t,s}) / Y_t \qquad (6.3)$$

Remember that the neoclassical approach suggests that trade linkage will be an important driver of success, whereas the game theoretic contributions that were discussed in the previous section suggest otherwise as the gains and losses of the target will typically not be in the payoff matrix of the sender.

The second impact variable is time. Duration can only be observed *ex post*. So it is worth stressing that this chapter's aim is rather modest. The intention cannot be to guide the selection of potentially successful cases. Rather the goal is to understand *ex post* what the drivers have been of historical success and failure rates and to see how this reflects upon the sometimes contradicting theories that we discussed in the previous sections. Indeed, the influence of time is not *a priori* clear. The earlier literature (Daoudi and Dajani, 1983, Brady 1987 and Hanlon and Omond, 1987) stressed that total damage increases over time, missing the points that, first, bygones are bygones and, second, that substitution and flexibility increase over time thus reducing the impact of sanctions to some extent. These points would seem to be very relevant from an empirical point of view, but modern theories explain, as discussed, that time can also add to sanction success because it takes time to negotiate and to learn.

Regarding the time variable, it is important to note that the outcome of a number of sanctions cannot be determined yet as these sanctions were still 'ongoing' at the moment that the database was constructed.[16] Inclusion of these cases in the estimations may bias the results. First, the duration of the sanction is underestimated. Second, ongoing sanctions are typically seen as failures. Some sanctions indeed take very long to succeed. The sanctions against the South African Apartheid system are an example. Thus it is important that we do our estimations both for the full sample and for a smaller sample that excludes the ongoing cases.

Another point that was often made in the older literature (see, for example, Leyton-Brown, 1987, p. 308) relates to the difficulty of ending unsuccessful sanctions without an awkward loss of face. The implied tendency of ineffective sanctions to last for long periods, however, is no longer confirmed by the data. Interestingly, as illustrated in Figure 6.4, duration of ineffective sanctions has significantly decreased over time (duration of successful sanctions shows no time trend).

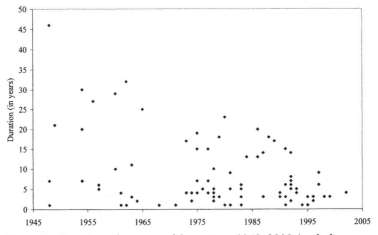

Figure 6.4 Duration of unsuccessful sanctions 1945–2005 (excluding ongoing sanctions)

Public Choice Variables

The inclusion of the target's political system at the start of the sanctions is straight-forward and deploys a standard international political science data source: Polity IV (discussed in the appendix to this chapter). This data source provides an 'autocracy score' and a 'democracy score' for a specific country in a specific year. Subtracting the autocracy score from the democracy score yields a summary measure. These measures can be used in different specifications so as to test the robustness of the specification.

Public Choice, moreover, implies that the design of sanctions matters, as their impact on interest groups in the target and in the sender will differ. Thus it is relevant to include the type of sanction (boycott, embargo, financial sanctions) as an explanatory variable.

Other Explanatory Variables

Several variables will be used to check the impact of obvious factors. It is easier to win from a small country (approximated by the ratio of the sender's GDP and the target's GDP); simpler sanctions (with goals that can be more easily reached) are more prone to succeed. Co-operation with the sender or hindrance (sanction-busting) should be considered of course.

Table 6.3 Summary of explanatory variables (excluding ongoing cases)

Explanatory variables	N	Mean	SD
Core model			
Absolute trade linkage (%)	148	29.3	21.7
Proportional trade linkage (%)	147	7.4	1.1
Sanction duration (years)	153	6.6	7.7
Autocracy score (index 1–10)	153	3.6	3.2
Democracy score (index 1–10)	153	2.8	3.5
Financial variables			
Financial Sanctions (dummy)	146	0.8	0.4
Aid to GDP (%)	152	0.6	3.7
Co-operation, sanction busting, smuggling			
Co-operation with sender (dummy)	146	0.3	0.4
Hindrance of sender (dummy)	146	0.2	0.4
Area (10^{-6})	145	0.7	1.6
Political variables			
Prior relations (index 1–3)	153	2.1	0.8
GDP sender to GDP target (ratio)	149	1.7	6.4
Reputation (number of sanctions in 10 year)	153	1.5	1.2
Moderate goal (dummy)	153	0.2	0.4
Target is political and economic instable	146	0.3	0.4
P.M. *Ex post* costs to GDP (%)	153	1.9	3.4

Likewise smuggling (to be proxied by the target's area) reduces the success rate, political and economic instability of the target increases the probability of success, and so on. Of particular relevance may be the issue that the financial dimension is lacking from our core equation so that it may be pertinent to analyze whether financial sanctions or the impact of aid are important. The appendix discusses the merits and definitions of the data that have been used in this exercise.

All in all our core equation will include three variables for (absolute or proportional) trade linkage between sender and target, duration of the sanction and the political system (democracy *vs.* autocracy) and will be tested against the alternative variables that were summarized in Table 6.3.

4 EMPIRICAL RESULTS

Table 6.4 summarizes the econometric results for the small quasi-reduced form equation. The results are satisfactorily from a statistical point of view as the co-efficients are generally speaking significant at the usual 95% confidence level and better. The model 'predicts' the right outcome in roughly 70% of the cases, thus beating alternative forecasting strategies such as tossing a coin or always predicting a failure. It should, however, be noted that the percentage of false positives is rather high and in the range of 37–41%.

As a point of reference (also in relation to the findings of Hufbauer et al. 2008) the first column reports results for a specification of the estimated equation that – 'erroneously' – uses the sender's *ex post* costs of sanctions as an explanatory variable. The other columns in the table show the results for our preferred indicators of potential damage (absolute and proportional trade linkage, respectively) and do so both for the unrestricted data set and for the limited set of cases that were not ongoing. These four specifications are theoretically to be preferred and perform better than the *ex post* cost variant on statistical grounds.

The estimates show that the probability that an economic sanction succeeds in changing the target's behaviour is higher, the larger the pre-sanction trade linkage, the more democratic and open the target's political system and the shorter the sanction period. This can be illustrated by means of the elasticities that we can derive for the hypothetical average sanction on the basis of the third and fifth specification (which exclude the ongoing cases). This hypothetical sanction is a case in which the explanatory variables assume the averages reported in Table 6.3, so absolute trade linkage is 29.3%, proportional trade linkage is 7.4%, sanction duration is 6.6 years and the autocracy score is 3.6 points. Substituting these values and using the estimated co-efficients that are reported in Table 6.4 into equation 6.1 we can derive that the probability that this hypothetical 'average case' ends successfully is about 40%. Next we can calculate how an increase by 1% influences this probability. An increase of trade linkage increases the probability by 0.2 percentage points while an increase in sanction duration and the autocracy score yield a reduction by 0.2 and 0.3 percentage points, respectively.

Table 6.4 Success of sanctions: LOGIT estimates for the quasi-reduced form equation of the success score of sanctions 1946–2000

	Cost *ex post*	Absolute Trade Linkage		Proportional Trade Linkage	
Ongoing sanctions	yes	yes	no	yes	No
Number of observations	172	166	148	161	147
(Potential) cost variable	11.2	1.1	1.6	3.5	3.8
	(4.5)	(0.6)	(0.7)	(1.6)	(1.7)
	{0.01}	{0.08}	{0.02}	{0.03}	{0.02}
Sanction period	−0.70	−0.69	−0.70	−0.68	−0.68
(log number of years)	(0.19)	(0.18)	(0.20)	(0.19)	(0.20)
	{0.00}	{0.00}	{0.00}	{0.00}	{0.00}
Autocracy score	−0.11	−0.11	−0.13	−0.15	−0.12
	(0.06)	(0.06)	(0.06)	(0.06)	(0.06)
	{0.06}	{0.04}	{0.03}	{0.01}	{0.04}
Constant term	0.33	0.27	0.25	0.44	0.39
	(0.31)	(0.36)	(0.37)	(0.33)	(0.34)
	{0.29}	{0.45}	{0.51}	{0.19}	{0.26}
Log likelihood	−96.2	−93.2	−83.8	−90.3	−84.6
Errors Type I (False Positive)	41%	38%	40%	37%	40%
Errors Type II (False Negative)	27%	26%	27%	25%	28%
Percent correct	70%	71%	70%	71%	69%

Notes
(standard errors in parenthesis)
{two-tail significance test in brackets}
Errors Type I and Type II in per cent of cases $\pi>0$ and $\pi<0$, respectively.

Next consider Table 6.5 which summarizes the results of a set of extended core equations (for specifications that either use proportional or absolute trade linkage, respectively). The table reports co-efficients and significance levels for variables that were added in order to control for factors such as sanction-busting and international co-operation, the status of diplomatic relations before the imposition of sanctions and the sender's reputation as an executioner of threats. These extensions also provide an additional test for the robustness of the estimated core equation.

Table 6.5 Extending the core equation

Added variable	Trade linkage variable	
	Proportional	Absolute
Financial variables		
Financial Sanctions	0.60	0.41
	{0.21}	{0.39}
Aid to GDP	0.25	0.15
	{0.25}	{0.32}
Co-operation, sanction-busting, smuggling		
Co-operation with sender	0.60	0.22
	{0.17}	{0.59}
Hindrance of sender	−0.03	−0.01
	{0.95}	{0.99}
Area	−0.20	−0.24
	{0.20}	{0.15}
Political variables		
Prior relations	0.50	0.60
	{0.05}	{0.04}
GDP sender to GDP target	−2.35	−2.88
	{0.43}	{0.61}
Reputation	−0.01	−0.01
	{0.46}	{0.61}
Moderate goal	0.62	0.69
	{0.17}	{0.12}
Political and economic instability	0.62	0.47
	{0.15}	{0.25}

Note: {two-tail significance test in brackets}

Generally speaking, the signs of the co-efficients conform to *a priori* expectations, with the exception of the estimated parameter for the ratio of sender-GDP-to-target-GDP that is, however, not significant and, as argued in the Appendix, may to some extent reflect selection bias in the Hufbauer et al. data-bases. Anyhow, the addition of these variables does not add much value thus validating the parsimonious estimation approach that was followed in this chapter. The only significant parameter relates to the pre-sanction relations between sender and target, but its significance is reduced to almost virtually zero if this variable is added to the core equation *in combination* with the other potentially relevant explanatory variables that were mentioned in Table 6.3, implying that the pre-sanction relations index, so to say, at best captures some aspects of other explanatory variables while it is also possible that the correlation is simply spurious.[17]

All in all the core equation provides a good empirical shorthand description of the key factors behind success and failure of economic sanctions since the Second World War.

5 CONCLUSIONS AND DISCUSSION

Occam's razor appears to be useful for the field of economic sanctions: parsimony has led to a simple yet highly significant explanation. This contrasts with many statistical analyses of the Hufbauer et al. data set, the most recent example being the Appendix to Hufbauer et al. (2008, pp. 181–92) in which 78% of the reported co-efficients are insignificant (and for the significant co-efficients the interpretation is often ambiguous because the outcome of a sanction is not influenced according to the estimate, while the contribution of the sanction to that outcome is significant).[18] The estimates in this chapter show that economic and 'non-economic' public choice variables play a significant role in the explanation of the outcome of sanction episodes. In particular the findings refute by implication theories that assume that no relationship exists between the outcome of sanctions and objective characteristics of sanction episodes, such as punishment, signalling and symbolism (compare Bonetti 1998, pp. 805–6) as well as the empirical relevancy of the Robinson Crusoe Fallacy that we discussed earlier, at least in the context of economic sanctions.[19]

This implies that sanctions can be effective instruments in international politics, because they result in a change of behaviour provided that the economic and political conditions are being met. This is to say, that the successes that have appeared (34% of the cases over the period 1946–2002) should not be considered as mere accidents but can be explained theoretically. From a policy perspective the findings show that economic analysis (in tandem with political science) has a relevant role to play in the selection of cases as well as in the design of the actual measures that are considered. It is true that not all explanatory variables that are included in our core model can be used in the selection of cases, as the duration of sanctions is essentially a variable that can only be observed *ex post* (this argument, incidentally, also pertains to the use of the *ex post* cost by Hufbauer et al.)[20] The point, however, is that the core model supports the notion that economic theory can help to identify the variables that are relevant such as pre-sanction trade linkage and the extent to which changes of the production structure are possible.

It is further noteworthy that these quantitative results are essentially the same as the results that were derived from the earlier data sets of Hufbauer et al.. This is relevant because about two thirds of the observations in the 2008 edition are new or revised (see Figure 6A.1 in the data appendix that follows this chapter) and this suggests that the results are robust. Moreover substantial structural breaks could be expected to occur regarding the efficacy and effectiveness of the use of economic relationships in an international context that is rapidly changing due to the end of the super power conflict, increasing globalization and an increasing use of multilateral sanctions. Indeed, the end of the Cold War (and the sanctions against Saddam Hussein) seem to have served as a starting point for a true proliferation in the use of economic sanctions as an instrument of foreign policy (*cf.* Bergeijk 1995c). Table 6.6 shows that the average annual number of imposed sanction increased by 50–70%, when we compare the pre-1990 and the post-1990 period.[21]

Table 6.6 Key characteristics pre-1990, post-1990 and for 1946–2002

	1946–1989		1990–2002		1946–2002	
Ongoing sanctions	yes	no	yes	no	yes	no
Number of sanctions	113	103	59	50	172	153
Annual average	2.6	2.3	4.5	3.8	3.7	3.3
Share of successes	32%	34%	39%	40%	34%	36%
Trade linkage						
absolute	22%	23%	45%	45%	29%	29%
proportional	6%	6%	11%	10%	8%	7%
Period (years)	8.9	7.8	4.2	4.1	7.3	6.6
Share of instable targets	21%	24%	48%	45%	30%	30%

Source: Calculations based on Hufbauer et al. (2008); see also the Data Appendix

The upshot of Table 6.6 is that there has been an increase in the use of sanctions, but that this has not deteriorated the success rate of the instrument as the share of successes increased by some 6 to 7 percentage points.

One obvious reason suggested by Table 6.6 is that this is a result of a better case selection as is shown by the doubling of trade linkage and the share of instable targets (which was identified as a significant variable in earlier studies) and the halving of the sanction period (which was mainly achieved for failure cases; see Figure 6.4.) This of course begs the question why the application of sanctions has become more intelligent. It may be the case that empirical research encourages learning and further improvements of case selection. If so, further research should show a further increase in success rate.

A new insight developed in this chapter is the notion of the importance of the target's political structure. Sanctions against dictatorships and other autocratically-ruled targets have a substantially lower probability of succeeding. Another insight relates to factors that were found to be empirically relevant in investigations of the 1990 data set, but no longer are found to be significant. A good example is the sender's reputation which after econometric experimentation was approximated by the number of prior sanctions in a decade. The loss of significance for this variable may be related to the fact that it was an unsatisfactory measure for a difficult concept (compare Bonetti 1998), but it may also be the case that the fact that many post-1990 sanctions have been imposed by new players such as the UN for whom the track record mattered less. Also this is a matter for further research.

As a final remark it is worth pointing out that we would not have known what we know today about the application of negative sanctions and the conditions for their success if Hufbauer and Schott had not started their data collection effort in the 1980s. Unfortunately, a comparable data set does not exist for the use of positive sanctions as a tool for foreign policy. We will thus by necessity limit our analysis of positive sanctions in the next chapter to the theoretical domain since empirical generalizations are not yet possible. The experience with the Hufbauer et al. data sets suggests that an effort to build a comparable data set for positive sanctions would be a wise investment with large expected payoffs for both science and policy.

NOTES

[1] Typically economic sanctions are formulated as international quantity restrictions of the flows of goods, services and capital although from a purely economic point of view prices could also be used as an instrument (see Spindler 1995).

[2] Incidentally, Farmer (2000) argues that the Hufbauer et al. methodology overestimates the actual impact of sanctions.

[3] Often sanctions fail because checks on the observance of the economic measures at the borders are simply impossible, as in the case of the sanctions against disintegrating Yugoslavia in the early 1990s. Moreover, many sanctions can only come about after long-lasting and laborious international consultation; a general characteristic of EU decision making on international political activities. Sometimes the costs of effective sanctions are too large for the sender so that diplomacy never gets beyond the stage of angry words without decisiveness.

[4]   Other classifications such as the one proposed by Smeets (1992), who distinguishes between success and efficacy, essentially boil down to the same. One always has to distinguish the question of whether damage can be done from the question of whether potential disutility will influence behaviour. Further note that compliance is not the only objective of sanctions. Punishment may be an equally important aim (Nossal 1989). Other goals include: subversion, deterrence (of other countries than the target), international symbolism and domestic symbolism; see Lindsay (1986).

[5]   It is often assumed that the free availability of goods that are covered by the sanctions on the target's markets indicates a lack of effectiveness and, consequently, a failure. The absence, however, of formal rationing activities can occur if the market mechanism functions properly. A decrease in the supply of goods feeds into higher prices, reducing the quantity demanded until a new equilibrium between demand and supply is reached. Accordingly, the market mechanism automatically distributes the goods among the population in the most efficient way and a formal rationing scheme will only be necessary if the rise in prices is deemed socially unacceptable.

[6]   See, for example, K. Elliott et al., 'Judging from History, the Anti-Saddam Sanctions Can Work', *International Herald Tribune*, December 11, 1990.

[7]   Note that this pertains to the Hufbauer et al. 1990 data set.

[8]   I ignore specific utility enhancing attributes of the sanctions, that is 'rally-around-the-flag'-effects or signalling effects that may influence the schedules of opposition and rulers. Such effects have been discussed and analyzed by other authors. Criticism will only be directed against the domestic government if the targeted regime falters (Lindsay 1986, p.162). If the regime has a stable position, it may actually utilise the threat for its own purposes. According to Scolnick (1988) in addition to transference of intra-group hostility, increased public support may bolster the target state's government and may enhance both its short-run and its long-run material capacity to resist, thus deepening the enmities between target and sender, and economic sanctions will not call forth the desired result. My point is not that such effects are unimportant. I ignore these effects in order to clarify the impact of autocratic and democratic institutions as transparently as possible.

[9]   In Chapter 3 another, purely neoclassical, mechanism was identified because it was shown that the institutional characteristics of decision-making influence the extent of precautionary 'non-specialization'. Democracies are 'too open' and thus more vulnerable to sanction measures.

[10]   Note that if $\theta \to \infty$ so $\pi \uparrow 1$ and if $\theta \to -\infty$ so $\pi \downarrow 0$. Hence the logical restrictions on the dependant variable ($0 \leq \pi \leq 1$) are never violated.

[11]   The success score in this case equals or exceeds 9 (Hufbauer et al., 2008, p. 50). See also the discussion in the Appendix to this chapter.

[12]   Moreover, it is difficult to estimate the total costs that result from a sanction. In addition to the direct costs entailing financial and real outlays immediately related to the imposition of sanctions (such as rising transport costs), Losman (1972, pp. 28–30) identifies indirect costs due to dislocation and forced under-utilization of factors of production, and forgone potential. The latter relates to certain expected future economies of production and revenues that will no longer be realisable. To estimate these more comprehensive costs, however, one has to have either a complete macroeconomic model of the economy concerned or an applied trade

model of its detailed export and import relationships. Hufbauer et al. (2008, p. 105) restrict their analysis to the direct costs and believe that their numbers overestimate actual costs. Their procedure, however, yields a very rough underestimate of the potential welfare loss.

[13] However, both measures will be used because the proportional trade linkage measure might be corrupted by the fact that trade shares might rise relative to GDP when countries disconnect from world trade (Gatzke and Li 2003) or if trade to GDP is negatively correlated with political power (Mansfield and Pollins 2003) See also Mousseau et al. (2003), p. 292.

[14] Note that the exports from *A* to *B* should equal the imports in *A* from *B* in principle. Due to the registration issues discussed in the Appendix this is of course not always the case, so that the point of measurement (*A*'s trade statistics or *B*'s trade statistics) matters. Still the trade data of all trade partners can be useful to estimate absolute trade linkage for a target for which national statistics are not available or totally unreliable.

[15] Note that this is not the case in the Hufbauer et al. study implying that their trade variables can be corrupted by the impact of actual sanction measures (provided that the sanctions bite). Our measurement also helps solving the issue of causality.

[16] Incidentally the percentage of ongoing sanctions decreased from 20% in the 1990 data set to 8% in the 2008 data set of Hufbauer et al.

[17] Prior relations only remain significant in combination with the dummy variable for the goal of sanctions (which is insignificant and should not be included).

[18] The percentage of insignificant co-efficients (that is a less than 90% confidence level, see the Appendix of Bergeijk, 1994b) is 67% in Deheja and Wood (1992), 68% in Hufbauer et al. (1985) and 45–60% (depending on the specification) in Lam (1990). Only Bonetti (1998) attempts to estimate his model parsimoniously.

[19] Tsebelis's main message is and remains valid of course: especially in analyzing specific cases one needs to consider the reactions of targets and senders.

[20] It is of course possible to use simulation techniques for duration in order to arrive at estimates for the conditional probability that a sanction case will succeed.

[21] This is also illustrated by the UN's track-record. Before August 1990 only two UN sanctions came into force (against former Rhodesia and South Africa (aimed at changing the status quo *inside* these countries rather than at restoring the *international* status quo. Since 1990 the UN imposed sanctions against Iraq (1990), Yugoslavia (1991) Haiti (1991), Liberia (1992), Cambodia (1992), Libya (1992), North Korea (1993), Angola (1993), Rwanda (1994), Sierra Leone (1997), Afghanistan (1999), the DR Congo (2003) and Ivory Coast (2004).

Appendix 6A.1: Data Sources and Methodology

In this part we are concerned with qualitative and quantitative characteristics of economic sanctions. So this first section of the data appendix is probably the right place for a dull warning on the reliability of data about economic sanctions. Obviously, observations about international economic warfare and particular about trade and investment flows should not automatically be considered reliable.

This appendix considers a number of issues regarding the data that have been used and the proper way to analyse these data. One reason is that data from subject fields of three different sciences have to be combined into one data set. We will use foreign policy data, economic data and data on the political system. It pays to discuss these data, their construction and limitations so as to allow researchers that specialized in one of these fields a better understanding of the value of the research. First this appendix discusses the Hufbauer et al. (1985, 1990 and 2008) data sets. Then we move on to a discussion of the measurement issues related to economic variables such as trade (linkage) and income levels. The third section discusses the Polity III data set of international comparative composite data of the institutional features of political systems. The final section lists the data sources for other variables.

1 A CLOSER LOOK AT HUFBAUER ET AL.

Due to a lack of sufficiently comparable observations, empirical research on the subject of economic sanctions as a tool of foreign policy was not possible before the publication of *Economic Sanctions Reconsidered* by Hufbauer and Schott (1985). This seminal study provided a comprehensive and systematic treatment of 103 cases in which economic sanctions have been applied and offered a unique opportunity to put the sanction theory on an empirical footing. An update which appeared as Hufbauer, Schott and Elliott (1990) contained twelve additional cases and a critical re-evaluation of the cases that were discussed in the 1985 edition. It took almost two decades before the third edition was published by Hufbauer Schott, Elliott and Oegg (2008). The third edition presents evidence on 65 post-1990 cases and now also covers a decade of sanction after the Iraq war and the fall of the Iron Curtain (12 new pre-1990 sanction cases were also included in the third edition). Thus the third edition offers the possibility to investigate the more recent history which is relevant as the efficacy and efficiency of the sanction instrument may have been influenced by the sanctions against Saddam Hussein (a major sanction episode), by *Détente* and by the increasing speed of globalization (including the integration of China in the world economic system).

All in all the data set has been extended substantially and moreover 38 old cases were revised, so that almost two thirds of the observations are new or revised (Figure 6A.1). It is thus highly relevant to analyse this data set in order to see whether old findings and policy recipes are still valid.

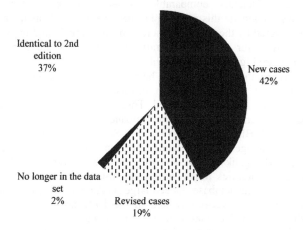

Figure 6A.1 Comparison of the 2nd and 3rd edition of Hufbauer et al.

Hufbauer et al. (2008, pp. 53–4) divide the sanction episodes into five categories, classified according to the major foreign policy objective sought by the sender country:

- to change the target's policies in a relatively modest way;
- to destabilise the target government;
- to disrupt a minor military adventure;
- to impair the military potential of the target country and;
- to change the target country's policies in a major way.

In the econometric investigation, however, I do not make a distinction as to the sender country's objectives (with one exception where I extend the core equation as reported in Table 6.5 and use a dummy variable that assumes the value 1 if the goal is 'moderate'). I do not take the objective into consideration in the core model for two reasons. First, an episode may have more than one objective. Destabilization presupposes a lesser goal, and attempts to impair the military power of an adversary usually encompass an explicit or implicit goal of destabilising the target country's government. Second, there are just not enough observations. There would only be some 40 cases per category and this impedes useful generalization in case the objectives are taken into account.[1]

Some specific methodological questions have been raised with respect to the major database on the efficacy of economic sanctions (Hufbauer et al. 1985, Hufbauer et al. 1990 and Hufbauer et al. 2008 – whenever possible I refer to the third edition). Bull (1984, p. 221), for example, wonders whether the data are sufficiently comparable to lend themselves for useful generalizations. In general this problem has become less acute as the number of sanctions covered by the study has increased substantially and the share of recent sanctions – for which comparatively better data are available – increased (compare Figure 6A.1 and Table 6.6).

More worrying, the database might be biased for several reasons.[2] First, obviously the most effective sanction threats could be underrepresented because they do not have to be applied. Thus some researchers expect that failure cases are overrepresented in the Hufbauer et al. databases (Tsebellis 1990, Smith, 1995, Blake and Klemm 2006). Second, countries that have a comparative advantage in the implementation of sanctions could be overrepresented (Bergeijk 1994b). Knowing they have little or no chance to succeed, specific countries might simply not use sanctions and hence be underrepresented in the database. Indeed large sender countries, most notably the United States, are over-represented in the Hufbauer et al. databases. Sanctions that only involve small non-anglosaxon countries have less chance of being picked up in international scholarly research due to cultural and language barriers.

Finally, the answer to whether a specific sanction case is indeed a success or a failure has to be based on judgements of several authors. Differences of opinion – of which Pape (1997) is a good example – are very probable, as, for example, Hufbauer et al. (2008, p. 49) admit:

> since foreign objectives often come in multiple parts, since objectives evolve over time, and since the contribution of sanctions to the policy outcomes is often murky, judgment plays an important role in assigning a single number to each element of the success equation.

The dependent variable in Hutbauer et al. is the success score of a sanction which is defined (Hufbauer et al. 2008, pp. 49–50) as the product of the assessments of the policy result (the extent to which the policy outcome sought by the sender country was in fact achieved) and of the sanction contribution to this result (the contribution made by sanctions to a positive outcome). So we may write the success score as:

$$Success\ score = Policy\ result \times Sanction\ contribution \qquad (6A.1)$$

Since both these assessments are each an integer from the interval 1 ('none') to 4 ('important') the success score adopts the values 1 , 2, 3, 4, 6, 8, 9, 12 and 16 only (see Table 6A.1).

Table 6A.1 The construction of the success score of economic sanctions

Element	Index
Policy result	
a) Failed outcome	1
b) Unclear, but possibly positice outcome	2
c) Positive outcome	3
d) Successful outcome	4
Sanction contribution	
a) Zero or negative contribution	1
b) Minor contribution	2
c) Modest contribution	3
d) Significant contribution	4

Source: Hufbauer et al. 2008.

The value of the success score is the subject of empirical investigations by Hufbauer et al. in which average scores are tabulated for potentially explanatory variables. Averages, however, are simply insufficient statistical means to describe the distribution of the subsets of sanction attributes; one would at least want to know the standard deviations before any valid conclusions can be drawn. Such simple counts, moreover, lead to wrong conclusions, because this approach fails to hold other potentially relevant variables constant. This implies the need to investigate the success score by means of multiple regression techniques.[3] Moreover, the question whether a sanction is a success or a failure essentially concerns a binary dependent variable ('yes' or 'no'; 1 or 0) implying an analysis on the basis of some kind of probability mechanism. According to Leitzel (1987, p. 287), 'the statistical evidence in support of the policy prescriptions that are formulated by Hufbauer et al. is scanty at best.' Bonetti (1991) discusses three additional objections to the multiple regression methodology in *Economic Sanctions Reconsidered*:

- there is no certainty that the relationships are linear additive as is assumed throughout;
- the definition of success is biased in favour of finding failures; and
- the predictive and explanatory power measured by significance tests and the standard error of the estimated equation is extremely poor.

All in all, their econometrics are not rightly applied and as a consequence not very instructive. This is especially disappointing since the Hufbauer et al. study has become the major reference work on the subject of economic sanctions. Hence the attempt to create an empirical basis for discussion of the efficacy of the economic instruments of diplomacy in Chapter 6.

2   THE ECONOMIC DATA

First, there is the general problem that 'normal' errors of measurement – that cause concern to all researchers – are very significant in studies about international trade and investment flows. As early as 1950, the problem that generally accepted economic figures often have very large error components was put to the fore by Morgenstern (1950). Since then much has been improved, but many inconsistencies still do exist in generally accepted figures on international transactions that are supplied by the national Statistical Offices and the international organizations such as the OECD and the IMF.[4] In addition, inaccuracies resulting from differences in definitions are quite probable since this part studies a period of 55 years and countries with very different economic systems in various stages of development.

Second, in so far as the figures have been supplied by the sanctioning and the target governments, the reliability is questionable. Hayes, for example, points to the fact that even before the South African authorities suspended publication of detailed trade statistics in 1986 'considerable aggregation in the statistics of the figures for certain "sensitive" items and trading partners prevented detailed analysis of the effects of sanctions on the South African economy' (Hayes 1988, p. 271). The subject of this study being economic warfare, it is important to realise that both sides may have an interest in distorting and/or incompletely supplying data (Harris 1968, p.8). Indeed, according to Baldry and Dollery (1992, pp. 1–2),

> artificially-engineered data paucities have generated problems facing researchers. Quite apart from the suppression of disaggregated trade and investment statistics by the South African authorities, nations, firms and individuals engaging in economic relationships with South Africa tend to disguise or understate the extent of their transactions.

South Africa is not unique in distorting trade statistics for strategic reasons. Governments that are supposed to impose economic sanctions often dictate the official trade statistics. Saudi Arabia, for example, reported in April 1989 that it was fully complying with the UN oil embargo of South Africa and this official view was reflected in the Saudi trade figures. The Shipping Research Bureau (1989) however, established that 76 oil tankers sailed from Saudi Arabia to deliver oil to South Africa in the years 1979–1987.[5]

Rather than adding observations to an earlier data set (Bergeijk 1994a), the data set on absolute and proportional trade linkages for the present empirical investigation has been reconstructed from scratch using data sets from the IMF (Direction of Trade Statistics), OECD (The World Economy: Historical Statistics) and the Penn World Tables.[6] In addition the detailed case descriptions in Hufbauer et al. 2008 often provided data that could be used to calculate trade linkage in the year prior to the sanction and in some cases where data on the target's national income were unavailable proportional trade linkage could be deduced from absolute trade linkage (for example when it is – almost – zero).

Data on the former East Bloc were (as in Bergeijk 1994a) taken from Joint Economic Committee (1985, Volume I, pp. 32–3, 126, 144 and 174).

3 POLITICAL SYSTEM DATA

The Polity IV dataset (http://www.systemicpeace.org/polity/polity4.htm) is used to describe the political system of the sanction target. Polity IV as its predecessor Polity III (Jaggers and Gurr, 1995) contains operational indicators of institutionalized authority characteristics. Over the post-Second World War period, Polity IV annually codes nine democracy and autocracy indicators for 162 countries (all independent countries that in the early 1990s had a population greater than 500,000).

Table 6A.2 illustrates which elements play a role in the coding. Aggregating these elements yields the 'autocracy score' and the 'democracy score' for a specific country in a specific year. Subtracting the autocracy score from the democracy score yields a summary measure ('relative democraticness').

Many empirical measures for political regimes have already been designed and applied by political scientists (see Inkeles 1991 for a useful review). Since economists are no experts on measuring 'democracy', it is important that the conceptual and empirical foundations of the data set that we use in our analysis are scientifically valid.

Table 6A.2 The construction of democracy and autocracy indicators in the Polity data set

Authority coding	Democracy score	Autocracy score
Competitiveness of political participation		
a) Competitive	3	0
b) Transitional	2	0
c) Factional	1	0
d) Restricted	0	1
e) Suppressed	0	2
Regulation of political participation		
a) Factional/restricted	0	1
b) Restricted	0	2
Competitiveness of executive recruitment		
a) Election	2	0
b) Transitional	1	0
c) Selection	0	2
Openness of executive recruitment		
a) Election	1	0
b) Dual: hereditary/election	1	0
c) Dual: hereditary/designation	0	1
d) Closed	0	1
Constraints on chief executive		
a) Executive parity or subordination	4	0
b) Intermediate	3	0
c) Substantial limitations	2	0
d) Intermediate	1	0
e) Slight to moderate limitations	0	1
f) Intermediate	0	2
g) Unlimited power of the executive	0	3

Source: Jaggers and Gurr (1995), p. 472.

Jaggers and Gurr (1995) compared the validity of Polity III's coding of regime types with seven conceptually and operationally different indicators developed by other political scientists. They find strong correlations (0.85 to 0.92) between Polity III and the other seven data sets, so that it seems safe to conclude that the Polity indicators describe 'democracy' satisfactorily.

4 OTHER DATA

Financial Variables

Aid in percent of GDP is from the DAC online database at http://www.oecd.org and in a few individual cases (if no OECD data were available) from the case descriptions in the Hufbauer et al. publications. Dummy variables for financial sanctions have been directly taken from Hufbauer et al. (2008, pp. 113–124, Table 4A1 to 4A5).

Co-operation, Sanction-Busting, Smuggling

Area (in square miles) is from The Economist Book Ltd., 1990, *The Economist Book of Vital World statistics: A Complete Guide to the World in Figures*, Hutchinson: London and updated for new cases using http://www.infoplease.com. Binary dummy variables for co-operation with and hindrance of the sender country, respectively were taken directly from Hufbauer et al. (2008, pp. 113–124, Table 4A1 to 4A5).

Political Variables

Prior relations between the sender and the target is a variable taken directly from Hufbauer et al. (2008, pp. 75–88, Tables 3A1 to 3A5). This is an index with values 1 antagonistic, 2 neutral, and 3 cordial. From the same tables a binary dummy variable was taken for the political and economic stability. The reputation variable (number of prior sanctions in a ten year period) has been constructed from the same source and if many sender countries were involved, the lead country's reputation was used. The ratio of sender GDP to target GDP has generally speaking been derived from the economic sources discussed in Section 2 of this appendix, but occasionally the ratio was taken from Hufbauer et al. (2008, pp. 113–124, Table 4A1 to 4A5).

Duration

Length of the sanction period is calculated from Hufbauer et al. (2008, pp. 113–124, Table 4A1 to 4A5). The Hufbauer et al. data set gives begin and end data of sanction episodes and the length of the sanction has been rounded upward to the nearest integer.

NOTES

[1] See Dashti-Gibson et al. (2001) for a logistic approach that splits the sample according to the sender country's objectives. Their investigation mainly serves to substantiate the point in the main text as they find no meaningful relationship.

[2] Kaempfer and Lowenberg (2007, pp. 894–8) provide a fair and detailed discussion of all potential sources of bias mentioned in the literature.

[3] Hufbauer and Schott (1985, pp. 99–102) accordingly seek to explain the success score using Ordinary Least Squares (OLS). Their regression model, however, is not appropriate. OLS cannot comply with the numerical restriction placed on the dependent variable. The 1990 edition does not contain an econometric analysis. The 2008 edition has an appendix in which logit models are estimated.

[4] See for recent studies about the inaccuracy of international economic observations for example IMF (1983, 1987 and 1992), World Bank (1991, p. 40), Yeats (1990 and 1992) and Bergeijk (1995a and b).

[5] See also Shipping Research Bureau, 1995.

[6] Earlier versions of the data set have been used at a replication and duplication project at the University of Amsterdam for undergraduates in econometrics. The empirical results have endured this particular hardship without problems.

7. The Expected Utility of Positive and Negative Economic Sanctions

Sometimes sanctions actually work before they are even implemented. In 1921 the League of Nations was asked only to consider punitive economic measures against the Yugoslavian military incursions into Albania. The government of Yugoslavia, however, informed the Conference of Ambassadors within one week after this request that it would withdraw its troops from Albania. More recently, in 1996, Mercosul members succeeded to prevent a *coup d'état* merely by threatening to dispel Paraguay from this Latin American customs union. These sanctions were not 'effective', as the economic sanctions did not go beyond the threat stage. So *ex post* there was no damage done. The cases, however, were highly successful and efficient as the targets changed their behaviour very quickly and the sender countries did not have to forego the welfare gains of international trade and investment. Admittedly, cases in which sanctions work *ex ante* are not often documented (Hufbauer et al. 2008, report 9 cases in the period 1946–2000, or about 5%), but more than 40% of the successful sanctions require less than one year and two thirds of the successful sanctions achieve compliance within the relatively short period of two years. Economic theory that wants to deal with rather quick and sometimes even immediate successes should essentially be able to cope with an *ex ante* analysis of strategic economic threats. This means that our theory has to deal with key features of uncertainty, such as expectations and risk preference.

At the start of the 1980s, however, the economic theory of economic sanctions typically was of a (comparative) static macroeconomic nature (see, for example, Kemp 1964, Porter 1979 and Frey 1984), and where the time dimension was part of the analysis this was only in the sense that the target economy was allowed to react by stock-piling or by other policies aimed at reducing its vulnerability to foreign economic pressure. A new strand of economic literature, however, developed in the mid-1980s which recognized that not only the implementation of economic sanctions but also the mere threat to use boycotts and embargoes could be an adequate foreign policy instrument.[1]

Hughes Hallett and Brandsma (1983) use a macroeconometric model of the post-war Soviet economy in order to assess the optimality of strategies in a dynamic and unrestricted non-cooperative game between East and West in the early 1980s. They show that the main economic weapon of the West against the Soviet Union is not the actually implemented embargo on technology and defence-related exports, but the threat of a future embargo on other goods as well. This is so because the optimal Soviet reaction to this risk causes a very rapid deterioration of the Soviet's foreign trade balance. In an early article (Bergeijk 1987), I developed an expected utility model of economic–military deterrence, much along the lines of the Logic of Choice proposed later by Baldwin (2000). One of the findings is that the threat of the 'stick' may lead to perverse results as an increase of the threat of disutility may actually induce non-compliance. Kaempfer and Lowenberg (1988) show within a public choice setting that sanctions that create little or no economic hardship can still generate political change, pointing out, for example, that a sanction with little economic impact on South Africa might be conductive to ending Apartheid. Using an equilibrium model of interest group competition within the target country Kaempfer and Lowenberg (1988, p. 768) argue that 'sanctions can communicate signals or threats, not necessarily entailing severe economic damage, which in turn produce policy changes'. Eaton and Engers (1992) consider a sender that periodically specifies conditions that the target must meet to avoid sanctions. They consider the possibility that sanctions have an overkill capacity and show that the deterrence effect of the threat of sanctions can be enough to let a target comply in order to avoid sanctions even if they are not currently in place. Indeed, Eaton and Engers (1992, p. 919) argue that the threat of sanctions probably plays a much greater role in the arena of international politics than their actual use in diplomatic relations seems to suggest.

1   THE SETTINGS: THREATS, PROMISES AND RATIONALITY UNDER UNCERTAINTY

The common characteristic of these 'new' models is that the sender countries utter a strategic threat consisting of the announcement that economic sanction measures will (possibly) be applied. If behaviour is altered the game ends and the sender attains its objective in the most cost-efficient way, since it does not have to bear the costs that result from the loss of some of the gains from international trade and investment.

Actually, this fits in the economic theory of strategic threats and reputation pioneered by Schelling ([1960] 1980) and Boulding (1962). They pointed out that if a threat is not sufficiently credible to change behaviour, punitive action has to be carried out. This is painful and costly for both the sender and the target since both parties will be unable to reap the full benefits of free and undisturbed trade and investment relations. Consequently, a sanction might be too costly to be carried out and the threat may appear false.

The question of whether the potential sanction damage will be administered or not cannot *a priori* be answered with certainty. More specifically, a sanction threat could best be defined as a statement creating an expectation that is conditional on the performance (or perhaps non-performance) of some activity (Boulding 1962, p. 253). The key word here is 'expectation': the value of a sanction threat that enters the target's utility function as an argument must be the result of the confrontation of potential damage and the subjective probability of this potential actually being administered upon misconduct. In addition uncertainty with respect to the goals of opposing countries is a major feature of the international threat system (Tinbergen 1985, p. 175). Indeed, as Schelling ([1960] 1980, p. 39) notes:

> In threat situations ... commitments are not altogether clear; each party cannot exactly estimate the costs and values to the other side of the two related actions involved in the threat.

This is why any theory of economic sanctions should not start from a deterministic setting; it has to deal with the stochastic outcome of situations in which economic sanctions have been applied. Since probabilities will be introduced one may prefer to speak about risk rather than uncertainty (Knight [1921] 1939). Throughout this analysis, however, I will consider uncertainty as a state of absent certainty.

The well-known von Neumann–Morgenstern ([1944] 1980) assumptions about expected utility can be used to construct indifference curves. By making different assumptions about the shape of the utility function it is possible to model distinct attitudes toward the risk that is typical of international threat situations and consequently of economic sanctions. The expected utility approach allows us to make a clear distinction between the *ex ante* expectations that guide decision making, and the outcomes *ex post* that are the results of those decisions. Presented with the choice between the mathematically expected payoff of a gamble in international politics and undergoing that particular gamble, the target might prefer the gamble. If the game is 'lost', the outcome *ex post* may seem irrational indeed. Thus the destruction of Iraq in the second Gulf War with hindsight induces one to question the rationality of Saddam Hussein. The decision, however, to get involved in a very risky gamble showing a very low or even negative expected outcome should not be considered irrational unless the highest possible outcome is less than the outcome that results if the gambler does not play.

The rational choice paradigm has also been questioned by Schrödt (1985, pp. 379–87). He sees only very limited scope for the concept of *homo economicus* in the analysis of international relations. Schrödt offers four arguments against (expected) utility maximization:

- the relative absence of testable propositions;
- the lack of practical relevance for policy makers of the main theoretical findings;
- the fact that decision making in international politics is often a group process so that the unitary actor hypothesis is violated; and
- the special characteristics of decision making in international politics (slow speed of reaction, inefficient information structures and so on) which may preclude maximizing behaviour.

While many of these points *a priori* would seem to be relevant to economic analysis in general, it is ultimately only the empirical testing of a theory that can shed light on the possible utility of a specific theory or analytical framework.[2] This is not to deny that purely political ends sometimes dictate the outcome of *ex ante* cost-benefit analysis (see Waltzer 1977, pp. 263–8). It all boils down to this: that the recognition of the inherent political boundaries of the problem does not impair positive economic analysis.

Many economic sanction theories do not distinguish between incentives and disincentives, because it is assumed that the target's opportunity costs of a penalty are equal to a reward of the same magnitude. That is to say, it is assumed that the opportunity costs of non-compliance coincide when a reward of $X is offered or a penalty of –$X is threatened. The symmetry of incentives and disincentives, however, breaks down both in a stochastic setting and for non-neutral attitudes toward risk. Moreover, as argued by Baldwin (1971), perceptions, time and conditionality influence positive and negative sanctions differently. In particular, the costs of implementation in combination with the prospects for success (and possibly side effects, after-effects and efficacy) may influence the extent and use of positive and negative sanctions differently. Reward and punishment are not merely two sides of the same coin (Lawson 1983, pp. 311–13). From a policy perspective this analytical distinction has the additional advantage that it enables us to give a better, more comprehensive analysis of the full range of policy options, which may also take the question of legitimacy into account. Consequently, it seems worthwhile to actually make the distinction and analyze both negative and positive economic sanctions.

In sum, the theory that will be developed in this chapter departs from the comparative static macroeconomic theory of economic sanctions through the combination of three elements. First, the decision process and the policy options of the target will be analyzed. Second, this will be done within a utility setting that acknowledges the uncertainty that is inherent in situations in which economic sanctions are being used. Third, we will analyze the possibility of rewarding behaviour that apparently conforms to the standards of the international community. So contrary to mainstream discussions, the analysis will incorporate both economic incentives and economic disincentives that are conditional on whether misconduct ceases or persists. Earlier studies analyse either the threat of trade disruption or situations in which the exact timing of the trade disruption is uncertain. These theories are either about the influence exerted by the target's awareness of the possibility of a boycott or an embargo and how this menace influences its behaviour, or about the target's behaviour given the certainty that economic measures will be deployed in the near future. The present analysis studies the possibility to omit misconduct and takes into account that even explicit threats need not be executed.

2 AN EXPECTED UTILITY MODEL OF ECONOMIC SANCTIONS

This section will introduce and discuss the structure of the expected utility model of economic sanctions and investigate the outcome space. The next section presents the comparative static analysis of the respective policy instruments in a formal model. The final section summarizes the main findings of the model exercises in a non-technical manner so that readers that want to skip the mathematical exposition can do so without many problems.

We will consider an international decision unit – the potential target of economic sanctions – that faces the possibility of a profitable act of misconduct. This act of misconduct, however, is heavily resented by the outside world. The target has the opportunity to be exclusively involved in neutral activities, which the outside world does not disapprove of or may even appreciate. The behaviour of the target is influenced, among other things, by the yields y_N (of neutral activities; one may think of it as the Gross Domestic Product of a country) and y_M (of misconduct; for example, the occupation of foreign territory).

Misconduct carries a premium M so that the yield of neutral activities $y_N = N$ is less than the yield of misconduct: $y_M = y_N + M$. Admittedly, the yield of misconduct often cannot be quantified unambiguously.[3] What are the benefits to the target country; what for example is the 'value' of acquiring a nuclear bomb? Some sorts of misconduct, such as expropriation of foreign assets, nationalization, illegitimate extensions of the territory and repudiation of foreign debt, have a clear economic dimension. In contradistinction, measurement of the premium of misconduct is very difficult if sanctions are aimed at the target's social structures. Perhaps the benefits to the elite of a specific power structure can be expressed in money, but clearly in other cases such as adherence to human rights the measuring rod of money loses its utility. Moreover, the yield of misconduct essentially amounts to the benefits of a particular policy as seen by those in power at a given moment. So the yield of the Communist Party's power structure seems to have been valued very differently by Brezhnev, Andropov or Chernenko and their ultimate successor Gorbachev.

Anyhow, even if the yield of misconduct is essentially intangible, administering sanction damage can influence the target's decision. In most cases the yield of misconduct lies outside the influence of the outside world. Hence M is considered to be an exogenous variable that cannot be influenced by the sanction sender(s).[4] The variables M and N are supposed to be independent of one another and a common denominator (for example money) is assumed, that allows aggregation of the dissimilar components that play a part in the choice situation.

The outside world in this model has two sanction instruments to influence the target's behaviour. The international community may threaten to use a negative sanction (with potential damage D) and may deploy a positive sanction (with a potential gain of S). It follows that the yield of misconduct is

$y_M = y_N + M - D$ if the threat is real or
$y_M = y_N + M$ if the threat is false.

In the case of a positive sanction the yield of neutral activities increases from N to $N + S$. Table 7.1 summarizes the target's choice set.

Table 7.1 Choice set

Target's choice	Sender's options	
	No sanction	Sanction
Neutral activities	$y_N = N$	Positive sanction: $y_N = N + S$
Misconduct	False threat $y_F = N + M$	Real threat $y_R = N + M - D$

The model offers a simplified representation of the international arena of politics only, as it obviously relates to a two-country model in which the passive sender–target relationship does not leave much room for dynamic interaction. The impact of the sanction is studied with the payoff matrix of Table 7.1 that summarizes the possible outcomes for the target, given its own choice and the sender's decisions.

Moreover, the parameters are exogenous to the target and we will not study the problem from the perspective of a dominant economic power. This assumption, a version of the small country assumption, is generally made in the analysis of economic sanctions (see, for example, Dekker 1973, Arad and Hillman 1979, Porter 1979 and Bergström, Loury and Person 1985). It is clear that the transparency of the analysis that thus results carries a cost as the theory is less general and less fit for the interpretation of the real world. Reality, however, is not bent too much since less than 10% of the cases in the Hufbauer et al. (2008) sanctions database pertain to situations where the target's GDP exceeds that of the sender (see also Table 6.3). Indeed in at least 80% of the cases the sender's GDP was at least ten times larger than the target's GDP giving credence to the small country assumption.[5]

Now it is assumed that the target derives utility u from the resulting yield, so that $u = u(y)$, where $u' > 0$. The value to the target of a certain amount of y_i is known as the *ex post* utility of outcome y_i. Since the yield of neutral activities is independent of the threat, it is implied that the utility generated by the conduct of neutral activities is known with certainty so that the *ex post* and the *ex ante* utility of neutral activities correspond.

$$u\{E(y_N)\} = E\{u(y_N)\} = u(y_N) = u(N) \qquad (7.1)$$

In order to model the target's decision whether or not to engage in misconduct, we need to assess the target's *ex ante* utility or the expected utility of the outcomes y_i and their associated probabilities of occurrence. So a function v is postulated which describes the *ex ante* utility that the target attaches to the uncertain outcome of misconduct. Let π denote the target's subjective probability ($0 < \pi < 1$) that the threat is real.

$$v = v[y_R, y_F; \pi, (1-\pi)] \qquad (7.2)$$

It is now possible to weigh the certain utility of neutral activities against the expected *ex ante* utility of the uncertain yield of misconduct. More specifically, if $v > u(y_N)$ the target will opt for misconduct. The function v will be based on the expected utility hypothesis that was originally developed by von Neumann and Morgenstern ([1944] 1980). The axioms that are the basic prerequisites for the construction of a von Neumann–Morgenstern utility index seem rather reasonable within the context of economic sanctions. Essentially this approach requires continuity, transitivity and strong independence of preferences over outcomes as well as a desire for a high probability of success. Moreover, it requires that the evaluation of a probability is based on the actual probability and not on the way the probability has been determined (that is it should not make a difference if π is a composite probability).[6] This is what we have first:

$$v = \pi \cdot u(y_R) + (1-\pi) \cdot u(y_F) \tag{7.3}$$

For a given value of the subjective probability, π, an indifference curve $v = u(y_N)$ can be drawn in outcome space, as illustrated in Figure 6.2. This curve represents the boundary line between those combinations (y_R, y_F) that lead to the misconduct option (above and to the right of the curve) and the area that represents the combinations of possible outcomes for which misconduct does not come off. Note that by definition $y_R > y_F$ and that the range of y_F is positive. It can easily be checked that regardless of the shape of the indifference curve, a point N^* on v exists where $M = D = S = 0$ and consequently $y_R > y_F = y_N = N$. The utility of the combination represented by N^* will be used as a yardstick to compare combinations of uncertain outcomes and for obvious reasons it will be called the certainty equivalent. The marginal rate of substitution in point N always equals $-\pi/(1-\pi)$.

Differentiating $v = u(y_N)$ while π is kept constant yields:

$$\pi \cdot u'(y_R) \cdot dy_R + (1-\pi) \cdot u'(y_F) \cdot dy_F = u'(y_N) \cdot dy_N \tag{7.4}$$

As long as we move along a specific indifference curve, the right hand side of equation 7.4 equals zero, so that the following expression for the slope of an indifference curve results:

$$-dy_F / dy_R = \pi \cdot u'(y_R)/\{(1-\pi) \cdot u'(y_F)\} \tag{7.5}$$

Shone (1981, pp. 38–9) argues that a utility function which is concave in the resulting yield ($u'' < 0$) leads to convex indifference curves in outcome space and implies a risk adverse or cautious decision making unit. In contradistinction a convex utility function $u'' > 0$) and the associated concave-to-the-origin indifference curves portray the risk preferer or risk lover. On the boundary the linear curve ($u'' = 0$) is found that expresses that the risk neutral target is only concerned with the utility of the mathematically expected outcome.

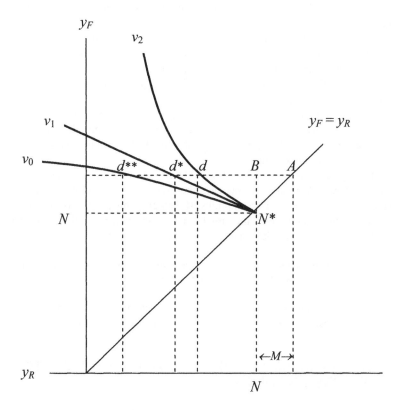

Figure 7.1 Indifference curves for risk aversion (v_2), risk neutrality (v_1) and risk preference (v_0)

Figure 7.1 shows three different indifference curves for the cases of risk preference (v_0), risk neutrality (v_1) and risk aversion (v_2). The linear indifference curve v_1 represents combinations (y_R, y_F) for which the weighted average (with π and $1-\pi$ as weights) equals N. It is quite intuitive that v_2 is the indifference curve for a risk averse target, because every point on v_2 is above and to the right of v_1, with the exception of the so-called certainty equivalent N^*. Since v_2 and v_1 represent equal levels of utility $u(N)$ for different risk preferences and since v_2 needs larger uncertain yields to arrive at this utility level, the target represented by indifference curve v_2 must attach negative utility to uncertainty. Consequently, this target is to be considered risk averse. Likewise v_0 portrays the risk lover. Observe that the curve for risk aversion approaches $y_R = 0$ asymptotically since it follows from equation 7.5, $y_R > 0$

and $u'' < 0$ that the marginal rate of substitution becomes negatively infinite as y_R tends to zero, from above.

Figure 7.1 also clearly shows that the area above an indifference curve represents combinations (y_R, y_F) that lead to the choice for misconduct. Consider for example, point A where by definition $v(N+M) > u(y_N) = u(N)$ or point B, which also will clearly result in the choice for misconduct because $v(B) = \pi \cdot u(N) + (1-\pi) \cdot u(N+M) > u(N)$.

Taking limits for $u'' \to \infty$ and $u'' \to -\infty$, it follows that points to the right of $y_R = N$ will trigger misconduct irrespective of both the attitude toward risk and the subjective probability π (note that in the limit v can be represented by a vertical line through point N^*).

Finally, a well-behaved target will always show up in our model if the condition $y_F < N$ applies. In this case the premium M would be negative; a situation ruled out by our assumptions. If, however, misconduct occurs while this condition is being met, the target is not acting in a rational way. In that case we observe, as did Schelling ([1960] 1980, p. 6) that:

> the rationality of the adversary is pertinent to the efficacy of threat, and that madmen ... can often not be controlled by threats.

It is only in this sense that irrationality (or madness) of statesmen would support the dismissal of the utility approach to the subject of this book.

3 THE ANALYSIS OF THE ECONOMIC INSTRUMENTS OF FOREIGN POLICY

The analysis concentrates on a utility maximizing actor that receives signals from the outside world that are aimed at influencing the target's behaviour. In order to keep the analysis as transparent as possible it is assumed that the target cannot utter meaningful (counter) threats. So the model deals with the typical case of a small (developing) country. In order to prevent misconduct the outside world may resort to a number of different instruments. In the first place the sanction threat can be enhanced. This can be achieved either by increasing potential sanction damage D or by enlarging the subjective probability π. The outside world may also try to influence the yield of neutral activities N. Finally, the possibility exists to reward or invite 'good behaviour' by means of a positive sanction S.

It should at this point be clarified that the concepts of both positive and negative sanctions are relative concepts, as the question of what constitutes a sanction to a large extent depends on the target's perception of the situation (Baldwin 1971). A promise not to kill if one behaves as requested may not be considered a positive sanction as it is a clear threat in the case of a hold-up. This implies that in practical policy making the sender should first establish the target's baseline in terms of its expected future value position. For example, reducing or ending a negative sanction that is actually being implemented may be considered as a reward. In this sense negative sanctions can be used to lay the groundwork for the subsequent use of positive sanctions:

> What (the sender) is doing in such situations is using the stick to shift (the target's) baseline so as to make the subsequent promise of a carrot more attractive (Baldwin 1971, p. 25).

The formal model that was developed and discussed in the previous section is designed to investigate the impact of the respective policy instruments. The positive analysis of these instrumental variables will focus on their contribution to the prevention or remedy of international misconduct.

Sanction Damage

The capacity to force economic costs upon an adversary by means of economic sanctions was first analyzed by Hirschman ([1945] 1980). He labelled this effect the 'influence effect'. In general the influence effect will depend on the target's problems if the sanctioning economy is no longer available as a market or a supplier. Hirschman ([1945] 1980, pp. 17–40) and Wolf (1983, pp. 404–5) give a prescription of how to achieve a large influence effect. The sender can increase the effectiveness of the sanction instrument (and simultaneously reduce its own vulnerability to foreign treats) by diversifying its exports both with respect to markets and with respect to goods. The sender should increase the number of trade partners on the import side as well and preferably import goods that are still in an early phase of production. Finally, trade partners with a low *per capita* income should be preferred and participation in transit trade should be stimulated. Next to this general prescription of how a country should shape its trade policy in order to get more influence and become less dependent, an important role is being played by the disutility which in an actual case can be brought to the fore in a relatively short period of time. The amount of disutility increases if more countries join the economic sanction measures, if a boycott complements an embargo (and *vice versa*) and if sanction measures for specific commodities and services are extended to include total bilateral trade and capital flows (lending, aid and so on). In addition the threat of sanction damage can also be increased by non-economic measures such as intensified surveillance and military blockades of physical trade flows.

The imposition or enlargement of a sanction threat is for given N, M and or π associated with a lower value of y_R and, consequently, with a decrease of the expected utility of misconduct. By attaching (additional) costs to misconduct, the sender tries to lower the economic attractiveness of misconduct. Negative economic sanctions decrease the expected utility of misconduct, inducing the target to another – more acceptable – mode of behaviour. In the outcome space of Figure 7.1 this shows up as a shift of all points (y_R, y_F.) to the left, while the locus of the curve $v = u(y_N)$ remains unchanged. Any point in (y_R, y_F)-space located at the right of this indifference curve prior to the expansion of D and shifting to the left of that indifference curve due to enlargement of D shows that the behaviour of the decision unit is effectively influenced and that misconduct is prevented or stopped. Irrespective of the attitude towards risk an increase in D dissuades from misconduct.

The qualitative result of a higher D leading for given N, M and π to a lower y_R does not change when different attitudes toward risk are assumed. There will, however, be different conclusions with respect to the efficient amount of potential disutility D. In the case of risk-aversion, represented by curve v_2 in Figure 7.1, a sanction threat that is associated with the length of dA will do. To a risk-neutral decision unit the condition $D > M/\pi$ will have to be met in order to prevent misconduct. It follows *a fortiori* that to contain a risk-loving daredevil just by increasing the potential sanction damage is an even more difficult task. In Figure 7.1 this is illustrated by the minimum value of D that prevents misconduct. The necessary threat increases from $d{*}A$ in the case of risk-neutrality (represented by curve v_1) to $d{**}A$ for risk-loving behaviour (curve v_0), as compared to dA for risk aversion.

The model, however, suggests that these observations are relevant only from the perspective that the threat may be too small. If a sanction threat is not credible enough to influence behaviour, the imposed sanction measures will also impose costs on the sender's economy. Superfluous threats in general would seem to achieve absolute deterrence and therefore need not be carried out. For some problems, however, economic sanctions simply are to be considered overkill. The argument that sanctions may be too large has a more general bearing. It is straightforward to show that any implementation of a successful sanction beyond the minimally required level leads to the desired co-operation but at the same time involves unnecessary costs for the sender. Just as too small a sanction will not lead to the desired result, too large a sanction leads to unnecessary (potential) welfare losses both for the sender and the target (Bergeijk and Marrewijk, 1994).

The Credibility of the Sanction Threat

The subjective probability $\pi = \pi(E|I)$ depends on the event E of which the probability is to be estimated ('Will the sanction actually be implemented?') and on I, the given information (also called the weight of evidence). The target may thus be influenced by information about the sender's intentions.

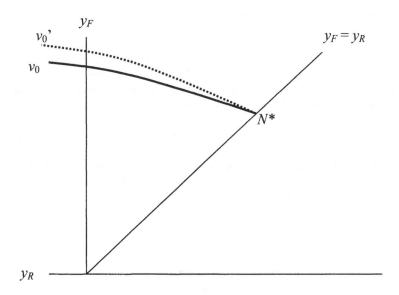

Figure 7.2 Increase in π (case of risk preference)

This information may be imparted explicitly as in the case of a diplomatic message, but it can also be communicated implicitly, for example, because similar kinds of misconduct have also been punished with negative economic sanctions in the past or because very strong verbal condemnations are issued suggesting that action may be taken upon misconduct. Graphically, an increase of π rotates the indifference curve $v = u(y_N)$ clockwise with point N^* serving as a hinge. This implies that increasing π reduces the willingness of the decision unit to antagonize the outside world (Figure 7.2).

Sometimes, however, the size of the threat may affect its credibility. This is not merely a theoretical possibility as the literature often suggests that superfluous sanctions are superior to limited threats (see, for example, Kaplow 1990). If such policy prescriptions are taken at face value, sanctions will exceed 'reasonable' levels and the target may not believe that the threat will be executed at all. Whenever the potential disutility becomes too large in relation to the kind of misconduct concerned, the subjective probability π may actually diminish if the threat is enlarged. Targets will have an opinion about the likelihood that sanction measures will actually be imposed. The target's leadership may balance the threat of punishment against the misdemeanours in international politics and may consider the threat of punishment as too big in relation to their wrongdoing. Indeed, ethics and legality are important issues in the application of UN sanctions and this would seem to require proportionality (see Hazelzet 1999 for an introduction into these issues[7]). Consequently, the target may ignore the threat as either unrealistic or unjust.

Now let $\pi = \pi(D)$ describe the relation between the subjective probability π and potential disutility D and assume the possibility of a range for $\pi = \pi(D)$ where $\pi'(D) < 0$. The effect of this hypothesis can best be studied with the following expression of v for given N, M and, consequently, $y_{F,0}$:

$$v = \pi(D) \cdot u(y_{F,0}-D) + (1-\pi(D)) \cdot u(y_{F,0}) \tag{7.6}$$

Next, differentiate v with respect to D. The resulting relation is definitely negative – implying that a larger sanction threat dissuades from misconduct – as long as $\pi'(D) \geq 0$. However, for $\pi'(D) < 0$ a perverse reaction might result if :

$$\pi' \{u(y_{F,0}-D) - u(y_{F,0})\} > \pi \cdot \partial u(y_{F,0}-D) / \partial(y_{F,0}-D) \tag{7.7}$$

in which case the enlargement of the sanction threat – contrary to *a priori* expectations – triggers misconduct. Note that this possibility of a counter productive negative sanction is only relevant for the enlargement of existing sanction threats because the condition of equation 7.7 will in general not be met if initially no sanction threat was uttered $(D = 0)$.

Neutral Activities

The yield of neutral activities in many instances cannot be influenced by the sender. Economic growth, for example, depends to a large extent on the target's domestic economic policies, on exogenous movements in the terms of trade, on developments in world trade and on capital market conditions. Such factors in general cannot be influenced by another country. Instances, however, do exist where the sender willingly facilitates economic activity in the target economy or – for example, by means of (military) action and sabotage – reduces the target's economic base. If this happens without any conditionality attached to it, the sender influences the yield of neutral activities, which have been defined as those activities of which the sender does not disapprove. Also where the sender does not consider the target's yield of neutral activities as an appropriate instrument for its foreign policy, it will be instructive to study both this specific country attribute and how changes in N influence the target's decision whether or not to comply.

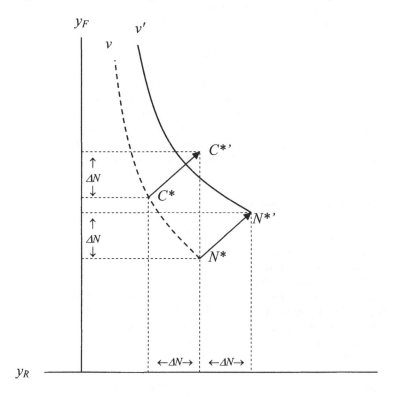

Figure 7.3 Unconditional increase in the yield of neutral activities for the case of risk aversion

In contradistinction to the results that have been derived so far, the impact of unconditional changes in the yield of neutral activities N depends on the target's attitude towards risk. This is illustrated in Figure 7.3 that shows the consequences of an increase of y_N by $\Delta N > 0$ for the case of a risk avers target. As both y_F and y_R increase by ΔN all points shift in outcome space parallel to the line $y_F = y_R$ with a vector of length $\Delta N \sqrt{2}$. At the same time, however, the curve $v=u(y_N)$ is shifting outwards. The flattened shape of the new indifference curve $v' = (N + \Delta N)$ ensues from the diminishing marginal utility ($u'' < 0$), that is associated with risk aversion. It follows that all points that were originally on $v = u(N)$ with the exception of point N^*, will emerge above and to the right of the new indifference curve, such as point $C^{*\prime}$ in Figure 7.3.

Therefore a reduction of the yield of neutral activities stops misconduct of a risk-averse target, while an increase in y_N calls forth undesirable behaviour from such an agent. This finding for the commonly considered case of risk aversion conforms to Marshall's ([1923] 1965, pp. 168–70) well known observation that the cessation of trade often implies a larger real loss to a poor than to a rich country. For a given premium M a rich risk-averse country (with large y_N) will be more inclined to opt for misconduct than a poor risk averse country (small y_N). The same type of analysis shows opposite results for risk loving targets. Perhaps more conforming to common sense is the finding that a higher value of y_N promotes neutral activities and that a reduction of this yield acts as an incentive to misconduct. Finally, as can easily be seen from equation 7.2, manipulation of N does not influence risk-neutral behaviour.

Positive Economic Sanctions

Finally, a positive sanction S is introduced. As pointed out by Newnham (2002), sanctions can be general – in the sense that friends are strengthened and enemies are weakened in order to condition them to future demands – or specifically linked to political demands. Positive sanctions may include flows of goods. American food aid, for example, often has a political character, as discussed by Eggleston (1987) and Thompson (1992). In many cases positive sanctions, however, pertain to intangible exchange such as the sharing of specific technologies and infrastructures.

Often positive sanctions entail international transfers of purchasing power. Allies are often bought, negative side effects of compliance can be compensated and misconduct is often commutable.[8] Some very visible – and specific – examples of such financial transfers are the $10–$25 billion 'reparation payments' that the Gulf Co-operation Council offered in 1982 to persuade Iran to end its war against Iraq, the Dutch development aid programme to its former colony Surinam in the 1980s (aimed at restoring and stabilising – democratic – government rule), the $1 billion aid programme that international donors in 1993 pledged to make available to Haiti in 1993 once its political crisis was solved and President Aristide was reinstated, and the Japanese aid to the restructuring economies of Mongolia, Cambodia, Central Asian republics of the former Soviet Union and Vietnam with explicit statements by the Japanese Ministry of Finance in documentation regarding Official Development Assistance (Furuoka 2007). Engagement has a very long tradition in the German–Russia relationships (Newnham 2002), the

European Union's relationship with the restructuring economies in Central and Eastern Europe (as discussed in Chapter 1) and it has also been a relevant element in the US–China relations in the second half of the 1990s. Evaluating this case in economic statecraft, Mastanduno (2003, p. 185) concludes:

> If China does muster the combination of capabilities, intentions, and behaviour to mount a revisionist challenge the United States can react accordingly and mobilize for containment. In the meantime it can afford to experiment with economic engagement both for pragmatic reasons and with the hope of any gambler that long shots occasionally pay off.

Mastanduno's observation points out to the implicit message of positive sanctions that they will only be applied as long as the behaviour of the target economy is in agreement with the sender's political objectives. A key question, however, is under which conditions such sanctions may work.

Our model can shed some light on this issue. Analogous with the analysis of neutral activities it will be assumed that the utility of a positive sanction is known with certainty:

$$u\{E(y_N)\} = E\{u(y_N)\} = u(y_N) = u(N + S) \tag{7.8}$$

This assumption is satisfied whenever a set exists of economic activities that will automatically cease in the event of misconduct. This seems reasonable enough. Take, for instance military misconduct. Obviously, in that case the use of civilian flight paths and harbour facilities as well as the transfer of technology will certainly cease. Indeed, war cancels everything. Note that the yields of these activities are *a priori* known with certainty by the sender and by the target, as is the fact that they will be cancelled if misconduct occurs. As a logical consequence positive sanctions are certain to make neutral activities more attractive.

The indifference curve $v = u(y_N)$ in Figure 7.4 shifts outwards when a positive sanction is applied or increased, while the combinations (y_R, y_F) pertaining to misconduct do not move. This result is independent of the target's attitude towards risk. It is important to note that combinations (y_R, y_F) exist where positive sanctions can make a difference while the target's behaviour cannot be influenced by negative sanctions. This is true even if the threat is perfectly credible if not certain (that is for $\pi \to 1$) and for extreme attitudes towards risk (thus for $u'' \to \infty$ or $u'' \to -\infty$). This can, for example, be shown with regard to point D in Figure 7.4. This is so because points to the right of N^* (where $y_R > N$) will always call forth misconduct.

Indeed, an important finding of our analysis is that positive sanctions will provide the only instrument in cases where the (threat of) sanction damage cannot be enlarged. A positive sanction of S will shift the indifference curve outward from v to v' so that the behaviour can also be influenced in those cases that are represented by combinations in the shaded area in Figure 7.4.

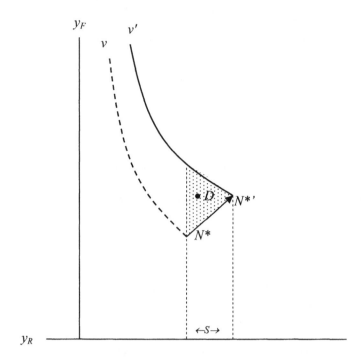

Figure 7.4 The impact of a positive sanction

4 SOME LESSONS FOR ECONOMIC STATECRAFT

Baldwin (1985) introduced the term 'economic statecraft' to indicate the political use that could be made of the economic instruments of foreign policy. Baldwin asserted that (1985, p. 4) 'the utility of economic techniques has been systematically underestimated since 1945'. In line with Baldwin, the analysis in the preceding sections showed that economic instruments can play a larger role in modern diplomacy provided that they are applied correctly. Chapter 6 substantiated this finding empirically for the case of negative sanctions.

As Table 7.2 summarizes, the positive analysis of sanctions in an expected utility setting in this chapter related to three distinct attitudes toward the risk that is inherent in situations in which international influence attempts are being made. The different approaches to risk – as moulded by different shapes of the target's utility function – cover a wide range of decision entities varying from cautious to risk-loving ones. The utility of the uncertain yield of misconduct is weighed against the certain but presumably lower yield of neutral activities and if the former exceeds the latter the decision to engage in misconduct is rational.

Table 7.2 Impact of the economic instruments on misconduct

	Risk aversion $u'' < 0$	Risk neutrality $u'' = 0$	Risk preference $u'' > 0$
Neutral activities N	+	0	–
Sanction damage D	–/+	–/+	–/+
Imposition (no prior threat)	–	–	–
Credibility π	–	–	–
Positive sanction S	–	–	–

In order to establish how the choice between misconduct and neutral activities can be influenced by diplomatic economic instruments, four instruments were distinguished and analysed. First, we investigated negative economic sanctions. The threat of economic punishment consists of two elements: the potential sanction damage D and the target's subjective probability π of this potential being actually used upon misconduct. A second category of variables consisted of the yield of misconduct M and the yield of neutral activities N. Finally, the analysis focused on positive sanctions S.

Conclusions and Caveats

Our conclusion is that the willingness of the target to antagonize the international community can only be unambiguously reduced by increasing the probability π, by the imposition of negative sanctions and by the imposition and enlargement of positive sanctions. This does not mean that misconduct is effectively prevented if these instruments are deployed, but that misconduct is made less attractive. The impact of both changes in the yield of neutral activities and of the increase of existing negative sanctions cannot be established *a priori* with certainty, as this impact depends on the attitude towards risk and the target's expectations formation process which in general cannot be observed before the sanction is actually imposed.[9] So the use of these instruments may be counter-productive and induce misconduct rather than correcting or preventing it. The analysis clarifies that positive and negative sanctions are not two sides of the same coin. Indeed, even if the target is completely convinced that negative sanctions will be imposed it may still be impossible for the sender to impose sufficiently large negative sanctions while positive sanctions at the same time may be able to accomplish compliance.

It is true that the model does not include reactions to threats and, consequently, the target economy is perhaps modelled too passively. A more active attitude, however, may very well lead to paradoxical results. Smith (1986), for example, develops a formal model of a multinational that has to decide whether and how to enter new markets. Should the firm export or should it invest in productive capital? Clearly this long-term decision is influenced by the multinational's expectations about the sender's trade policy, that is to say by this nation's reputation for the political use of restrictions on international trade and foreign direct investment. This implies that the maximum economic impact of negative economic sanctions (the *ex post* damage) can only be produced by a country that has a reputation for *not* deploying sanctions. Such a country would by definition be unable to influence a target since for this country $\pi = 0$. On the other hand, a country which is capable of expressing very credible threats because of a long history of imposed and executed sanctions will usually find it difficult to inflict damage on an adversary that in the same historical record finds an important incentive to invest in either countervailing power or reductions in its economic exposure. (This ambiguity may accidentally explain why the reputation variable did not turn out to be a significant determinant of the outcome of negative economic sanctions during the econometric investigations on which Chapter 6 reports.)

Another caveat concerns the fact that the analysis in this chapter has been *ex ante* so that it does not answer the question of whether a threat will be carried out or not. To answer this particular question one would have to model the sender's trade-off between both the direct and future costs and the direct and future benefits of its (in)activity. As these complex processes have not been included in the analysis one might want to dismiss the model as being too simple.

It should be granted, however, that despite its simplicity this model fits some of the main features of the international system very well, as it clarifies the distinction between the outcome of an *ex ante* expected utility calculation and the *ex post* real world outcome. Moreover, the theory offers a clear prescription of how the yield of neutral activities should be manipulated in order to prevent misconduct. The attitude of the target country towards risk not being known for certain, it follows that rewards in international politics will only be effective if they are conditional. Hence the analysis within a stochastic utility setting also offers an explanation for the failure of those international policies that offer profitable possibilities unconditionally.

The Political Economy of Economic Diplomacy

The phenomenon of an increase in conditional stochastic disutility (threat of punishment) possibly leading to a perverse result (a larger extent of misconduct) is important. It is essentially this possibility of both a negative and a positive marginal impact of the deterrent concerned that impairs the suitability of negative economic sanctions, unless initially no threat was uttered. Indeed, in keeping peace with a potential adversary one should avoid subjecting this adversary to economic pressures, humiliation or threats as long as he keeps peace (Fischer 1984, p. 84). Obviously, if a military strategy is complemented with economic warfare during peace time, the value of peace for the other side is reduced.[10] In the same vain Mastanduno (2003, p. 185) remarks that any

> economic containment effort is likely to be viewed ... as provocative. It would create a self-fulfilling prophecy by giving ... incentives to pursue a more confrontational foreign policy.

More importantly, threats introduce uncertainty with respect to the impact of the economic instruments of modern diplomacy, implying a reduction of the effective availability of policy instruments for peaceful conflict resolution. Recent game theoretic analyses suggest that negative sanctions may not be able to sustain an international system in the long run. Tsebelis (1990) shows that modification of the target's payoffs by means of negative sanctions does not influence the level or the frequency of violations of international standards in super games. This conclusion is valid under a wide range of assumptions about the available information, the continuity of choices and the rules of the game. Bonetti (1994) analyses negative sanctions as an iterated discrete time war of attrition in which sunk cost accounting explains the persistence and frequency of sanction episodes. He shows that rational nations may be reticent to engage in economic warfare because they tend to fight for too long. Bonetti argues that positive sanctions and diplomacy may provide the only viable and robust substitutes to the traditional policy techniques of warfare or armed deterrence.[11]

Moreover, as the marginal impact of the manipulation of the unconditional yield of neutral activities depends on the *a priori* unknown attitude of the threatened decision unit towards risk, it follows that changes in unconditionally offered yields associated with unobjectionable behaviour cannot deliver the target's change of behaviour with certainty. Ungar and Vale (1985/86, p. 236) cite the fact that no conditions had been imposed on

South Africa in exchange for US favours as the main reasons for the failure of President Reagan's 'constructive engagement' policy *vis-à-vis* the Apartheid regime. An efficient deployment of positive sanctions requires that the desired change in the target's behaviour is anatomised in subsets of attainable changes. As South Africa moved toward a non-racial society the necessity emerged to reward Pretoria by rolling back cultural, economic and political sanctions in order to keep the reforms acceptable for the white population. Such incentives may help to keep a country on the right track, because once accepted they provide a potential means for negative sanctions once more. Thus the order in which negative sanction measures are rolled back must depend on the extent of reversibility. Negative cultural and political sanctions should be ended first as they can be easily re-imposed. Trade sanctions are less appropriate as positive sanctions, but still more appropriate than capital sanctions since the conditionality of investment, credit and aid is negligible as reversal of such transactions is hardly possible. Likewise sanctions on (nuclear) technology and arms should be ended only in the final stage of the 'sanction game'.

This implies that in the international system, conditional threats and unconditional rewards are inferior to both conditional rewards and unconditional decreases of the yield of misconduct. The failure of unconditional exchanges focuses attention on the need to design mutually beneficial economic relations that emphasise conditionality, implying that exchanges should be reversible or mutually beneficial. Trade in this respect may be superior to aid and direct investment, since capital flows are most often one-way traffic and, moreover, money that crossed the target's border is by definition no longer conditional upon the target's behaviour.

Hirsch (1981, p. 49) argues that economic instruments, policies and transactions should be directed at stabilizing and safeguarding peace between (potential) belligerents. Our analysis clarifies an important lesson for economic diplomacy, namely that the achievement of such a 'balance of prosperity' requires that the benefits of bilateral co-operation are substantial and that the realization of these benefits is conditional on continued co-operation.

NOTES

[1]   With respect to the impact on the target economy this 'new' approach to economic sanctions to a large extent follows the economic analysis that underpins the economic argument for national defence tariffs (see Section 2 in Chapter 2). Indeed Srinivasan (1987, p. 347) reviewing this literature stresses that the threat of sanctions is more often used than the actual imposition of economic hardship.

[2] See Isard (1988), especially pp. 121–75, on the cognitive framework for individual and group behaviour and decision making under psychological stress and crisis conditions. See, moreover, Haney, Hertzberg and Wilson (1992) for a laboratory experimental test of the differences between unitary actors and advisory models. They conclude (p. 632) that 'the unitary actor model is on the right track. Such a model does not do great harm to model the larger questions. Compare also Sandler (1992) on collective action theory which is grounded in maximizing models and pursues the problems of decision making by group processes.

[3] In addition it may not be clear what exactly disputable behaviour or misconduct is. Much depends on one's position. Black and Cooper (1989, p. 192 *n*.), for example, argue that the analysis of the sender's motivations may be applicable for the target's behaviour as well.

[4] The yield of misconduct can of course change in time. See, for example, Simon (1989) for an analysis that shows that land and other productive resources in general are no longer worth acquiring at the cost of war. Obviously, a smaller M will always reduce the incentives for misconduct.

[5] Incidentally, these numbers are rather stable and did, for example, not differ between the 2nd and 3rd edition of the study by Hufbauer et al. (1990 and 2008, respectively)

[6] The five basic axioms can be summarized as follows. Let $X > Y$ denote that X is preferred to Y. Let π be the probability of receiving i and $L(X;\pi)$ be a lottery of receiving X with probability π. Then we may write the requirements as:

- Transitivity: $A > B$ and $B > C$, then $A > C$
- Continuity: a π exists such that $B = \{A, C; \pi, (1-\pi)\}$
- Strong independence: if $B > A$ and C is any other prospect, then it follows that $\{B, C; \pi, (1-\pi)\} > \{A, C; \pi, (1-\pi)\}$
- Preference for high probability of success: if $A = B$ and $v_A > v_B$ then it follows that $L(A, \pi_A) > L(B, \pi_B)$
- Compound probabilities: $L\{L(B; \pi_1), \pi_2\} = L\{L(B; \pi_2), \pi_1\}$

See for useful succinct introductions into and discussions of the economic theory of expected utility: Henderson and Quandt, 1971, especially pp. 42–9, and McKenna 1986, especially pp. 21–5.

[7] An interesting and comprehensive treatment of the international law aspects regarding positive and negative economic sanctions is provided by Picchio Forlati (2000, esp. pp. 200–9)

[8] See Hower (1988) on the utility of extra instruments in containing international conflict.

[9] See, however, Bergeijk and Marrewijk (1995) for a model that incorporates Bayesian learning by the target of economic sanctions.

[10] See also Manacsa (2008) for an analysis of the relationship between negative sanctions and war based on Hufbauer et al. data.

[11] However, as pointed out by Bornstein (1968), positive economic sanctions definitely provide not a panacea and may, for example, not be fit for military situations, especially if states are to be convinced that they have to sacrifice what they consider to be the requirements of both their national security and their sovereignty.

PART IV

Policy Conclusions and Further Research

8. An Agenda for Economic and Commercial Diplomacy

Economic realism is a powerful antidote to political enthusiasm. In the international economic arena the visions of politicians are often impressive, gestures are spectacular and the tempo of change is assumed to be high. In reality the economic scope for improvement is often small in the short term. Economic processes exhibit considerable inertia. Consequently, economic reality often seems to lag behind political dreams. A clear discrepancy exists, however, between on the one hand the globalization of production and the international co-operation that are almost tangible in multinational corporations, and on the other hand, world politics where the colour of one's passport often completely dominates affairs. Too many problems are still being dealt with from a national – and all too often nationalistic – point of view. Remedies are mainly sought in domestic policies which in many cases actually distort international exchange.

Globalization is at the basis of the network of nations, as economies are linked through international trade in goods and services, through capital flows (foreign direct and portfolio investment, lending and aid) and increasingly through the migration of labour. Globalization, on the one hand, is a source of substantial welfare gains. On the other hand, opening up of its economy makes a nation vulnerable to foreign pressure. International interdependence is also the basis for economic warfare and it may create diplomatic conflicts, for example between the United States and Japan over Japanese cars or between the European Union and the United States over agriculture. Policies that in the past could rightly be considered as purely domestic, such as government procurement, may now generate external effects on other countries and lead to international diplomatic conflicts. In this light the change in governance of the world trading from 'embedded liberalism' towards national treatment (that is regulatory harmonisation) is understandable although perhaps not economic efficient (Woolcock 2002). At the same time a trend towards a greater weight for national interests in strategies on internationalization can be witnessed in a great many countries.

Globalization of both consumption and production has clear benefits that are not always fully recognized in the political decision making processes. International exchange enhances efficiency both because comparative advantages and economies of scale can be exploited more fully and because international competition is an important incentive for firms to minimize costs and to develop new products and new production techniques. In addition to the specialization and competition effects of international trade, interdependence and the mutual benefits that derive from international exchange are important economic incentives to reduce international political and military conflicts in the long run. It is thus no option to sit back and relax and simply let the economics prove international political ideas to be false. Indeed, many political activities and gestures carry an important price tag – although these costs are all too often invisible to the untrained and/or non-economic eye.

In a sense the discussions in the previous chapters have tried to uncover that price tag for a number of elements of the broad field of economic diplomacy, including positive and negative sanctions and the most important instruments of commercial diplomacy, such as state visits, the network of embassies and consulates and export promotion agencies.

This discussion is both timely and necessary because many new theories and empirical regularities appear to have emerged since the mid-1990s. Firm level data have become available and this has stimulated new theories about trade, specialization and productivity. The new era of globalization (and the end of the superpower conflict) in combination with the emergence of new and significant players in the world economic system have changed our perspectives on openness, institutions and growth. Economic and political equilibria are shifting due to the changing gravity of globalization. The scope and range of the instruments of economic diplomacy are positively correlated with the intensity of the international economic relationships (an autarkic country is invulnerable to economic sanctions) and therefore the changing pattern of the centres of economic gravity due to globalization is a complicating factor for diplomacy. Such changes in the geography of the world economic system have a direct impact on national security issues and hence on foreign policy. And the 'Death of Distance' appears to have been announced too early. The world is not flat and distance is an increasingly important driver of the geographic pattern of international trade and investment.

With so much change happening, it is hardly surprising that we have learned that our knowledge about the real world is much less perfect than we had previously thought. The first section of this chapter deals with this imperfectness suggesting a research agenda for students of economic diplomacy and (bilateral) trade and investment flows. The second section discusses some policy implications against the back ground of imperfect knowledge and analyzes as a case study the increasing use of negative economic sanctions. The final section reflects on the analysis and applications of economic diplomacy.

1 A THOUSAND AND ONE Ph.D TOPICS

This book developed out of a Ph.D. thesis and I hope that it in its turn may provide inspiration for others. On the basis of the available empirical and theoretical literature, I would in particular single out three themes for further investigation that appear to be highly relevant from the perspective of the needs of both policy and science. These three issues are:

- heterogeneity,
- causality, and
- bias.

In addition to these general themes, a number of specific extensions with respect to the available methodologies, new dependant variables, longer and different time periods and other data sets are suggested by the previous chapters. Let us consider these general themes and specific extensions and the research questions that they imply.

Heterogeneity

A recurring theme in this book has been that a large (and often growing) extent of heterogeneity exists under the veil of the averages and estimated co-efficients that have been reported in the literature on international economic relationships. Obviously many empirical researchers are aware of this heterogeneity and increasingly report accordingly about their findings (see Table 8.1). Typically they find different levels of significance and occasionally even different signs of the estimated co-efficients for the OECD countries, the emerging markets and the developing countries. Political scientists have noted similar heterogeneity with respect to, for example, the impact of democracy on international relations (see, for example, Mousseau et al. 2003).

While this observation is increasingly being recognized and reported in the empirical literature, we still do not know much about the actual drivers behind the apparently diverging country experiences. Indeed, institutions, economic policies, culture, geography and even religion have been suggested as explanatory variables for heterogeneity. But we do know that due to globalization the extent of heterogeneity in the world economic system has increased and will probably continue to do so in the next decades.

Table 8.1 Reported heterogeneity in international economic relations

	Study	This book	
		Chapter	Section
Distance effects	Fratianni and Kang 2006b	1	4
FDI	Fortanier 2008	2	5
Embassies, consulates	Yakop 2009	5	3
Export promotion	Lederman et al. 2006;	5	3
	Veenstra 2009		

Thus it is important that further research takes this heterogeneity seriously. Ideally all reported econometric results on policy instruments in international relationships should be checked and given the number of available studies in international politics and international economics a promising research agenda is ahead. It is, however, not only the new empirical regularities where new knowledge can be produced. Equally important and interesting will be the much more complex analyzes that have to be made about policy implementation and the mix of instruments.

A serious complicating factor has to be noted. The currently most intensively used empirical tool, the gravity analysis, may not be appropriate due to the endemic use of country-fixed effects in the econometrics which actually filter out all country-specific and possibly policy-induced heterogeneity. Methodological solutions have been suggested (see, for example, Baier and Bergstrand 2009), but it will in addition pay to use other methodologies, either those techniques that have already been used in applied analysis (a number of these were reviewed in Chapter 2) or new and innovative approaches. After all, only by applying different methods to the same problem can the researcher grasp the robustness of his findings. In sum, heterogeneity implies many substantive empirical, methodological and theoretical research questions on the agenda regarding economic and commercial diplomacy.

Causality

A second recurring theme in this book has been the considerable ambiguity regarding the (interpretation of) causality of the econometrically established relationships. Do stronger economic ties reduce political conflicts between nations or does less (more) conflict increase (decrease) trade)? Does the network of embassies and consulates shape a country's trade pattern or is the geography and importance of trade partners a key determinant of the decision for the location of diplomats? Do exporters become more productive or does a firm have to be more productive before it can export? It seems that causality is a much more difficult problem in the international field, perhaps due to the interplay between economic and political factors. Chapter 2 suggests that many of these twin questions may actually be two sides of the same coin. Anyhow, solving the causality issue is not the panacea for the lacking synthesis between international politics and international economics. Unambiguously establishing causality may actually be beyond the reach of what science presently can do, but it is a very important topic – also for policy making – and the scientific debate on causality should thus be rigorous and intensive.

Importantly, a number of studies have already explicitly addressed the issue of causality, but only for a limited number of bilateral relationships and pre-1990 periods. Much more evidence (that is broader data sets that deal with or include other countries and cover more recent periods) is needed before judgements about the robustness of the established causality become possible and trustworthy. Actually, research may show that causality depends on the institutional settings and/or economic frame works that characterise periods in time or causality may be partly geographically determined. Theories may simply not be wrong or right but relevant or irrelevant depending on specific conditions of time and place.

The conclusion of this discussion, however, is that causality also will generate a substantive research agenda.

Bias

The body of knowledge about economic and commercial diplomacy that was discussed and developed in this book has another curious but not often noted aspect, namely its bias with respect to positive and negative interactions. As discussed in Chapters 4 and 5 the empirical evidence that is produced by economists working on the use and impact of the foreign service in the post-1990 world trade system is mainly limited to positive diplomatic exchanges, and in particular the diplomatic and commercial infrastructures. In contrast the empirical evidence on the use of economic relationships as a tool to achieve foreign policy goals is by and large limited to the use of negative sanctions, while we know little about the determinants of failure and success of positive sanctions (Caruso, 2003, p. 4).[1]

It would be important to have a clearer vision on the economic costs of the negative political instruments of diplomacy, that is hostile interaction. The literature provides pre-1990 estimates that require urgent updating. Moreover, research has tended to focus on the impact of fatal military interaction (for which unambiguous data are available) thus neglecting the nuances of more grey areas between war and peace that, however, will influence the expectations of consumers, firms and governments and thus the extent of international specialization as we saw in Chapter 3.

For these reasons further research – in particular comprising detailed analysis that uses more recent non-binary data to investigate conflict's impact on trade – would seem to be promising. Moreover, data collection and the combination of existing data sets will be important. As pointed out in Chapter 6, further research and an investment in a data set should help to provide a better understanding of the potential use of positive sanctions as foreign policy tools. Actually this would require a major effort by the international scientific community that deserves a high place on the agenda.

Further Extensions

The knowledge that has been built with the existing empirical studies on economic and commercial diplomacy and the conflict–trade nexus could be strengthened further by a number of extensions. Although this section tends to duplicate some of the arguments that were already put on the table it is worth to systematically list why and where available and existing knowledge can be strengthened simply by applying available methodologies.

- *Update earlier studies*. The studies of the 1980s and early 1990s that used non-binary data for conflict and co-operation derived from the COBDAB and WEIS database need to be updated in order to also cover post-1990 observations on conflict and co-operation.[2]
- *Extend the number of years*. Some topics such as the impact of export promotion agencies and the network of embassies and consulates have only been investigated satisfactorily for a limited number of years (and often only for a single year).
- *Use other indicators as explanatory variables*. Where studies have deployed binary data (such as the occurrence of war) more gradation could be provided, because economic diplomacy is probably more relevant in non-extreme situations. Events data could be constructed from other sources than previously deployed.
- *Increase country coverage*. This could be particularly relevant for the impact of state visits where the international scientific community has so far only provided data regarding four countries. Moreover, a number of the regularly quoted studies deal with the major economic powers only.
- *Study other forms of economic interaction* An important new field would be the impact of incoming and outgoing flows of foreign direct investment. The enormous increase since the early 1990s in the

volume of international investment flows and its impact on conflict and peace has so far not been explored by researchers.

All in all it seems reasonable to assume that a lot of new and relevant knowledge can be built regarding the different aspects of economic diplomacy. Investment in the collection and construction of data and the fuller exploration of data sources (especially those of other disciplines) will probably have a large intellectual return.

2   POLICY MAKING WITHOUT PERFECT KNOWLEDGE

The message of the previous section is definitely not that policy making is impossible because we do not know enough. The upshot is essentially that policy making should not take everything for granted and recognize the inherent uncertainties. Policy makers should recognize the upside and the downside risks, discount the imperfectness of the knowledge base and exercise judgement. According to Geelhoed (1997, p. 178) policy makers

> do not need to know everything. We do not need the perfectly logical analysis. We need guidance and we need it now. We do not need so much light that every little corner of a problem can be investigated. We simply need sufficient and sufficiently reliable knowledge in order to prevent falling from the stairs or bumping against a blind wall. Indeed, if we can prevent the most serious policy errors, the policy generally speaking is not bad at all.

It is thus worth considering what can already be concluded both on the basis of the present stock of knowledge and from what we know about the white spots in that knowledge base. Let us start by considering some of the consequences of the less than perfect empirical literature and then discuss some problems, where theory might add valuable and reliable inputs

Policy and the Empirics of Economic Diplomacy

At least three consequences follow directly from the imprecision of our knowledge. First of all, policy makers should be aware that really not much scientifically established empirical knowledge is available about the way they should actually deal in concrete cases. General correlations and probabilities may even provide the wrong guidance in concrete cases. Much of the reported correlations disappear (and sometimes even change sign) as soon as the level of development of economies is taken into account. An interesting example that directly illustrates the policy relevance is provided by the utility of embassies and consulates. Rose (2007) showed econometrically that this network of international diplomacy matters and this result was substantiated in Chapter 5 for a larger set of exporting countries and a more recent year. Veenstra (2009), however, shows for the OECD countries that this network only matters for the bilateral trade relationship with low and middle income countries. Policy makers that have to prioritize diplomatic activities should thus give a greater weight to non-OECD markets when they have to take decisions about the location of diplomats. This heterogeneity is the more relevant because indications exist that observed instabilities in previously established econometric relationships may have been induced by the new phase of globalization that seem to have had a clear impact on behaviour in the international arena (compare for example Table 6.6 that reports on the key characteristics of 113 pre-1990 and 59 post-1990 punitive sanctions). Another example is Li's (2006) finding that the end of the Cold War significantly shifted the FDI-curve. The policy conclusion of substantial and increasing international heterogeneity is that a one-size-fits-all approach is thus not appropriate. Economic diplomacy and commercial policy will have to take country characteristics into account when the design of policies and the mix of policies are considered.

Secondly, some of the causality issues have clear implications for policy making. The 'chicken or egg' question regarding productivity and export at the microeconomic level implies that policy instruments should not be made freely available to all firms but only to those that are sufficiently productive and prepared to successfully meet the competition of the world market. It is also important to understand better whether the location of consulates and embassies is a result of intensive trade relations or whether diplomats actually reduce bilateral barriers to international trade. If trade follows the flag, then the benefits of an embassy will normally exceed its costs. The available econometric solutions (such as the use of instrumental variables) are not yet very satisfactorily. Moreover, closing an embassy or a consulate is traditionally a very strong negative political signal in international diplomacy and the resulting extent of hysteresis in the number and location of embassies and consulates makes a time series approach problematic.[3] The trade–conflict nexus may, however, be less problematic from a policy perspective as trade and co-operation should perhaps move in tandem. It would seem logical that the royal road to reduce conflict is the simultaneous combination of diplomatic co-operation, friendly political exchanges and intensifying trade and investment relationships.

Thirdly, the asymmetry with respect to what we do and do not know about on the one hand, positive or co-operative exchange and on the other hand, hostile or non-co-operative exchange implies that our empirical evaluation of the diplomacy–trade nexus and the trade–diplomacy nexus can be seriously distorted. This has at least two implications of which policy makers should be aware. The bias in our present knowledge also relates to the pro-active re-active dimensions of economic diplomacy (Figure 8.1) and thus the tendency may be to meet short-term problems with negative interaction where positive reactions might be more appropriate.

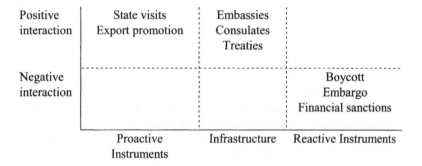

Positive interaction	State visits Export promotion	Embassies Consulates Treaties	
Negative interaction			Boycott Embargo Financial sanctions
	Proactive Instruments	Infrastructure	Reactive Instruments

Figure 8.1 Available empirical knowledge

Moreover, this distortion in our knowledge base about the costs and benefits of economic diplomacy and international economics suggests that the 'markets' for economic and commercial diplomacy may not be in balance. Indeed such disequilibrium may be one of the drivers behind both the substantial growth in state visits (positive exchange), punitive economic sanctions (negative exchange) and the growth of export promotion agencies.[4] In some cases a reduction of negative political exchanges should be more appropriate. The anti-Islam film 'Fitna' that was published by the Dutch MP Geert Wilders in 2008 is an example of such a negative communication that neglected the potentially damaging impact of the political (essentially domestic) message on the economic relations of the Netherlands with the Muslim world.

In sum policy makers and politicians should be aware that the alternative of positive economic sanctions might require further attention essentially because the costs of negative interaction tend to be neglected or forgotten. Let us by way of illustration consider what this means for the concrete case of the increasing use of negative sanctions as an instrument of foreign policy.

The Costs of Negative Sanctions

Deploying negative sanctions often comes down to fighting a political conflict by trampling on consumers and firms that have relatively little outstanding with the political differences of opinion. Economic sanctions are essentially the heaviest non-military instrument in international conflict resolution. Their use should be restricted to those exceptional cases where other, possibly more appropriate, diplomatic measures have been exhausted – at least to the level where their opportunity costs are equal to those of negative sanctions. In reality, however, one observes that political decision making often neglects other options (Bergeijk 1995c). This bias towards negative economic sanctions *vis-à-vis* purely political measures and positive sanctions is particularly worrying since international politics that resorts to economic warfare and economic surveillance more often, increases trade uncertainty and this yields a suboptimal allocation of factors of production. Indeed, interdependence and the mutual benefits that derive from international exchange are important economic incentives to reduce international political and military conflicts in the long run. Sanctions undermine this positive contribution of international economic exchange. Such hidden, but real costs of international diplomacy are generally not considered with the implication that scarce resources are being wasted.

A more balanced situation could be achieved if future empirical research uncovers the costs and benefits of the considered activities in the field of diplomacy on international trade and investment. But economists can already do better and clarify the costs of considered instruments using theory to guide policy makers. In addition to the direct welfare consequences of the increased use of economic sanctions, they can point out the indirect impact of the increasing use of negative economic sanctions on the world trade system. Sanctions also influence the economic opportunities of countries that are in no way involved in the international conflict. These are the external effects of economic sanctions that do not play a role in the cost-benefit analysis of either the sanction's target or the sender country and may be called the hidden costs of economic sanctions (Bergeijk and Marrewijk 1994). The problem is not so much that the probability of a specific country becoming a target of economic sanctions increases, since a potential target can influence this probability by behaving in accordance with the international standards set by the international community (or specific sender countries). Rather the problem of (global) trade uncertainty derives from the fact that political risk spreads through the world economic system as the overall probability increases that every country's trade partners will become the subject of economic sanctions. Moreover, in many cases the impact of boycotts and embargoes will spill-over to the trade partners (and to the trade partners' trade partners and so on). This will induce countries to specialize to a lesser extent and to limit their external trade in order to reduce the risk of foreign trade restrictions in the future. Chapter 3 highlighted the trade-off between on the one hand, the probability that the international gains from trade can actually be reaped and on the other hand, the extent of these gains. This trade-off may substantially change the global pattern of trade, especially since the target's firms may be able to reap monopoly profits in markets that are sheltered by the rest of the world's sanction measures. Lowenberg (1993) argues that domestic firms will then no longer have an incentive to lobby for liberalization of the objectionable policy. Firms will prefer to reinforce that policy in order to get a bigger chunk of the sanction rents for themselves. The result is that an increase in the use of sanctions may put economies on a more inward-looking track with a reduction of the world's potential for international trade as a logical consequence.

So in the end, other, presumably innocent countries will suffer from the trade disruption that is aimed at specific 'ill-mannered' countries. Although gains from trade still do exist in such a scenario, the welfare gains decrease substantially below the level in a deterministic (or simply a less uncertain) trade setting. In this way the general (and possibly endogenous) trade uncertainty, that results if international politics resorts to economic warfare and economic surveillance more often, may change the global patterns of production and comparative advantage. The implied sub-optimal allocation of the factors of production is a substantial hidden cost that should be taken into account in any policy analysis or policy recommendation of the use of economic relationships as a source of international power.

Logic of Choice

The case of negative sanctions illustrates the three main points of the 'logic of choice', formulated by Baldwin (2000). First, choice requires consideration of all policy alternatives (including the null alternative of inaction). In foreign policy these alternatives comprise the use – possibly in different degrees – of (combinations of) military force, positive and negative sanctions and other diplomatic activities that strengthen thrust or express discontent. Second, this set of available options should be evaluated in terms of costs and benefits. Third, these instruments should therefore not be formulated as goals but as a means to reach pre-specified goals. For example, the policy goal should not be the imposition of an economic sanction but the change in behaviour that is sought with that sanction. Having defined the goal, economic and political scientists can help to determine which instrument of combination will in the most cost efficient way realise the goal – taking political constraints into account, of course. Typically such analyses could be casts in terms of a cost benefit analysis. Importantly, the choice amongst alternatives may be distorted when the extent of uncertainty and measurement is not the same for the cost and benefit components of these instruments. But improper measurement *per se* is not prohibitive for the 'logic of choice' because it 'matters only to the extent that it differs from bias in studying success rates of alternative techniques of statecraft'. The 'logic of choice', however, also has lessons for other subfields of economic diplomacy. For example, with regard to commercial diplomacy this suggests that caution should be exercised with respect to the instruments for which empirical impact estimates are not yet available (and obviously, the implied research question is that these instruments should be analyzed empirically). Also relevant is that the costs and benefits of purely political diplomatic activities are by and large unknown. The 'logic of choice' implies that these political instruments have not been used in an optimal and rational way.

3 THE ART OF ECONOMIC DIPLOMACY

It is difficult to imagine a subject field that requires more strongly the need to apply the 'art' rather than the 'science' of economics. Policy-relevant applied work on economic and commercial policy has to be done in a context of many uncertainties and should always recognize the importance of non-economic aspects. The student of international economic relationships is probably well advised to follow Schumpeter's (1954, p. 12) recommendation to first of all master economic history (which Schumpeter considers more important than the other two fundamental fields of economics, that is statistics and theory). Indeed, a good grasp of economic history and the history of economic thought is essential because a command of historical facts is necessary to understand economic phenomena and because studying history is the best method to understand how economic and non-economic 'facts are related to one another and how the various social sciences *should* be related to one another' (Schumpeter 1954, p. 13 original emphasis). Moreover, history provides the perspective that is necessary to be able to see the underlying trends that determine the future playing field for economic diplomacy.

Since a good decade, bilateralism has gained respectability in policy quarters and among academics probably under the influence of a shift in the issues that have been addressed in the multilateral trade negotiations under the auspices of the WTO. Typically the attention has shifted from border taxes and restrictions on the volumes of exported and imported products towards national regulations and institutional arrangements. This drive towards national treatment is understandable in the light of the fact that increasingly the combined impact of regulation in the domestic market and in partner countries exceeds that of the combined effects of the barriers to trade and invest that traditionally had been the focal point of trade negotiations as we discussed in Chapter 4. Perhaps it is even true that bilateralism has never been away and survived under the veil of globalization and multilateralism.[5] Bilateral economic diplomacy and commercial policies can be beneficial from a welfare point of view if they lead to a reduction of border effects and solve market failures that frustrate the international division of labour. The only way to know if this is the case is to investigate the trade creation *versus* trade diversion aspects of such activities. If trade is diverted (so that trade of other countries is reduced) then economic diplomacy boils down to government failure. Fortunately, the instruments of bilateral economic diplomacy and commercial diplomacy are also associated with an increase in import flows so that the impact of these instruments extends beyond the Mercantilist's zero-sum game. This general finding, however, needs to be checked in concrete cases.

This book did not really deal with the economic diplomacy that is taking place in the international organizations (although we have occasionally touched upon the subject). This is not because such activities are unimportant. On the contrary, the efforts of economic diplomacy that strengthen the multilateral approach to world trade and global investment are essential for our well-being, especially at the present junction in time. So it is probably right to add a few words on the multilateral governance of free trade and investment. During the Second World War institutional arrangements were proposed to safeguard the post-war economy. These Bretton Woods institutions (IMF, World Bank and GATT, which later became the WTO) aimed at a world order that could prevent a repetition of the 1930s that was aggravated by (in so far as it did not result from) a wave of protectionism and beggar-thy-neighbour policies. The focus of this book on bilateral diplomatic and economic relationships thus should not blur the fact that free trade is essential to survive the credit crisis that hit the global economy.

The benefits of the Bretton Woods institutions were hoped to extend beyond economic stabilization and prevention of the errors of the Great depression. The spirit of Bretton Woods was also to prevent a repetition of the great wars. Recent empirical research for the years 1885–1992 shows that a clear contribution was delivered:

> The pacific benefits of democracy, economic interdependence, and international organizations are all the more apparent if they are compared to the effects of alliances and a preponderance of power – the elements stressed in realist theories of international politics. Surprisingly, alliances do not reduce the likelihood of interstate disputes, even fatal ones, when the influences of (democracy, economic interdependence and membership of international organizations) and previous dyadic conflicts are held constant. ... Efforts to consolidate democracy, increase interdependence, and create a network of international organizations, our results suggest, should have greater benefits (...that) policymakers should incorporate in their strategy for peace. (Oneal *et al* 2003, p. 388)

For the near future it is important to point out that the multilateral governance of the world trade system is offering protection of small and medium-sized countries and new entrants to the world market. This is so because only the large economies can benefit from strategic trade policies and economic warfare, while the rest of the world is to be the victim. Ultimately, however, unilateral trade policies will reduce world demand for the products of the country that is trying to regulate its foreign trade. Hence in the long run an open multilateral trade system is in the interest of all countries.

It is the multilateral approach that offers a first line of defence against increasing bilateralism and protectionism and against power politics of other countries. It provides the institutional and economic background against which trade, investment, and conflict resolution can be reconciled.

NOTES

[1]   A clear example is that the topic of positive sanctions or rewards is not explicitly covered in the *Handbook of Defense Economics* (Sandler and Hartley 2007) although this pays a lot of attention to peace economics and the economics of peace making.

[2]   No continuous time series is available for events data. COPDAB covers 1948–78, WEIS covers 1966–92 and VRA presently covers 1990–2001. A useful discussion is Polacheck and Seiglie 2007, pp. 1032–39.

[3]   The approach (pioneered by Maurel and Afman 2007) to study the effect of newly established embassies and consulates in countries that enter into the world economic system (such as the countries that formerly were part of the Soviet Union) seems promising, but may also run into difficulties because these countries will already *ceteris paribus* experience a substantial increase in bilateral trade and investment.

[4]   These trends are illustrated in Figures 1.1 and 4.1.

[5]   This suggests an alternative explanation of Figure 1.1 that shows the fourfold increase in the use of economic sanctions and the eightfold increase in state visits.

References

Adler–Karlsson, G., 1982, 'Instruments of Economic Coercion and Their Use', in F.A.M. Alting von Geusau and J. Pelkmans (eds), *National Economic Security: Perceptions, Threats and Policies,* Tilburg; John F. Kennedy Institute, pp. 160–82.

Aldrich, J. and F.D. Nelson, 1984, *Linear Probability and Probit Models,* London: Sage Publications.

Alexander, C. and K. Warwick, 2007, 'Governments, Exports and Growth: Responding to the Challenges and Opportunities of Globalisation' *The World Economy*, pp. 177–94.

Anderson, J.E. and E. van Wincoop, 2003, 'Gravity with Gravitas, A Solution to the Border Puzzle', *American Economic Review,* **93** (1), pp. 170–92.

Anderson, J.E. and E. Van Wincoop, 2004, 'Trade Costs', *Journal of Economic Literature*, **42**, pp. 691–751.

Andreasen, U., 2008, 'Reflections on Public Diplomacy after the Danish Cartoon Crises: From Crisis Management to Normal Public Diplomacy Work', *The Hague Journal of Diplomacy*, **3**, pp. 201–7.

Arad, R.W. and A.L. Hillman, 1979, 'Embargo Threat, Learning and Departure from Comparative Advantage', *Journal of International Economics*, **9**, pp. 265–75.

Aspin, L,, 1991, 'The Aspin Papers; Sanctions, Diplomacy, and War in the Persian Gulf', *Significant Issues Series*, **13** (2), Washington, DC: Centre for Strategic and International Issues.

Aw, B.Y., M.J. Roberts and D.Y. Xu, 2008, 'R&D Investments, Exporting, and the Evolution of Firm Productivity', *American Economic Review,* **98** (2), Papers & Proceedings, pp. 451–6.

Azar, E.E., 1980, 'The Conflict and Peace Data Bank (COPDAB) Project', *Journal of Conflict Resolution*, **24** (1), pp. 143–52.

Baier, S.L. and J.H. Bergstrand, 2009, '*Bonus Vetus* OLS: A Simple Method for Approximating International Trade-Cost Effects using the Gravity Equation', *Journal of International Economics*, **77** (1), pp. 77–85.

Bailey, N.A. and C. Lord, 1988, 'On Strategic Economics', *Comparative Strategy*, **7**, pp. 93–7.

Baine, N. and S. Woolcock, 2003, *The New Economic Diplomacy: Decision Making and Negotiation in International Economic Relations*, Aldershot: Ashgate Publishing Ltd.

Baldry, J.C. and B.E. Dollery, 1992, 'Investment and Trade Sanctions Agaianst South Africa in a Model of Apartheid,' *UNE Working Papers in Economics*, No. 1, University of New England

Baldwin, D.A., 1971, 'The Power of Positive Sanctions', *World Politics*, **24** (1), pp. 19–38.

Baldwin, D.A., 1985, *Economic Statecraft*, Princeton: Princeton University Press.

Baldwin, D.A., 2000, 'The Sanctions Debate and the Logic of Choice', *International Security*, **24** (3), pp. 80–107.

Baldwin, R., 2006, *The Great Unbundling(s)*, Economic Council of Finland: Helsinki.

Baldwin, J. and Gu, W., 2004, 'Trade Liberalization: Export-Market Participation, Productivity Growth, and Innovation', *Oxford Review of Economic Policy*, **20** (3), pp. 372–92.

Balkan, E.M., 1992, 'Political Instability, Country Risk and Probability of Default', *Applied Economics*, **24** (9), pp. 999–1008.

Bayard, T.O., J. Pelzman and J.F. Perez-Lopez, 1983, 'An Economic Model of United States and Western Controls on Exports to the Soviet Union and Eastern Europe', in Joint Economic Committee, *Soviet Economy in the 1980s: Problems and Prospects* Congress of the United States: Washington, DC, pp 507–55.

Berg, M van den, M. de Nooij, H. Garretsen en H.L.F. de Groot, 2008, 'MKBA buitenlandinstrumentarium' (Cost-benefit Analysis of Trade Policy Instruments, in Dutch), SEO Report 2008–64, SEO: Amsterdam.

Bergeijk, P.A.G. van, 1987, 'A Formal Treatment of Threats: A Note on the Economics of Deterrence', *De Economist*, **135** (3), pp. 298–315.

Bergeijk, P.A.G. van, 1989a, 'Success and Failure of Economic Sanctions', *Kyklos*, **42** (3), pp. 298–315.

Bergeijk. P.A.G. van, 1989b, 'Trade and Diplomacy: An Extension of the Gravity Model in International Trade Theory', *Institute of Economic Research Memorandum*, No. 320, Groningen: University of Groningen.

Bergeijk, P.A.G. van, 1991, 'International Trade and the Environmental Challenge,' *Journal of World Trade*, **25** (6), pp. 105–15.

Bergeijk, P.A.G. van, 1992, 'Diplomatic Barriers to Trade', *De Economist*, **140** (1), pp. 44–63.

Bergeijk, P.A.G. van, 1994a, *Economic Diplomacy, Trade and Commercial Policy: Positive and Negative Sanctions in a New World Order*, Edward Elgar: Cheltenham, UK.

Bergeijk, P.A.G. van, 1994b, 'Effectivity of Economic Sanctions: Illusion or Reality?', *Peace Economics, Peace Science, and Public Policy*, **2** (1), pp. 24–35.

Bergeijk, P.A.G. van, 1995a, 'The Accuracy of International Economic Observations', *Bulletin of Economic Research*, **47** (1), pp. 1–20.

Bergeijk, P.A.G. van, 1995b, 'The Oil Embargo and the Intellectual: The academic debate on economic sanctions against South Africa', in Shipping

Research Bureau (ed.), *Oil Sanctions Against South Africa: The Full Story*, Amsterdam University Press: Amsterdam, 1995, pp. 338–45.

Bergeijk, P.A.G. van, 1995c, 'The Impact of Economic Sanctions in the 1990s', *The World Economy*, **18** (3), pp. 443–55.

Bergeijk P.A.G. van, R.J. Berndsen and W.J. Janssen (eds), 2000, *The Economics of the Euro Area,* Edward Elgar: Cheltenham, UK.

Bergeijk, P.A.G. van, and R. Fenthur, 2008, 'Hoe en wanneer zijn economische sancties effectief? (How and When are Economic Sanctions Effective?, in Dutch), *Internationale Spectator*, **62** (6), pp. 359–63.

Bergeijk, P.A.G. van and R.C.G. Haffner, 1996, *Privatisation, Deregulation and the Macroeconomy*, Edward Elgar: Cheltenham, UK.

Bergeijk, P.A.G. van and D.L. Kabel, 1993, 'Strategic Trade Theory and Trade Policy', *Journal of World Trade*, **27** (6), pp. 175–86.

Bergeijk, P.A.G. van and B.W. Lensink, 1993, 'Trade, Capital and the Transition in Central Europe', *Applied Economics*, **25**, pp. 891–903.

Bergeijk, P.A.G. van and C. van Marrewijk, 1994, 'Economic Sanctions: A Hidden Cost of the New World Order', in M. Chatterji, H. Jager and A. Rima (eds), *Economics of International Security: Essays in Honor of Jan Tinbergen*, Macmillan: London, pp. 168–82.

Bergeijk, P.A.G. van and C. van Marrewijk, 1995, 'Why Do Sanctions Need Time to Work? Adjustment, Learning and Anticipation', *Economc Modelling*, **12** (2), pp. 75–86.

Bergeijk, P.A.G. van, and H. Oldersma, 1990, 'Détente, Market-oriented Reform and German Unification. Potential Consequences for the World Trade System', *Kyklos* **43** (4), pp. 599–609.

Bergeijk, P.A.G. van, and H. Oldersma, 2006, 'Terrorism and Trade', *Aelementair* **6** (1), pp.12–15.

Bergstrand, J.H. 1985, 'The Gravity Equation in International Trade: Some Microeconomic Foundations and Empirical Evidence', *Review of Economics and Statistics*, **67** (1), pp. 474–81.

Bergstrand, J.H., 1989, 'The Generalized Gravity Equation, Monopolistic Competition, and the Factor-proportions Theory in International Trade', *Review of Economics and Statistics*, **71**, pp. 143–52.

Bergström, C., G.C. Loury and M. Persson, 1985, 'Embargo Threat and the Management of Emergency Reserves', *Journal of Political Economy*, **93**, pp. 26–42.

Bernard, A.B. and J.B. Jensen, 1999, 'Exceptional Exporter Performance: Cause, Effect or Both?', *Journal of International Economics*, **47** (1), pp. 1–25.

Bernard, A., and Jensen, J.B., 2004a, 'Exporting and Productivity in the USA', *Oxford Review of Economic Policy*, **20**, pp. 343–57.

Bernard, A., and Jensen, J.B., 2004b, 'Why Some Firms Export', *Review of Economics and Statistics*, **86** (2), pp. 561–69.

Bernard, A.B. S.J. Redding and P.K. Schott, 2008, 'Comparative Advantage and Heterogeneous Firms', *Review of Economic Studies*, **74** (1), pp. 31–66.

Bernard, A.B. and J. Wagner, 2001, 'Export Entry and Exit by German Firms', *Weltwirtschaftliches Archiv*, **137** (1), pp. 105–123.

Bhagwati, J.N., 1991, *Political Economy and International Economics*, Collected Writings V, Cambridge MA: MIT Press.

Bhagwati, J.N., 1992, 'The Threats to the World Trading System', *The World Economy*, **15** (4), pp. 433–56.

Bhagwati, J.N. and T.N. Srinivisan, 1976, 'Optimal Trade Policy and Compensation Under Endogenous Uncertainty: The Phenomenon of Market Disruption', *Journal of International Economics*, **6**, pp. 317–36.

Bhagwati J.N. and T.N. Srinivasan, 1982, 'The Welfare Consequences of Directly-unproductive Profitseeking (DUP) Lobbying Activities: Price versus Quantity Distortions,' *Journal of International Economics*, **13** (1), pp. 33–44.

Biesebroeck, J. van, 2005, 'Exporting Raises Productivity in Sub-Saharan African Manufacturing Firms', *Journal of International Economics*, **67** (2), pp. 373–91.

Bikker, J.A., 1982, *Vraag-aanbodmodellen voor stelsels van geografisch gespreide markten toegepast op internationale handel en ziekenhuis-opnames in Noord-Nederland*, (Demand and Supply Models of Geographically Delineated Markets with Applications to International Trade and Hospitalisations in the Northern Part of the Netherlands; in Dutch), PhD Thesis, Free University: Amsterdam.

Bikker, J.A., 1987, 'An International Trade Flow Model With Substitution: An Extension of the Gravity Model', *Kyklos*, **40**, pp. 315–37.

Bikker, J.A., 2007, 'An Extended Gravity Model with Substitution Applied to International Trade Flows', paper presented at 'The Gravity Equation Or: Why the World is not Flat', University of Groningen, 19 October 2007.

Black, P.A. and J.H. Cooper, 1989, 'Economic Sanctions and Interest Group Analysis; Some Reservations', *South African Journal of Economics*, **57** (2), pp. 188–93.

Blake, C.H. and N. Klemm, 2006, 'Reconsidering the Effectiveness of International Economic Sanctions: An Examination of Selection Bias', *International Politics*, **43**, pp. 133–149.

Blomberg, S.B. and G.D. Hess, 2006, 'How Much does Violence Tax Trade?', *Review of Economics and Statistics*, **88** (4), pp. 599–612.

Bonetti, S., 1991, 'Sanctions and Statistics: Reconsidering *Economic Sanctions Reconsidered*', *Discussion Paper 9103*, University of St. Andrews, UK.

Bonetti, S., 1994, 'The Persistence and Frequency of Economic Sanctions', in M. Chatterji, H. Jager and A. Rima (eds), *Economics of International Security: Essays in Honor of Jan Tinbergen*, Macmillan: London, pp. 183–93.

Bonetti, S., 1998, 'Distinguishing Characteristics of Degrees of Success and Failure in Economic Sanctions Episodes', *Applied Economics*, **30**, pp. 805–13.

Bornstein, M., 1968, 'Economic Sanctions and Rewards in Support of Arms Control Agreements', *American Economic Review*, **58** (2), Papers & Proceedings, pp. 417–27.

Boulding, K.E., 1962, *Conflict and Defense – A General Theory* New York: Harper.

Bremer, S.A. (ed.), 1987, *The Globus Model: Computer Simulation of Worldwide Political and Economic Developments*, Frankfürt am Main Campus Verlag.

Brady, L.J., 1987, 'The Utility of Economic Sanctions as a Policy Instrument', in D. Leyton-Brown (ed.), *The Utility of International Economic Sanctions*, New York: St. Martins, pp. 297–302.

Brakman, S., R. Gigengack and C.J. Jepma, 1988, 'The Speed of Adjustment as a Measure for Competitiveness', *Austrian Economic Papers*, **1** (3), pp. 161–78.

Brown, D. K., A.V. Deardorff and R.M. Stern, 2002, 'Computational Analysis of Multilateral Trade Liberalization in the Uruguay Round and Doha Development Round', in A. Mattoo and R.M. Stern (eds), *India and the WTO*, Washington, DC: World Bank and Oxford University Press, pp. 13–46.

Brzoska, M., 2008, 'Measuring the Effectiveness of Arms Embargoes', *Peace Economics, Peace Science and Public Policy*, **14** (2), article 2.

Brun, J.-F., C. Carrère, P. Guillaumont and J. de Melo, 2005, 'Has Distance Died?', *The World Bank Economic Review*, **19** (1), pp. 99–120.

Bull, H., 1984, 'Economic Sanctions and Foreign Policy', *The World Economy*, **7** (1), pp. 218–22.

Butter, F.A.G. den and R.H.J. Mosch, 2003, 'Trade, Trust and Transaction Costs', *Tinbergen Institute Working Paper No. 2003-082/3*, TI: Amsterdam.

Cairncross F., 1997, *The Death of Distance*, Cambridge MA: Harvard Business Publications.

Cantillon, R., 1755, *Essai sur la nature du commerce en géneral*, (Essay on the Nature of International Commerce in General; in French) http://www.econlib.org/library/NPDBooks/Cantillon/cntNT.html.

Carbaugh, R.J., 1989, *International Economics*, 3rd edition, Wadsworth: Belmont.

Carter, B.E., 1988, *International Economic Sanctions,* Cambridge, MA: MIT Press.

Caruso, R., 2003, 'The Impact of International Economic Sanctions on Trade An Empirical Analysis', *Peace Economics, Peace Science and Public Policy*, **9** (2), article 2.

Cataquet, H., 1985, 'Country Risk Analysis: Art, Science and Sorcery?', in H.J. Krümmel (ed.), *Internationales Bankgeschäft,* Beihefte zu *Kredit und Kapital,* H8, Berlin.

Chang, Y.-C., S.W. Polachek and J. Robst, 2004, 'Conflict and Trade: The Relationship between Geographic Distance and International Interactions', *Journal of Socio-Economics,* **33,** pp. 491–509.

Charlton, A. and Davis, N., 2007, 'Does investment promotion work?', *The B.E. Journal of Economic Analysis & Policy,* **7** (1), 42: 1–19.

Citron, J. and G. Nickelsburg, 1987, 'Country Risk and Political Instability', *Journal of Development Economics,* **25,** pp. 385–92.

Collini, S., D. Winch and J. Burrow, 1983, *That Noble Science of Politics. A Study in Nineteenth-Century Intellectual History,* London: Cambridge University Press.

Cortright D. and G.A. Lopez, 2002, *Sanctions and the Search for Security,* London: Boulder.

Daoudi, M.S. and M.S. Dajani, 1983, *Economic Sanctions: Ideals and Experience,* Boston, MA: Routledge & Kegan.

Dashti-Gibson, J. P. Davis and B. Radcliff, 2001, 'On the Determinants of the Success of Economic Sanctions: An Empirical Analysis', *American Journal of Political Science,* **41** (2), pp. 608–18.

Deardorff, A.V., 1995, 'Determinants of Bilateral Trade: Does Gravity Work in a Neoclassical World?', *NBER Working Paper W5377* NBER: Cambridge, MA.

Dehejia, R.H. and B. Wood, 1992, 'Economic Sanctions and Econometric Policy Advise: A Cautionary Note', *Journal of World Trade,* **26,** pp. 73–84.

Dekker, P.G., 1973, 'Economische oorlogvoering: Enige opmerkingen over boycot en embargo' (Economic Warfare: A Note on Boycott and Embargo, in Dutch), *De Economist,* **121** (4), pp. 387–402.

Dekker, P., S. Ederveen, H. de Groot, A. van der Horst, A. Lejour, B. Straathof, H. Vinken and C. Wennekers, 2006, 'Divers Europe', *European Outlook* 4, SDU: The Hague.

Delgado, M.A., J.C., Fariñas and S. Ruano, 2002, 'Firm Productivity and Export Markets: A Non-parametric Approach', *Journal of International Economics,* **57,** pp. 397–422.

Denters, E. and J. Klijn, 1991, *Economic Aspects of a Political Settlement in the Middle East: The Dynamics of Self-determination,* Amsterdam: VU University Press.

Dewit, G., 2001, 'Intervention in Risky Export Markets: Insurance, Strategic Action or Aid?', *European Journal of Political Economy,* **17** pp. 579–92.

Diamond, P.A., 1967, 'The Role of the Stock Market in a General Equilibrium Model with Technological Uncertainty', *American Economic Review,* **57,** pp. 171–9.

Disdier, A. and K. Head, 2008 'The Puzzling Persistence of the Distance Effect on Bilateral Trade', *Review of Economics and Statistics*, **90**, pp. 37–48.

Dixit, A., 1990, 'Trade Policy with Imperfect Infromation', in R.W. Jones and A.O. Krueger (eds), *The Political Economy of International Trade: Essays in Honor of Robert E. Baldwin*, Basil Blackwell: Oxford and Cambridge, MA, pp. 9–24

Döhrn, R. and A.R. Milton, 1992, 'Zur künftigen Einbindung der osteuropaïschen Reformländer in der Weltwirtschaft' (On the Integration into the World Economy of the Reforming Countries in Eastern Europe, in German), *RWI-Mitteilungen*, **43**, pp. 19–40.

Dollar, D., 1992, 'Outward-oriented Developing Economies Really do Grow More Rapidly: Evidence from 95 LDCs 1976–85', *Economic Development and Cultural Change*, **40**, pp. 523–44.

Dorussen, H. and J. Mo, 2001, 'Ending Economic Sanctions: Audience Costs and Rent-Seeking as Commitment Strategies', *Journal of Conflict Resolution*, **45** (4), pp. 395–426.

Drazen, A., 2000, *Political Economy in Macroeconomics*, Princeton: Princeton University Press.

Duguid, P., 2007, 'The Making of Methuen: The Commercial Treaty in the English Imagination', *Mimeo*. University of California.

Eaton, J. and M. Engers, 1992, 'Sanctions', *Journal of Political Economy*, **100** (5), pp. 899–928.

Edwards, S., 1998, 'Openness, Productivity and Growth: What Do We Really Know?', *Economic Journal*, **108** (1), pp. 383–98.

Eggleston, R.C., 1987, 'Determinants of the Levels and Distribution of PL 480 Food Aid: 1955–79', *World Development*, **15** (6), pp. 797–808.

Erickson, B.H., 1975, *International Networks: The Structured Webs of Diplomacy and Trade,* Sage professional papers in international studies 02–036, Beverly Hills and London: Sage Publications.

Estevadeordal, A. And A.M. Taylor, 2008, 'Is the Washington Concensus Dead? Growth, openness and the great liberalization 1970s–2000s', *NBER Working Paper 14264*, Cambridge, MA: NBER.

Ethier, W.J., E. Helpman and J.P. Neary (eds), 1993, *Theory, Policy and Dynamics in International Trade: Essays in honor of Ronald W. Jones*, Cambdrige, MA: Cambridge University Press.

Evenett , S. and W. Keller, 2002, 'On Theories Explaining the Success of the Gravity Equation', *Journal of Political Economy*, **110** (2), pp. 281–316.

Ezran, R., C. Holmes and R. Safadi, 1992, 'How Changes in the CMEA Area may Affect International Trade in Manufactures' *World Bank PRIT Working Papers Series* WPS 972, Washington, DC: World Bank.

Farmer, R.D., 2000, 'Costs of Economic Sanctions to the Sender', *World Economy* **23** pp. 93–117.

Feder, G, 1982, 'On Exports and Economic Growth', *Journal of Development Economics*, **12**, pp. 59–72.

Feenstra, R.C., Markusen, J.R. and Rose, A.K. (2001), 'Using the Gravity Equation to Differentiate among Alternative Theories of Trade', *Canadian Journal of Economics*, **34** (2), pp. 430–47.

Felipe. J. and M. Vernengo, 2002, 'Demystifying the Principles of Comparative Advantage', *International Journal of Political Economy*, **32** (4), pp. 49–75.

Fischer, D., 1984, *Preventing War in the Nuclear Age*, Totowa: Rowman & Allanheld.

Fortanier, F., 2008, *Multinational Enterprises, Institutions and Sustainable Development*, Ph.D Thesis, University of Amsterdam: Amsterdam.

Francois, J., H. van Meijl and F. van Tongeren, 2003, 'Economic Benefits of the Doha Round for the Netherlands', *Agricultural Economic Research Institute Report 6.03.02*, LEI: Wageningen.

Frankel, J.A. and D. Romer, 1996, 'Trade and Growth: An Empirical Investigation', *NBER Working Papers 5476*.

Frankel, J.A., 1997, *Regional Trading Blocs in the World Economic System*, Washington, D.C.: Institute for International Economics.

Fratianni, M. and H. Kang, 2006a, 'International Terrorism, International Trade and Borders', *Mimeo.,* Indianapolis: Indiana University.

Fratianni, M. and H. Kang, 2006b, 'Heterogeneous Distance-elasticities in Trade Gravity Models', *Economics Letters*, **90**, pp. 68–71.

Frey, B.S., 1984, *International Political Economics*, Oxford: Basil Blackwell.

Frey, B.S. and S. Lüchinger, 2003, 'How to Fight Terrorism: Alternatives to Deterrence', *Defence and Peace Economics*, pp. 237–49.

Frey, B.S., S. Lüchinger and A. Stutzer, 2004, 'Calculating Tragedy: Assessing the Costs of Terrorism', *CESifo Working paper 1341*, CESifo: Munich.

Frey, B.S. and F. Schneider, 1986, 'Competing Models of International Lending Activity', *Journal of Development Economics*, **20**, pp. 225–45.

Freytag,, A, J.J. Krüger and F. Schneider, 2006, 'The Origins of Terrorism', www.econ.jku.at/Schneider/TerrorPaperJanuar06.pdf.

Friedman, M. and R. Friedman, 1980, *Free to Choose: A Personal Statement*, New York: Harcourt Brace Jovanovich.

Friedman, T.L., 2005, *The World is Flat*, London: Penguin.

Fryges, H. and J. Wagner, 2007, 'Exports and Productivity Growth – First Evidence from a Continuous Treatment Approach', *Discussion Paper no. 07-032*, ZEW: Mannheim.

Furuoka, F., 2007, 'Japan's Positive and Negative Aid Sanctions Policy Toward Asian Countries Case Studies of Thailand and Indonesia', *Mimeo.* Universiti Malysia: Sabah.

Gasiorowski, M.J., 1986, 'Economic Interdependence and International Conflict: Some Cross National Evidence', *International Studies Quarterly*, **30**, pp. 23–38.

Gatzke E. and Q. Li, 2003, 'Measure for Measure; Concept Operationalization and the Trade Interdependence–Conflict Debate', *Journal of Peace Research*, **40** (5), pp. 553–71.

Geelhoed, L.A., 1997, 'The Policy-maker's Demand for Economic Analysis' in P.A.G. van Bergeijk, A.L. Bovenberg, E.E.C. van Damme and J. van Sinderen (eds), *Economic Science and Practice: The Roles of Academic Economists and Policy-makers*, Edward Elgar: Cheltenham, UK, pp. 166–80.

Gil-Pareja, S., R. Llorca-Viveroa and J. A. Martínez-Serrano, 2007, 'The Impact of Embassies and Consulates on Tourism', *Tourism Management*, **28**, (2), pp. 355–60.

Grampp, D., 1987, 'Peace and Trade: The Classical *vs*. the Marxian View', in H. Visser and E. Schoorl (eds), *Trade in Transit*, Dordrecht: Kluwer, pp. 17–31.

Grauwe, P de and F. Camerman, 2002, 'How Big are the Big Multinational Companies?, *Mimeo.*, University of Leuven: Louvain.

Greenaway, D. and R. Kneller, 2004, 'Exporting and Productivity in the United Kingdom', *Oxford Review of Economic Policy*, **20** (3), pp. 358–71.

Greenaway, D. and R. Kneller, 2007, 'Industry Differences in the Effect of Export Market Entry: Learning by Exporting?', *Review of World Economics*, **143** (3), pp. 416–32.

Griffin, K. and J. Gurley, 1985, 'Radical Analysis of Imperialism, the Third World, and the Transition to Socialism: A Survey Article', *Journal of Economic Literature*, **23** (3), pp. 1089–1143.

Griffith, R., S. Redding and H. Simpson, 2008, 'Technological Catch-up and the Role of Multinationals', paper presented at the HIS 50th anniversary conference 'Are cities more important than countries?', Erasmus University Rotterdam, 31 October.

Grosso, J.L. and T. Smith, 2005, 'From Lord Boycott to Mickey Mouse; A Classification Model to Analyse the Impact of Consumer Boycotts around the World', *European Journal of Scientific Research*, **9** pp. 51–7.

Guiso, L., P. Sapienza and L. Zingales, 2004, 'Cultural Biases in Economic Exchange', *NBER Working Paper 11005*, Cambridge, MA: NBER.

Guttentag, J.M. and R.J. Herring, 1986, 'Dysaster Myopia in International Banking', *Essays in International Finance 164*, Princeton University Press: Princeton.

Hamilton, C.B. and L.A. Winters, 1992, 'Opening Up International Trade with Eastern Europe', *Economic Policy*, **14**, pp. 77–116.

Hazelzet, H., 1999, 'Assessing the Suffering from "Successful" Sanctions: An Ethical Approach', in W. van Genugten and G.A. de Groot (eds), *United Nations Sanctions*, Intersentia: Antwerpen, pp. 71–96.

Haney, P.J., R.Q. Herzberg and R.K. Wilson, 1992, 'Advice and Consent: Unitary Actors, Advisory Models, and Experimental Tests', *Journal of Conflict Resolution*, **36** (4), pp. 603–33.

Hanlon, J. and R. Omond, 1987, *The Sanctions Handbook*, Harmondsworth: Penguin.

Harris, P.B., 1968, 'Rhodesia: Sanctions and Politics', *Rhodesian Journal of Economics*, **2**, pp. 5–20.

Harris, R. and Q.C. Li, 2005, *Review of the Literature: The Role of International Trade and Investment in Business Growth and Development,* London: DTI.

Harris, R.I.D. and C. Robertson, 2001, 'Research Project on DT Industrial Support Policies. Contract A: An analysis of current DTI industry support patterns': available at http://www.gla.ac.uk/harris/dti¬a.pdf.

Harris, S. and C. Wheeler, 2005, 'Entrepreneurs' Relationships for Internationalization: Functions, Origins and Strategies', *International Business Review*, **14**, pp. 187–207.

Havrylyshyn, O. and L. Pritchett, 1991, 'European Trade Patterns After the Transition', *World Bank PRE Working Papers Series* WPS 748, Washington, DC: World Bank.

Hayes, J.P., 1988, 'Divided Opinions on Sanctions Against South Africa', *The World Economy*, **11** (2), pp. 267–80.

Head, K. and T. Mayer, 2007, 'Illusory Border Effects: Distance Measurement Inflates Estimates of Home Bias in Trade', *Mimeo.*, Université de Paris, Paris.

Head, K. and J. Ries, 2006, 'Do Trade Missions Increase Trade', *Saunder School of Business Working Papers*, University of British Columbia.

Heydon, K., 2008, "The OECD: An Epistemic Community in Evolution", *Mimeo.*, London: LSE.

Heckscher, E.F., 1955, *Mercantilism*, second revised edition: London (originally published in 1931).

Hegre, H., 2003, 'Development and the Liberal State. What Does It Take to Be a Trading State', in Schneider, G., K. Barbieri and N.P. Gleditsch (eds), *Globalization and Armed Conflict,* Lanham, UK: Rowman & Littlefield, pp. 205–32.

Helble, M., 2007, 'Border Effect Estimates for France and Germany Combining International trade and Intranational Transport Flows', *Review of World Economics*, **143** (3), pp. 433–63.

Helpman, E. and A. Razin, 1978, *A Theory of International Trade under Uncertainty*, Academic Press: New York.

Helpman, E., 1987, 'Comment on "The National Defense Argument for Government Intervention in a Changing World"', in R.M. Stern (ed.), *U.S. Trade Policies in a Changing World Economy*, Cambridge, MA: MIT Press, pp. 370–3.

Henderson, J.M. and R.E. Quandt, 1971, *Microeconomic Theory: A Mathematical Approach,* 2nd edition, New York: McGraw–Hill.

Hermele, K. and B. Odén, 1988, 'Sanction Dilemmas; Some Implications of Economic Sanctions against South Africa', *Discussion Paper 1,* Scandinavian Institute of African studies: Uppsala.

Hertel, T.W., W. Martin, C.F. Bach and B. Dimaranan, 1999, 'Growth, Globalisation and Gains from the Uruguay Round', *World Bank Policy Research Working Paper Series 1614,* Washington, DC: World Bank.

Hervé, K, I., Koske, N. Pain and F Sédilot, 2007, 'Globalisation and the Macroeconomic Policy Environment', *Economics Department Working Papers No.5,* Paris; OECD

Herz, N., 2001, 'Better to Shop than to Vote?', *Business Ethics A European Review,* **10** (3), pp. 190–93.

Hirsch, S., 1981, 'Peace Making and Economic Interdependence' *The World Economy,* **4**, pp. 407–17.

Hirschman, A.O., 1980, *National Power and the Structure of Foreign Trade,* expanded edition, Los Angeles: University of California Press. (First published in 1945).

Hobson, J.A., 1988, *Imperialism: A Study,* 3rd edition, London: Allen & Unwin (First published in 1902).

Hoekman, B. and B Smarzynska Javoricik, 2004, 'Policies Facilitating Firm Adjustment to Globalization', *Policy Research Working Paper 3441,* Washington, DC: World Bank.

Hont, I., 1990, 'Free Trade and the Economic Limits to National Politics: Neo-Machiavellian Political Economy Reconsidered', in J. Dunn (ed.), *The Economic Limits to Modern Politics,* Cambridge, MA: Cambridge University Press, pp. 41–121.

Hower, G. 1988, 'The Effects of Cooperation on Crisis Outcome', paper presented at the 3rd world congress of the Peace Science Society (International), University of Maryland.

Hufbauer, G.C. and J.J. Schott, 1985, *Economic Sanctions Reconsidered: History and Current Policy,* Peterson Institute for International Economics: Washington, DC.

Hufbauer, G.C., J.J. Schott and K.A. Elliott, 1990, *Economic Sanctions Reconsidered,* 2nd edition, Peterson Institute for International Economics: Washington, DC.

Hufbauer, G.C., J.J. Schott, K.A. Elliott and B. Oegg, 2008, *Economic Sanctions Reconsidered,* 3rd edition, Peterson Institute for International Economics: Washington, DC.

Hughes Hallett, A.J. and A.S. Brandsma, 1983, 'How Effective Could Sanctions Against the Soviet Union Be?', *Weltwirtschaftliches Archiv,* **119**, pp. 498–522.

Hummels, D. and J.A. Levinson, 1995, 'Monopolistic Competition and International Trade: Reconsidering the Evidence', *Quarterly Journal of Economics,* **110** (3), pp. 441–87.

Hutchison, T., 1988, *Before Adam Smith. The Emergence of Political Economy 1662–1776,* Oxford: Basil Blackwell.

Hyrkkanen, M., 1987, 'Free Trade and Contract as Alternatives to Imperialsim and the Arms Race: The Case of Eduard Bernstein', in V.

Harle (ed.), *Essays in Peace Studies,* Aldershot: Avebury, UK, pp. 167–80.

Inkeles, A. (ed.), 1991, *On Measuring Democracy,* New Brunswick: Transaction Books.

International Monetary Fund (IMF), 1983, 'Statistical Asymmetry in Global Current Account Balances', in *World Economic Outlook,* IMF: Washington, DC, pp. 161–7.

International Monetary Fund (IMF), 1987, *Report on the World Current Account Discrepancy,* IMF: Washington, DC.

International Monetary Fund (IMF), 1992, *Report on the Measurement of International Capital Flows,* IMF: Washington, DC.

International Study Group on Exports and Productivity, 2007, 'Exports and Productivity: Comparable Evidence for 14 countries', *Research Paper 2007/41,* Levrhulme Centre for Research on Globalisation and Economic Policy: Nottingham.

Intrilligator, M.D., 1987, 'Comments on "The National Defence Argument for Government Intervention in Foreign Trade"', in R.M. Stern (ed.), *U.S. Trade Policies in a Changing World Economy,* Cambridge, MA: MIT Press, pp. 364–9.

Isard, W., 1954, 'Location Theory and Trade Theory; Short-run Analysis', *Quarterly Journal of Economics,* **68** (2), pp. 305–20.

Isard, W., 1988, *Arms Races, Arms Control and Conflict Analysis. Contributions from Peace Science and Peace Economics,* Cambridge, MA: Cambridge University Press.

Italianer, A., 1994, 'Wither the Gains from European Economic Integration?', *Revue Economique,* **45** (3), pp. 689–702.

Jaggers, K. and T.R. Gurr, 1995, 'Tracking Democracy's Third Wave with the Polity III Data', *Journal of Peace Research,* **32** (4), pp. 469–82.

Johnston, S., 2006, 'What are the Main Problems with TDI's Current Use?', paper presented on European Trade Economists Network, 22 September.

Joint Economic Committee, 1985, *Soviet Economy in the 1980s: Problems and Prospects,* Congress of the United States: Washington, DC.

Jolly, R., L. Emmerij, D. Ghai and F. Lapeyre, 2004, *UN Contributions to Development Thinking and Practice,* United Nations Intellectual History Project Series, Bloomington and Indianapolis: Indiana University Press.

Kaempfer, W.H. and A.D. Lowenberg, 1986, 'A Model of the Political Economy of International Investment Sanctions: The Case of South Africa', *Kyklos,* **39** (3), pp. 377–96.

Kaempfer, W.H. and A.D. Lowenberg, 1988, 'The Theory of International Economic Sanctions: A Public Choice Approach', *American Economic Review,* **78** (4), pp. 768–93.

Kaempfer, W.H. and A.D. Lowenberg, 1992, *International Economic Sanctions: A Public Choice Perspective,* Westview Press: Boulder, CO.

Kaempfer, W.H. and A.D. Lowenberg, 2007, 'The Political Economy of Economic Sanctions', in T. Sandler and K. Hartley (eds), *Handbook of*

Defense Economics: Defense in a Globalized World, Elsevier: Amsterdam, pp. 867–912.

Kaempfer, W.H., A.D. Lowenberg and W. Mertens, 2004, 'International Economic Sanctions Against a Dictator', *Economics & Politics*, **16** (1), pp. 29–51.

Kaplow, L., 1990, 'A Note on the Optimal Use of Non-monetary Sanctions', *Journal of Public Economics*, **42**, pp. 245–7.

Kemp, M.C, 1964, *The Pure Theory of International Trade*, Englewood Cliffs: Prentice Hall.

Kennedy, P.M., 1989, *The Rise and Fall of the Great Powers. Economic Exchange and Military Conflict from 1500 to 2000*, New York: Vintage Press.

Keohane R.O. and J.S. Nye, 1977, *Power and Interdependence*, Boston, MA: Little, Brown.

Keshk, O., B.M. Polins and R. Reuveny, 2004, 'Trade Still Follows the Flag: The Primacy of Politics in a Simultaneous Model of Interdependence and Armed Conflict', *Journal of Politics*, **66** (4), pp. 1155–79.

Keynes, J.M., 1984, *The Economic Consequences of the Peace*, Collected Writings II, London: Macmillan. (First published in 1919).

Keynes, J.M., 1986, *The General Theory of Employment, Interest and Money*, Collected Writings VII, London: Macmillan (First published in 1936).

Khan, H.A., 1988, 'Impact of Trade Sanctions on South Africa: A Social Accounting Matrix Approach', *Contemporary Policy Issues*, **6**, pp. 130–40.

Kindleberger, C.P., 1970, *Power and Money: The Economics of International Politics and the Politics of International Economics*, New York: Basic Books.

Kindleberger, C.P., 1986, 'International Public Goods without International Government', *American Economic Review*, **76** (1), pp. 1–13.

Knight, F.H., 1939, *Risk, Uncertainty and Profit*, London (First published in 1921).

Knorr, K., 1975, *The Power of Nations: The Political Economy of International Relations*, New York: Basic Books.

Kofman, P., J.-M. Viaene and C.G. de Vries, 1990, 'Primary Commodity Prices and Exchange-rate Volatility', in L.A. Winters and D. Sapsford, (eds), *Primary Commodity Prices: Economic Models and Policy*, Cambridge MA, Cambridge University Press, pp. 213–32.

Kostecki, M. and O. Naray, 2007, 'Commercial Diplomacy and International Business', *Discussion Papers in Diplomacy*, Netherlands Institute of International Relations 'Clingendael': The Hague.

Kox, H., 2008, 'Heterogenous Firms in Dutch Exports', paper presented at the workshop Internationale handel en transport in Nederland, CBS Voorburg, June 12.

Krautheim, S., 2007, 'Gravity and Information: Heterogeneous Firms, Exporter Networks and the "Distance Puzzle"', *Mimeo.*, Florence: European University Institute.

Krugman, P., 1996, 'Making Sense of the Competitiveness Debate', *Oxford Review of Economic Policy*, **12** (3), pp. 17–25.

Lam, S.L., 1990, 'Economic Sanctions and the Success of Foreign Policy Goals', *Japan and the World Economy*, **2**, pp. 239–48.

Lankhuizen, M., G.J. Linders and H.L.F. de Groot, 2008, 'Distance and the Mode of Serving Markets', *TI Discussion paper* [in print], TI: Amsterdam.

Larsen, H., 2006, 'The Danish Mohammed Cartoon Crisis and the Role of the EU', paper for the BISA annual Conference, University of Cork, December 18.

Law, J., 1705, *Money and Trade Considered. With a Proposal for Supplying the Nation with Money*, Andrew Anderson, Avelon Project at Yale Law School, http://www.yale.edu/lawweb/avalon/econ/mon.htm.

Lawson, F.H., 1983, 'Using Positive Sanctions to End International Conflicts: Iran and the Arab Gulf Countries', *Journal of Peace Research*, **20** (4), pp. 311–28.

Leamer, E.E., 2007, 'A Flat World, a Level Playing Field, a Small World After All, or None of the Above? A Review of Thomas L. Friedman's The World is Flat', *Journal of Economic Literature*, **45** (1), pp. 83–126.

Leamer E.E., and R.M. Stern, 1970, *Quantitative International Economics*, Boston, MA: Allyn and Bacon.

Lederman, D., M. Olarreaga en L. Lucy Payton, 2006, 'Export Promotion Agencies: What Works and What Doesn't?', *World Bank Policy Research Working Paper* 4044, Washington, DC: World Bank.

Leitzel, J., 1987, 'Hufbauer, G.C. and Schott, J.J.: Economic Sanctions Reconsidered: History and Current Policy (Review)', *Kyklos*, **40** (1), pp. 286–8.

Lenin, V.I., 1967, 'Report on Concessions Delivered to the R.C.P. [B] Group at the Eighth Congress of Soviets [December 21, 1920]', in C. Leiteisen (ed.), *Lenin on Peaceful Coexistence*, Moscow: Progress Publishers, pp. 72–95.

Lensink, B.W. and P.A.G. van Bergeijk, 1991, 'The Determinants of Developing Countries' Access to the International Capital Market', *Journal of Development Studies*, **28** (1), pp. 86–103.

Lewer, J.J. and H. van den Berg, 2003, 'How Large Is International Trade's Effect on Economic Growth', *Journal of Economic Surveys*, **17** (3), pp. 363–96.

Leyton-Brown, D. (ed.), 1987, *The Utility of International Economic Sanctions*, New York: St. Martin's Press.

Li, Q. 2006, 'Political Violence and Foreign Direct Investment' in M. Fratianni (ed.), *Regional Economic Integration,* Research in Global

Strategic Management Volume 12, Amsterdam: Elsevier North Holland, pp. 225–50.

Li, Q. and D. Schaub, 2004, 'Economic Globalisation and Transnational Terrorism', *Journal of Conflict Resolution*, **48** (2), pp. 230–58.

Linder, S.B., 1961, *An Essay on Trade and Transformation,* Stockholm: Almqvist and Wiksell.

Linders, G.-J., 2006, *Intangible Barriers to Trade*, PhD. Thesis, Vrije Universiteit: Amsterdam.

Linders, G.-J., H.L.F. de Groot and P. Nijkamp, 2004, 'Locality Matters: Myths and Facts on the New Economy', in J. Poot (ed.), *On the Edge of the Global Economy*, Edward Elgar: Cheltenham, UK, pp. 27–48.

Linders, G.-J., A. Slangen, H.L.F. de Groot and S. Beugelsdijks, 2005, 'Cultural and Institutional Determinants of Bilateral Trade Flows', Tinbergen Discussion Paper, *TI2005-074/3*, TI: Amsterdam and Rotterdam.

Lindsay, J.M., 1986, 'Trade Sanctions as Policy Instruments: A Re-examination', *International Studies Quarterly*, **30**, pp. 153–73.

Linnemann, H., 1966, *An Econometric Study of International Trade Flows,* Amsterdam: North Holland.

Lloyd, T., O. Morrissey, G. Reed, 2001, 'Estimating the Impact of Anti-dumping and Anti-cartel Actions Using Intervention Analysis', *Economic Journal*, **108** (447), pp. 458–76.

Losman, D.L., 1972, 'The Effects of Economic Boycotts', *Lloyds Bank Review*, No 106, pp. 27–41.

Lowenberg, A.D., 1993, 'Comment' in B. Heydra (ed.), *The Use of Economic Sanctions in Trade and Environmental Policy*, OCFEB: Rotterdam.

Lundborg, P., 1987, *The Economics of Export Embargoes: The Case of the US–Soviet Grain Suspension*, London: Croom Helm.

Maclean, J., 1988, 'Marxism and International Relations: A Strange Case of Mutual Neglect', *Millennium*, **17**, pp. 295–319.

Manacsa, R.C., 2008, 'When Are Senders Serious? Examining the Incidence of War Between Sanction Adversaries, 1914–2003', *Mimeo.*, University of North Texas.

Mansfield, E.D. and J.C. Pevehouse, 2003, 'Institutions, Interdependence, and International Conflict', in Schneider, G., K. Barbieri and N.P. Gleditsch (eds), *Globalization and Armed Conflict*, Lanham: Rowman & Littlefield, pp. 233–50.

Mansfield, E.D. and B.M. Pollins (eds), 2003, *Economic Interdependence and International Conflict: New Perspectives on an Enduring Debate*, Michigan Studies in International Political Economy, Ann Arbor: The University of Michigan Press.

Marinov, R., N. Rocha and V. DiNino, 2008, 'Trade Liberalization and New Exporters' Size', *The B.E. Journal of Economic Analysis & Policy,* **8** (1), http://www.bepress.com/bejeap/vol8/iss1/art10.

Marrewijk, C. van, 1992, 'Trade Uncertainty and the Two-Step Procedure: The Choice of Numéraire and Exact Indexation', *De Economist*, **140** (3), pp. 317–27.

Marrewijk, C. van and P.A.G. van Bergeijk, 1990, 'Trade Uncertainty and Specialization: Social versus Private Planning', *De Economist*, **138** (1), pp. 15–32.

Marrewijk, C. van and P.A.G. van Bergeijk, 1993, 'Endogenous Trade Uncertainty: Why Countries May Specialize Against Comparative Advantage', *Regional Science and Urban Economics*, **23** (4), pp. 681–94.

Marshall, A., 1965, *Money, Credit and Commerce*, New York: Reprints of Economic Classics (First published in 1923).

Mastanduno, M. 2003, 'The Strategy of Economic Engagement: Theory and Practice', in E.D. Mansfield, and B.M. Pollins (eds), *Economic Interdependence and International Conflict: New Perspectives on an Enduring Debate*, Michigan Studies in International Political Economy, Ann Arbor: The University of Michigan Press, pp. 175–86.

Marx, K. and F. Engels, 1928, *Das Kommunistische Manifest*, 5th edition, Vienna (First published in 1848).

Maurel, M., and E. Afman, 2007, 'Diplomatic Relations and Trade Reorientation in Transition Countries', paper presented at 'The Gravity Equation Or: Why the World is not Flat', University of Groningen, 19 October 2007.

Mayer, W., 1977, 'The National Defense Tariff Argument Reconsidered', *Journal of International Economics*, **7**, pp. 363–77.

McCallum, J., 1995, 'National Borders Matter: Canada–US regional trade Patterns', *American Economic Review*, **85** (3), pp. 615–23.

McCann, P. and Z. J. Acs, 2008, 'Globalisation: Countries, Cities and Multinationals', paper presented at the HIS 50th anniversary conference 'Are Cities More Important than Countries?', Erasmus University Rotterdam, 31 October.

McKenna, C.J., 1986, *The Economics of Uncertainty*, Brighton, UK: Wheatsheaf.

Melitz, M., 2003, 'The Impact of Trade on Intra-industry Reallocations and Aggregate Industry Productivity', *Econometrica*, **71**, pp. 1695–725.

Menkveld, P.A., 1991, *Origin and Role of the European Bank for Reconstruction and Development*, London: Graham & Trotman.

Mill, J.S., 1968, *Principles of Political Economy with Some of Their Implications to Social Philosophy*, Collected Works II, London: Routledge (First published in 1840).

Morgan, T.C. and V. Schwebach, 1995, 'Economic Sanctions as an Instrument of Foreign Policy: The Role of Domestic Politics', *International Interactions*, **21** (3), pp. 247–263.

Morgenstern, O., 1950, *On the Accuracy of Economic Observations*, Princeton University Press: Princeton.

Morrow, J.D., R.M. Siverson, and T.E. Tabares, 1998, 'The Political Determinants of International Trade; The Major Powers 1907–90', *American Political Science Review*, **92** (3), pp. 649–61.

Moser, C., T. Nestmann and M. Wedow, 2006, 'Political Risk and Export Promotion: Evidence from Germany', *Discussion Paper Series 1: Economic Studies No 36/2006*, Deutsche Bundesbank: Frankfurt am Main.

Mousseau, M., H. Hegre and J. Oneal, 2003, 'How the Wealth of Nations Conditions the Liberal Peace', *European Journal of International Relations*, **9** (2), pp. 277–314.

Murshed, S.M. and D. Mamoon, 2010, 'The Consequences of Not Loving Thy Neighbour as Thyself: Trade, Democracy and Military Expenditure Explanations Underlying India-Pakistan Rivalry', *Journal of Peace Research*, forthcoming.

Neary, P.J., 2004, 'Europe on the Road to Doha', *CESinfo Economic Studies*, **50** (2), pp. 319–32.

Neumann, J. von and O. Morgenstern, 1980, *Theory of Games and Economic Behavior*, Princeton: Princeton University Press (First published in 1944).

Newnham, R.E., 2002, *Deutsche Mark Diplomacy: Positive Sanctions in German–Russian Relationships*, Penn State Press: Pensylvania.

Nicoletti, G., S. Golub, D. Hajkova, D. Mirza and K.-Y. Yoo, 2003, 'Policies And International Integration: Influences On Trade And Foreign Direct Investment', *Economics Department Working Papers 359*, OECD: Paris.

Nitsch, V., 2007, 'State Visits and International Trade' *World Economy* **30** (4), pp. 1797–816.

Nitsch, V. and D. Schumacher, 2004, 'Terrorism and International Trade: An Empirical Investigation', *European Journal of Political Economy*, **20** (2), pp. 423–33.

Nossal, K.R., 1989, 'International Sanctions as International Punishment', *International Organization* **43**, pp. 301–22.

O'Brien, D. 1976, 'Custom Unions: Trade Creation and Trade Diversion in Historical Perspective', *History of Political Economy*, **8** (4), pp. 540–63.

Olson, R.S., 1979, 'Economic Coercion in World Politics. With a Focus on North–South Relations', *World Politics*, **31** (4), pp. 471–94.

Oneal, J.R., B. Russett and M.L. Berbaum, 2003, '*Causes* of Peace: Democracy, Interdependence, and International Organizations, 1885–1992', *International Studies Quarterly*, **47**, pp. 371–93.

Ottaviano, G.I.P. and T. Mayer, 2007, *The Happy Few: Internationalisation of European Firms, New Facts Based on Firm Level Evidence*, Bruegle Blueprint; Brussels.

Pape, R. 1997, 'Why Economic Sanctions Do Not Work', *International Security*, **22**, (2), 1997, pp. 90–136.

Pen, J., 1967, *A Primer on International Trade*, New York: Random House.

Pen J., 1994, 'Harmony and Conflict in International Relations', preface to P.A.G. van Bergeijk, *Economic Diplomacy, Trade and Commercial*

Policy: Positive and Negative Sanctions in a New World Order, Edward Elgar: Cheltenham, UK, pp. *xiii–xiv*.

Pevehouse, J.C., 2003, 'Trade and Conflict: Does Measurement Make a Difference', in E.D. Mansfield and B.M. Pollins (eds), *Economic Interdependence and International Conflict: New Perspectives on an Enduring Debate*, Michigan Studies in International Political Economy, Ann Arbor: The University of Michigan Press, pp. 239–53.

Picchio Forlati, M., 2000, 'The Present State of Research Carried Out by the English-speaking Section of the Centre for Studies and Research' in *Economic Sanctions in International Law*, Centre for Studies and Research in International Law and International Relations, Marinus Nijhoff: The Hague.

Pindyck, R.S. and D.J. Rubinfeld, 1991, *Econometric Models and Economic Forecasts*, 2nd edition, New York: McGraw Hill.

Pisu, M., 2008, 'Export Destinations and Learning-by-exporting: Evidence from Belgium', *National Bank of Belgium Working Paper 150*, Nationale Bank van Belgie: Brussel.

Ploeg, R. van der and S. Poelhekke, 2008, 'Growth, Foreign Direct Investment And Urban Concentrations: Unbundling Spatial Lags', paper presented at the HIS 50th anniversary conference 'Are Cities More Important than Countries?', Erasmus University Rotterdam, 31 October.

Polachek, S.W., 1980, 'Conflict and Trade', *Journal of Conflict Resolution*, **24** (1), pp. 55–78.

Polachek, S.W., 1992, 'Conflict and Trade: An Economic Approach to Political International Interactions', in W. Isard and C.H. Anderton (eds), *Economics of Arms Reduction and the Peace Process*, Amsterdam: Elsevier, pp. 89–120.

Polachek, S.W. and J.A. McDonald, 1992, 'Strategic Trade and Incentives for Cooperation', in M. Chatterji *et al.* (eds), *Disarmament, Economic Conversion and Management of Peace*, Preager: Westport, pp. 273–84.

Polachek, S.W. and C. Seiglie, 2007, 'Trade, Peace and Democracy: An Analysis of Dyadic Dispute', in T. Sandler and K. Hartley (eds), *Handbook of Defense Economics: Defense in a Globalized World*, Elsevier: Amsterdam, pp. 1017–74.

Pollins, B.M., 1989a, 'Does Trade Still Follow the Flag?', *American Political Science Review*, **85**, pp. 465–80.

Pollins, B.M., 1989b, 'Conflict, Cooperation and Commerce' *American Journal of Political Science*, **33**, pp. 737–61.

Pomery, J., 1984, 'Uncertainty in Trade Models', in R.W. Jones and P.B. Kenen, (eds) *Handbook of International Economics*, Amsterdam: North-Holland, pp. 419–65.

Porter, M. E., 1990, *The Competitive Advantage of Nations*, London and Basingstoke, UK: MacMillan.

Porter, R.C., 1979, 'International Trade and Investment Sanctions: Potential Impact on the South African Economy', *Journal of Conflict Resolution*, **23** (4), pp. 579–612.

Rae, D. and M. Sollie, 2007, 'Globalisation and the European Union: Which Countries Are Best Placed To Cope?', *Economics Department Working Paper No. 586*, OECD: Paris.

Ratnapala, S. 2003, 'Moral Capital and Commercial Society', *The Indepent Review*, **8** (2), pp. 213–33.

Reekie, D., 1987, 'The Economics of Apartheid Politics', *Economic Affairs*, **7**, pp. 10–3.

Reuveny, R., 2000, 'The Trade and Conflict Debate; A Survey of Theory, Evidence and Future Research', *Peace Economics, Peace Science and Public Policy*, **6** (1), pp. 23–49.

Reuveny, R., 2003, 'Measuring Conflict and Cooperation: An Assessment', in E.D. Mansfield and B.M. Pollins (eds), *Economic Interdependence and International Conflict: New Perspectives on an Enduring Debate*, Michigan Studies in International Political Economy, Ann Arbor: The University of Michigan Press, pp. 254–69.

Ribeiro, A.M.C.A., 2007, 'A evolução do paradigma diplomático: a emergência da diplomacia económico – o casa Português' (The Evolution of the Diplomatic Paradigm: The Emergence of Economic Diplomacy – The Case of Portugal, in Portuguese) Masters Thesis, Lisbon: Technical University.

Ricardo, D., 1962, *The Principles of Political Economy and Taxation*, London: Everymans Library (first published in 1817).

Richardson, L.F., 1960, *Arms and Insecurity. A Mathematical Study of the Causes and Origins of War*, London: Atlantic Books.

Richardson, N.R., 1978, *Foreign Policy and Economic Dependence*, Austin University of Texas Press.

Rodriguez, F. and D. Rodrik, 2000, 'Trade Policy and Economic Growth: A Skeptic's Guide to the Cross-national Evidence', in B. Bernana and K. Rogoff (eds), *NBER Macroeconomic Annual 2000*, Cambridge, MA: NBER.

Roemer, J.E., 1977, 'The Effects of Sphere of Influence and Economic Distance on the Commodity Composition of Trade in Manufactures', *Review of Economics and Statistics*, **59**, pp. 318–27.

Rose, A., 2004, 'Do We Really Know that the WTO Increases Trade?', *American Economic Review*, **94** (1), pp. 98–114.

Rose, A., 2007, 'The Foreign Service and Foreign Trade: Embassies as Export Promotion', *The World Economy*, **30** (1), January, pp. 22–38.

Rosecrane, R., 1986, *The Rise of the Trading State. Commerce and Conquest in the Modern World*, New York: Basic Books.

Ruffin, R.J., 1974, 'International Trade under Uncertainty', *Journal of International Economics*, **4**, pp. 243–59.

Sachs, J.D. and A. Warner, 1995, 'Economic Reform and the Process of Global Integration', *Brookings Papers on Economic Activity*, no 1, pp. 1–118.

Sandler, T., 1992, *Collective Action: Theory and Applications*, Brighton, UK: Harvester Wheatsheaf.

Sandler, T. and K. Hartley (eds), 2007, *Handbook of Defense Economics: Defense in a Globalized World*, Elsevier: Amsterdam,

Saner, R. and L. Yiu, 2003, 'International Economic Diplomacy: Mutations in Post-Modern Times', *Discussion Papers in Diplomacy no. 84*, Netherlands Institute of International Relations 'Clingendael', The Hague.

Sayrs, L.W., 1988, 'Reconsidering Trade and Conflict: A Qualitative Response Model with Sensoring', *Conflict Management and Peace Science*, **10** (1), pp. 1–19.

Sayrs, L.W., 1990, 'Expected Utility and Peace Science: An Assessment of Trade and Conflict', *Conflict Management and Peace Science*, **11** (1), pp. 17–44.

Schelling, T.C., 1980, *The Strategy of Conflict*, Harvard: Harvard University Press (First published in 1960).

Schiavo-Campo, S., 1978, *International Economics. An Introduction to Theory and Policy*, Cambridge, MA: Winthrop.

Schneider, F. and B.S. Frey, 1985, 'Economic and Political Determinants of Foreign Direct Investment', *World Development*, **13** (2), pp. 161–75.

Schneider, G., K. Barbieri and N.P. Gleditsch (eds), 2003, *Globalization and Armed Conflict*: Lanham: Rowman & Littlefield.

Schneider, G. and G.G. Schultze, 2003, 'The Domestic Roots of Commercial Liberalism: A Sector-Specific Approach', in G. Schneider, K. Barbieri and N.P. Gleditsch (eds), *Globalization and Armed Conflict*, Lanham: Rowman & Littlefield, pp. 103–22.

Scolnick, J.M., 1988, 'How Governments Utilize Foreign Threats', *Conflict*, **8**, pp. 12–21.

Schrödt, P.A., 1985, 'Adaptive Precedent-Based Logic and Rational Choice: A Comparison of Two Approaches of the Modelling of International Behavior', in U. Luterbacher and M.D. Ward (eds), *Dynamic Models of International Conflict*, Boulder, CO: Lynne Rienner, pp. 373–400.

Schultz, C.E., 1989, *On the Rationality of Economic Sanctions*, Oslo: Norwegian Institute of International Affairs.

Schumpeter, J.A., 1954, *History of Economic Analysis*, London: Allen & Unwin.

Schumpeter, J.A., 1966, *Capitalism, Socialism, and Democracy*, 2nd edition, London: Unwin (First published in 1943).

Segura-Cayuela, R. and J.M. Vilarrubia, 2008, 'The Effects of Foreign Service on Trade Volumes and Trade Partners', Working paper 0808, Banco de España: Madrid.

Seeler, H.J., 1982, 'Wirtschaftssanktionen als zweifelhaftes Instrument der Außenpolitik' (Economic Sanctions as Dubious Instrument of Foreign Policy, in German) *Europa-Archiv*, **20**, pp. 611–18.

Shipping Research Bureau, 1989, *Newsletter on the Oil Embargo Against South Africa* Nr 15/16.

Shipping Research Bureau (ed.), 1995, *Oil Sanctions Against South Africa: The Full Story*, Amsterdam University Press: Amsterdam, 1995.

Shone, R., 1981, *Applications in Intermediate Microeconomics*, Oxford: Martin Robertson.

Sideri, S., 1970, *Trade and Power: Informal Colonialsim in Anglo-Portuguese Relationships*, Ph. D Thesis University of Amsterdam, Amsterdam University Press: Amsterdam.

Simon, J.L. 1989, 'Lebensraum: Paradoxically, Population Growth May Eventually End Wars', *Journal of Conflict Resolution*, **33** (1), pp. 164–80.

Sinderen, J. van and P.A.G. van Bergeijk, 1994, 'European Economic Integration: A Force Against Nationalism', *Current Politics and Economics of Europe*, **4** (4), 269–82.

Skylakakis, T., 2006, 'The Importance of Economic Diplomacy', *The Bridge*, http://www.bridge-mag.com/magazine/.

Smeets, M. 1990, 'Economic Sanctions Against Iraq: The Ideal Case?', *Journal of World Trade*, **24** (6), pp. 105–20.

Smeets, M. 1992, 'Efficacy of Economic Sanctions, with Special Reference to Iraq and Yugoslavia', paper presented at the Tinbergen Institute's Congress 'Economics on International Security', The Hague, May, 22.

Smith, Adam, 1976, *An Inquiry into the Nature and Causes of the Wealth of Nations*, Canna's edition, Claredon Press: Oxford (First published in 1776).

Smith, Alasdair, 1986, 'East West Trade, Embargoes and Expectations', *CEPR Discussion Paper 139*, CEPR: London.

Smith, Alisdair, 1995, 'The Success and Use of Economic Sanctions', *International Interactions*, **21** (3), pp 249–45.

Spero, J. (J. Edelman-Spero), 1977, *The Politics of International Economic Relations*, London: Allen & Unwin.

Spindler, Z.A., 1995, 'The Public Choice of "Superior" Sanctions', *Public Choice*, **85** (3–4), pp. 205–26.

Srinivasan, T.N., 1987, 'The National Defense Argument for Government Intervention in Foreign Trade', in R.M. Stern (ed.), *U.S. Trade Policies in a Changing World Economy*, Cambridge, MA: MIT Press, pp. 337–63 and 374–5.

Straathof, B., 2008, 'Gravity with Gravitas: Comment' *CPB Discussion Paper 111*, CPB: The Hague.

Strange, S., 1998, *States and Markets*, 2nd edition, London: Continuum.

Subramanian, A., 1992, 'Trade Measures for the Environment', *The World Economy* **15**, pp. 135–52.

Summary, R.M., 1989, 'A Political-Economic Model of U.S. Bilateral Trade', *Review of Economics and Statistics*, **71** (1), pp. 179–82.

Thompson, P.B., 1992, *The Ethics of Aid and Trade: U.S. Food Policy, Foreign Competition, and the Social Contract*, Cambridge, MA: Cambridge University Press.

Tinbergen, J., 1962, *Shaping the World Economy – Suggestions for an International Economic Policy*, Twentieth Century Fund: New York.

Tinbergen, J., 1985, 'De economie van de oorlog' (The Economics of War, in Dutch), *Economisch Statistische Berichten*, **70**, pp. 172–5.

Tsebelis, G., 1989, 'The Abuse of Probability in Political Analysis: The Robinson Crusoe Fallacy', *American Political Science Review*, **83**, pp. 77–91.

Tsebellis, G., 1990, 'Are Sanctions Effective: A Game Theoretic Analysis', *Journal of Conflict Resolution*, **34** (1), pp. 3–28.

Tolley, G.S. and J.D. Wilman, 1977, 'The Foreign Dependence Question', *Journal of Political Economy*, **85**, pp. 323–47.

Ungar, S.J. and P. Vale, 1985/86, 'South Africa: Why Constructive Engagement Failed', *Foreign Affairs*, **64**, pp. 234–58.

Veenstra, M.-L. van, 2009, 'The Effectiveness of Export Promotion by the Foreign Service or by Export Promotion Agencies: A Quantitative Analysis', M.A. Thesis Erasmus University Rotterdam.

Wacziarg, R. and K. Horn Welch, 2003, 'Trade Liberalization and Growth: New Evidence', *NBER working papers 10152*.

Wagner, J., 2007, 'Exports and Productivity: A Survey of the Evidence from Firm Level Data', *The World Economy*, **30** (1), pp. 60–82.

Wallensteen, P., 2000, 'A Century of Economic Sanctions: A Field Revisited', *Peace Research Papers No. 1*, Department of Peace and Conflict Research: Uppsala.

Waltzer, M., 1977, *Just and Unjust Wars*, New York.

Wang, Z.K. and L.A. Winters, 1991, 'The Trading Potential of Eastern Europe', *CEPR Discussion Paper Series* 610, London: CEPR.

Weck-Hannemann, H. and B.S. Frey, 1992, 'The Contribution of Public Choice Theory to International Political Economy', in C. Polychroniu (ed.), *Perspectives and Issues in International Political Economy*, Westport: Praeger, pp. 38–58.

Weede, E. 2004, 'The Diffusion of Prosperity and Peace by Globalization', *The Independent Review* **9** (2), pp. 165–86.

Went, R., 2002, *The Enigma of Globalization: A Journey to a New Stage of Capitalism*, Routledge Frontiers of Political Economy No. 43, Routledge: New York and London.

Went, R., 2003, 'Globalization in the Perspective of Imperialism', *Science Society*, **66** (4), 473–97.

Wilde, J.H. de, 1991, *Saved from Oblivion: Interdependence Theories in the First Half of the 20th Century*, Aldershot, UK: Darmouth.

Wilkinson, T.J. and L.E. Brouthers, 2000, 'An Evaluation of State Sponsored Promotion Programs', *Journal of Business Research*, **47**, pp. 229–36.

Wolf, T.A., 1983, 'Choosing a U.S. Trade Strategy Towards the Soviet Union', in Joint Economic Committee, *Soviet Economy in the 1980s: Problems and Prospects,* Congress of the United States: Washington, DC, pp. 400–418.

Wolfe, R., 2003, *The Making of the Peace: The OECD in Canadian Economic Diplomacy,* International Economic Relations Division (External Affairs and International Trade) Canada Centre for International Relations, Queen's University: Kingston.

Woolcock, S. 2002, 'The Changing Nature of Trade Diplomacy' paper for the BISA panel on economic diplomacy in the 21st century, LSE and Kings College, Cambridge, UK, December.

World Bank 1991, *World Development Report 1991*, Washington, DC: World Bank.

World Bank, 2007, *Global Economic Prospects: Managing the Next Wave of Globalization,* Washington, DC: World Bank.

World Trade Organization, 2007, *World Trade Report,* WTO: Geneva.

Yakop, M. and P.A.G. van Bergeijk, 2007, 'The Weight of Economic Diplomacy: Measurement and Policy Issues', paper presented at 'The Gravity Equation or: Why the World is not Flat', University of Groningen, 19 October.

Yakop, M., 2009, 'The Weight of Economic Diplomacy', M.A. Thesis University of Amsterdam; Amsterdam.

Yanikkaya, H., 2002, 'Trade Openness and Economic Growth: A Cross-country Empirical Investigation', *Journal of Development Economics*, **72**, pp. 57–89.

Yeats, A.J., 1990, 'On the Accuracy of Economic Observations: Do Sub-Saharan Trade Statistics Mean Anything?', *World Bank Economic Review*, **4**, pp. 135–56.

Yeats, A.J., 1992, 'Can a Manufactured Good Cease to be a Manufactured Good Merely by Crossing a National Frontier?', *Bulletin of Economic Research*, **44** (3), p. 199–219.

Index

Adler-Karlsson, G. 117
Africa, country-specific knowledge
    and comparative advantage 92
Aldrich, J. and F. Nelson 126
Alexander, C. and K. Warwick 82
Algeria, bilateral trade to GDP ratios
    102, 104
Anderson, J. and E. van Wincoop 20,
    77, 97
Andreasen, U. 17
Arad, R. and A. Hillman 65, 153
Aspin, L. 120
Australia
    bilateral trade to GDP ratios 13,
        102, 104, 106
    distance effect in economic trade 12
Austria
    bilateral trade to GDP ratios 13,
        102, 104, 106
    distance effect in economic trade 12
    terrorism and tourism 41
Aw, B. et al. 75
Azar, E. 37, 39–40

Baier, S. and J. Bergstrand 176
Bailey, N. and C. Lord 24
Baine, N. and S. Woolcock 14–15,
    17
Baldry, J. and B. Dollery 142
Baldwin, D. 20, 24, 116, 118, 120,
    148, 150, 156–7, 164, 183
Baldwin, J. and W. Gu 75
Balkan, E. 42
Bangladesh, bilateral trade to GDP
    ratios 102, 104
banking industry 42, 81
Bayard, T. et al. 120
Belgium

bilateral trade to GDP ratios 13,
    102, 104, 106
country-specific knowledge and
    comparative advantage 92
distance effect in economic trade 12
Bergstrand, J. 96, 176
Bergström, C. et al. 31, 153
Bernard, A. et al. 75
Bernard, A. and J. Jensen 75, 89, 92
Bernard, A. and J. Wagner 78
Bhagwati, J. 1, 28, 47
Bhagwati, J. and T. Srinivasan 29, 47,
    70
Biesebroeck, J. van 92
Bikker, J. 35, 97
bilateral trade flows
    and economic and commercial
        diplomacy, agenda for 184–5
    and embassies and consulates 94–5,
        176
    to GDP ratios 13, 101–3, 104,
        106–9
    variance, and hostile and
        cooperative behaviour 39–40
    see also commercial policy and
        economic diplomacy, effect on
        bilateral trade flows; trade and
        conflict; trade uncertainty and
        trade disruption
Black, P. and J. Cooper 169
Blake, C. and N. Klemm 140
Blomberg, S. and G. Hess 7, 40, 41
Bonetti, S. 8, 133, 135, 137, 141, 167
border effects
    distance effect in economic trade
        9–14, 176
    and market failures 77–82
    and network improvement 78, 80

reduction and government policy
111
Bornstein, M. 61, 170
Boulding, K. 148, 149
boycotts 115, 117, 119, 121, 157, 181,
182
see also economic sanctions
Brady, L. 127
Brakman, S. et al. 91–2
Brazil, bilateral trade to GDP ratios
102, 104
Bremer, S. 38
Bretton Woods institutions 185
Brown, D. et al. 15
Brun, J.-F. et al. 20
Brzoska, M. 116
Bull, H. 140

Cairncross, F. 9
Canada
bilateral trade to GDP ratios 13
border effects 77
distance effect in economic trade 12
state visits, impact of 88
TFP growth 75
and trade intensity of manufactured
goods 41
Cantillon, R. 69
Carbaugh, R. 120
cartels
and competition protection 92
and embargoes 118
Carter, B. 46, 47
Caruso, R. 177
Cataquet, H. 42
Central and Eastern Europe
diplomatic exchange, effects of 40
restructuring 14, 18, 163
Chang, Y.-C. et al. 20
Charlton, A. and N. Davis 112
Chile, bilateral trade to GDP ratios
102, 104
China
bilateral trade to GDP ratios 13
cultural and institutional
background international
conflict settlement 4

distance effect in economic trade
12, 14
state visits, importance of 87
trade shares 4
US economic engagement 163
Citron, J. and G. Nickelsburg 42
Colbertism 69
Collini, S. et al. 24
colonization, and trade and conflict
26–7
commercial and economic diplomacy,
agenda for *see* economic and
commercial diplomacy, agenda
for
commercial policy and economic
diplomacy, effect on bilateral
trade flows 93–112, 180, 184–5
bilateral trade to GDP ratios 13,
101–3, 104, 106–9
country selection in model 101
development level impact 105–11
distance in model 97, 100, 104
economic data used 100
embassy and consulate data 100–1,
103–5, 106, 107, 108–9, 181
embassy and consulate share in
relation to bilateral distance
94–5, 176
empirical results 103–5
and export promotion agencies
93–5, 176, 178, 181
export promotion data 100, 103–5
gravity equation and empirical
regularities, incorporation of
97–8
gravity model overview 98–103,
176
gravity model, strengths and
weaknesses 97–8
per capita GDP, relevance of
106–8
staff numbers data 103–5, 107
see also economic and commercial
diplomacy, agenda for
commercial policy and economic
diplomacy, reasons for 69–92
border effects *see* border effects

capital market imperfections, reasons for 81–2
country risk 81–2
country-specific knowledge and comparative advantage 80, 83, 86, 87
creation or diversion of trade 70
directly unproductive profit seeking (DUP) 70
embassies and consulates and international networking 83–6, 90, 178, 179–80
and export *see* export
financial barriers 81–2
free trade and GDP 71–3
globalization and Total Factor Productivity (TFP) 75–6
information barriers and government intervention 81, 97
information barriers, network effects and externalities 79–81
international networking 83–91
internationalization of firms, entry factors in 75
labour mobility, changing perspective of 77
macroeconomic trade benefits 71–3
market failure and competition effect 78–9
market failure and government intervention 78–9, 82
Mercantilism 69, 89, 91, 185
microeconomic trade barriers 74–7, 180
national regulations, importance of 73
new entrants and government aid 70
private sector visits and international networking 86, 89–90
productivity increase, reasons for 74–5, 77
R&D and profitability, effects of 75
state visits and international networking 3, 7, 86–9, 108, 178, 181
state visits, motivation for 88–9

trade barriers 77–8, 97
trade benefits 71–7
comparative advantage, and country-specific knowledge 80, 83, 86, 87
Conflict and Peace Database (COBDAB) 37, 178
conflict and trade *see* trade and conflict
consumers
boycotts, and economic diplomacy 16–17
and free trade and no-trade decision making 55–7
Cortright, D. and G. Lopez 16
cultural distance 4, 10, 80
Czech Republic, bilateral trade to GDP ratios 102, 104

Daoudi, M. and M. Dajani 116, 127
Dashti-Gibson, J. et al. 146
De Grauwe, P. and F. Camerman 16
de Wilde, J. 24
Deardorff, A. 96, 98
Dehejia, R. and B. Wood 8, 137
Dekker, P. 63, 153
Dekker, P. et al. 10
Delgado, M. et al. 92
den Butter, F. and R. Mosch 10
Denmark
bilateral trade to GDP ratios 13, 102, 104
cartoons and consumer boycotts 17
distance effect in economic trade 12
Denters, E. and J. Klijn 35
Dewit, G. 82
Diamond, P. 65
Disdier, A. and K. Head 10, 11
Dixit, A. 65–6
Döhrn, R. and A. Milton 36
Dominican Republic, bilateral trade to GDP ratios 102, 104
Dorussen, H. and J. Mo 121
Drazen, A. 46
Duguid, P. 20
East–West trade and *Détente* 36–7, 85, 96, 139, 147–8, 180

Eaton, J. and M. Engers 148
economic and commercial diplomacy,
    agenda for 173–86
  art of economic diplomacy 184–6
  and bilateral trade 184–5
  future research 174–9
  and globalization 173–4
  and logic of choice 183–4
  multilateral governance of free trade
    and investment 15, 185–6
  negative sanctions, costs of 181–3
  policy and empirics of economic
    diplomacy 179–81
  policy making without perfect
    knowledge 179–84
  see also commercial policy and
    economic diplomacy, reasons
    for
economic diplomacy
  bilateral trade to GDP ratios 13,
    101–3, 104
  and commercial policy, effect on
    bilateral trade *see* commercial
    policy and economic
    diplomacy, effect on bilateral
    trade flows
  conflict-trade relationship 5, 6–7
  and consumer boycotts 16–17
  costs and benefits of 182
  definition of 14–15, 17
  and distance effect in economic
    trade 9–14, 176
  and economic development,
    relationship between 86
  and economic sanctions 3, 8–9, 29,
    30, 57–8, 61
  and economic security 17–18
  empirical evidence for relevance of
    5–9
  export destinations and embassy
    influence 5, 7, 85
  and export promotion agencies 7,
    79–80, 93–5, 176, 178, 181
  and globalization 3–4, 5, 9–14
  history of 2–4, 18
  hostile and cooperative behaviour,
    and bilateral trade variance

    39–40
  and MNEs 15–16
  new challenges 1–20
  and non-state actors 14–17
  and political events, effect of 37–8
  and state visits 3, 7
  and terrorism 7, 17
  trends in 2–3
economic sanctions 115–46
  and aid to GDP 132
  boycotts 115, 117, 119, 121, 157,
    181, 182
  cooperation, sanction busting and
    smuggling 129, 130, 132, 145
  data sources and methodology
    138–46
  economic data used 142–3
  and economic diplomacy 3, 8–9, 29,
    30, 57–8, 61
  economics of 119–25
  effectiveness versus success 116–19
  embargoes 115, 116, 117, 118, 119,
    120–1, 157, 181, 182
  empirical results of study 130–3
  financial sanctions 115, 132, 181
  financial variables 129, 130, 131,
    145
  game theory 123–5, 126, 167
  identified threat cases 126
  ineffectiveness of 117–19, 124–5,
    128
  and interest groups 121–2, 183
  inverted trade liberalisation model
    120
  and market competition 120, 121
  negative 115–16, 147–70, 181–3
  political economy and public choice
    aspects 120–3
  political system data 143–5
  political variables 129, 130, 132,
    145
  positive 116, 147–70, 181
  public choice variables 128–9
  Robinson Crusoe Fallacy 124–5,
    133
  success, and democratic and
    autocratic institutions 122–3,

131, 135, 144
success drivers 125–30, 134, 141–2
time factors 123–4, 128, 131, 134,
    145–6
and trade liberalisation 119–20,
    183
trade linkage and time variables
    126–8, 130, 131–2, 134
and welfare reduction 119, 120,
    122, 123, 183
economic sanctions, expected utility
    of positive and negative 147–70
credibility of threat (weight of
    evidence) 159–60, 165–6
economic instruments of foreign
    policy analysis 156–64
enlargement threat and number of
    countries involved 157–8
and military misconduct 163
neutral activities and risk aversion
    160–2, 165–6, 167–8
and opportunity costs 150
political economy of economic
    diplomacy 167–8
political use of 164–8
positive economic sanctions 162–4,
    165–6, 167
and rational choice paradigm 150
sanction damage (influence effect)
    157–8
sanction size and loss of welfare to
    both sides 158
study model 151–6
target's perception of situation
    156–7
threat of sanctions, effect of
    148–51, 166, 167
uncertainty and expectation of
    sanction 149, 158, 159–60, 167
Ecuador, bilateral trade to GDP ratios
    102, 104
Eggleston, R. 162
Egypt, bilateral trade to GDP ratios
    102, 104
Elliott, K. et al. 136
embargoes 115, 116, 117, 118, 119,
    120–1, 157, 181, 182

see also economic sanctions
embassies and consulates
economic diplomacy and effect on
    bilateral trade flows 94–5, 176
and export destinations 5, 7, 85
and international networking 83–6,
    90, 178, 179–80
see also economic and commercial
    diplomacy, agenda for;
    economic diplomacy
environmental concerns
and consumer boycotts 16–17
and scarce resources 79
Erickson, B. 46
Estevadeordal, A. and A. Taylor 91
Ethier, W. et al. 111
EU
borders and distance effects 10, 14,
    77
European Bank for Reconstruction
    and Development (EBRD) 18
nationalism revival 35
policy experiment on trade and
    conflict 34–5
terrorism and tourism 41
trade shares 4
Europe, non-euro, trade shares 4
Evenett, S. and W. Keller 96
export
and comparative advantage 58–9,
    62
credit schemes 82
decisions and risk aversion 78, 83
destinations and embassy influence
    5, 7, 85
and international networking 78
premium percentages, UK 74
promotion activities 89–91, 100,
    103–5
promotion agencies 7, 79–80, 93–5,
    176, 178, 181
subsidies, effect of 70
Ezran, R. et al. 36

Farmer, R. 9, 135
FDI
and bilateral investment treaties 43

capital flows, conflict and
    cooperation 42–3, 44, 108, 180
and heterogeneity 176
impact of 178–9
and political instability 42–3, 44,
    108, 180
Feenstra, R. et al. 96
Felipe, J. and M. Vernengo 20
Fenthur, R. and P. van Bergeijk 8
Finland
    bilateral trade to GDP ratios 13,
        102, 104
    distance effect in economic trade 12
Fischer, D. 167
Fortanier, F. 43, 176
France
    bilateral trade to GDP ratios 13,
        102, 104, 106
    Colbertism 69
    distance effect in economic trade 12
    state visits, impact of 3, 87–8
Francois, J. et al 15
Frankel, J. 20
Frankel, J. and D. Romer 71
Fratianni, M. and H. Kang 6, 7, 20,
    176
free trade
    and GDP 71–3
    multilateral governance of 185–6
    trade liberalisation and economic
        sanctions 119–20, 183
    see also bilateral trade flows
Frey, B. 24, 28, 119, 120, 147
Frey, B. et al. 40–1
Frey, B. and F. Schneider 42, 44
Frey, B. and S. Lüchinger 34
Freytag, A. et al. 6
Friedman, M. and R. 25
Friedman, T. 9
Fryges, H. and J. Wagner 92
Furuoka, F. 162
future research
    bias of knowledge 177–8
    causality 176–7
    conflict and trade 111
    costs and benefits of economic
        diplomacy 182

and data collection 178
diplomatic activity and commercial
    policy 109
economic and commercial
    diplomatic activity, effect on
    trade and investment 109, 110
economic diplomacy and bilateral
    trade flows, instruments
    affecting 94
economic diplomacy,
    complementarities and
    substitution between 91
economic sanctions and sender's
    reputation 135
export decisions and risk aversion
    78
export promotion and trade flows
    91
FDI investment 178–9
gravity model 97
heterogeneity 175–6
success rate of economic sanctions
    135
suggestions for improving 178–9
TFP growth in France 75
trade and conflicts 45
trade creation, trade diversion and
    bilateralism 185

game theory, and economic sanctions
    123–5, 126, 167
Gasiorowski, M. 6, 32–3
Gatzke, E. and Q. Li 137
Geelhoed, L. 179
Germany
    bilateral trade to GDP ratios 13,
        102, 104, 106
    country-specific knowledge and
        comparative advantage 92
    distance effect in economic trade 12
    state visits, impact of 3, 87–8
    and trade intensity of manufactured
        goods 41
Gil-Pareja, S. et al. 6, 7, 85
globalization
    benefits of 173–4, 180
    and economic and commercial

diplomacy, agenda for 173–4
and economic diplomacy 3–4, 5,
  9–14
and terrorism 34
and Total Factor Productivity (TFP)
  75-6
Grampp, D. 25
Greece
  bilateral trade to GDP ratios 13
  distance effect in economic trade 12
  terrorism and tourism 41
Greenaway, D. and R. Kneller 69, 74,
  75, 92
Griffin, K. and J. Gurley 46
Griffith, R. et al. 92
Grosso, J. and T. Smith 16
Guiso, L. et al. 10
Guttentag, J. and R. Herring 46

Haffner, R. and P. van Bergeijk 76
Haiti, aid programme 162
Hamilton, C. and L. Winters 36
Haney, P. et al. 169
Hanlon, J. and R. Omond 127
Harris, P. 142
Harris, R. and Q. Li 80
Harris, S. and C. Wheeler 92
Havrylyshyn, O. and L. Pritchett 36–7
Hayes, J. 142
Hazelzet, H. 160
Head, K. and J. Ries 88
Head, K. and T. Mayer 77
Heckscher, E. 91, 96
Hegre, H. 34
Helble, M. 10
Helpman, E. 29, 65
Helpman, E. and A. Razin 48, 64, 65
Henderson, J. and R. Quandt 169
Hermele, K. and B. Odén 61
Hertel, T. et al. 15
Hervé, K. et al. 3–4
Herz, N. 16
Hirsch, S. 168
Hirschman, A. 24, 157
Hobson, J. 26
Hoekman, B. and B. Smarzynska
  Javoricik 79, 81

Hong Kong
  bilateral trade to GDP ratios 13
  distance effect in economic trade 12
Hont, I. 24
Hower, G. 169
Hufbauer, G. et al. 3, 8, 9, 117, 121,
  124, 125, 126, 130, 133, 134,
  135, 136, 137, 138–42, 143,
  145–6, 147, 153, 169
Hufbauer, G. and J. Schott 8, 135,
  138, 146
Hughes Hallett, A. and A. Brandsma
  147–8
Hummels, D. and J. Levinson 96
Hungary
  bilateral trade to GDP ratios 13,
    102, 104
  distance effect in economic trade 12
Hutchison, T. 24, 91
Hyrkkanen, M. 27

Iceland
  bilateral trade to GDP ratios 13
  distance effect in economic trade 12
India
  cultural and institutiona
    background and international
    conflict settlement 4
  Pakistan non-trade relationships 35
information barriers
  and government intervention 81, 97
  network effects and externalities
    79–81
Inkeles, A. 143
institutions
  characteristics, and trade and
    conflict 43, 80
  economic sanctions success, and
    democratic and autocratic
    institutions 122–3, 131, 135,
    144
  multilateral, and trade and conflict
    44–5
international networking
  commercial policy and economic
    diplomacy, reasons for 83–91
  and embassies and consulates 83–6,

90, 178, 179–80
MNEs 15–16
    and private sector visits 86, 89–90
    and state visits 3, 7, 86–9, 108, 178,
        181
    international trade relations, political
        dimensions 24–8
Intrilligator, M. 24
Iran, reparation payments 162
Iraq, sanctions against 115, 120, 134,
        139, 149
Ireland
    bilateral trade to GDP ratios 102,
        104
    distance effect in economic trade 12
Isard, W. 96, 97–8, 169
Israel
    bilateral trade to GDP ratios 102,
        104
    economic sanctions 118
    Palestine non-trade relationships 35
Italianer, A. 72
Italy
    bilateral trade to GDP ratios 13
    distance effect in economic trade 12

Jaggers, K. and T. Gurr 143–5
Japan
    aid programmes 162
    bilateral trade to GDP ratios 13
    distance effect in economic trade 12
    and trade intensity of manufactured
        goods 41
    trade shares 4
Johnston, S. 92
Jolly, R. et al. 27
Kabel, D. and P. van Bergeijk 65–6
Kaempfer, W. and A. Lowenberg 120,
        123, 146, 148
Kaempfer, W. et al. 123
Kaplow, L. 159
Kemp, M. 120, 147
Kennedy, P. 46, 91
Keohane, R. and J. Nye 46
Keshk, O. et al. 46
Keynes, J.M. 26
Khan, H. 61

Kindleberger, C. 24
Knight, F. 149
Knorr, K. 24
Kofman, P. et al. 47
Kostecki, M. and O. Naray 87
Kox, H. 92
Krautheim, S. 77–8
Krugman, P. 64, 82

Lam, S. 8, 137
Lankhuizen, M. et al. 10
Larsen, H. 17
Law, J. 69
Lawson, F. 150
Leamer, E. 20
Leamer, E. and R. Stern 98, 111
Lederman, D. et al. 6, 7, 90–1, 94, 95,
        100, 102, 105, 106, 176
Leitzel, J. 118, 141
Lenin, V. 27
Lensink, B. and P. van Bergeijk 46, 96
Lewer, J. and H. van den Berg 71–2
Leyton-Brown, D. 128
Li, Q. 42–3, 80, 137, 180
Li, Q. and D. Schaub 34
Li, Q. et al. 6, 7, 33
Linder, S. 108
Linders, G.-J. 10, 20
Linders, G.-J. et al. 97
Lindsay, J. 117, 136
Linnemann, H. 36, 96
Lloyd, T. et al. 92
Losman, D. 119, 136
Lowenberg, A. 120, 123, 146, 148,
        183
Lundborg, P. 33

Maclean, J. 26
Malaysia, bilateral trade to GDP ratios
        102, 104
Manacsa, R. 169
Mansfield, E. and B. Pollins 137
Mansfield, E. and J. Pevehouse 34
Marinov, R. et al. 75
Marrewijk, C. 30
Marrewijk, C. and P. van Bergeijk 58,
        65, 124, 158, 169, 182

Marshall, A. 162
Marx, K. 26, 27, 28
Mastanduno, M. 116, 163, 167
Maurel, M. and E. Afman 6, 7, 38, 40,
    85, 105, 186
Mayer, W. 30
McCallum, J. 77
McCann, P. and Z. Acs 15, 20
McKenna, C. 169
Melitz, M. 75
Menkveld, P. 18
Mercantilism 69, 89, 91, 185
Mexico
    bilateral trade to GDP ratios 13,
        102, 104
    distance effect in economic trade
        12
Mill, J.S. 25
MNEs
    and economic diplomacy 15–16
    free trade and no-trade decision
        making 55–7
Morgan, T. and V. Schwebach 126
Morgenstern, O. 53, 142, 149, 153,
    154
Morocco, bilateral trade to GDP ratios
    102, 104
Morrow, J. et al. 46
Moser, C. et al. 82
Mousseau, H. et al. 6, 137, 175
multilateral governance of free trade
    and investment 15, 185–6
Murshed, S. and D. Mamoon 20, 31,
    35
national defence tariff 23, 24, 28–31
Neary, P. 20
Netherlands
    bilateral trade to GDP ratios 13,
        102, 104
    country-specific knowledge and
        comparative advantage 92
    development aid programme in
        Surinam 162
    distance effect in economic trade 12
    'Fitna' film 181
    TFP growth 76
New International Economic Order

(NIEO) 27–8
New Zealand
    bilateral trade to GDP ratios 13
    distance effect in economic trade 12
Newnham, R. 162, 163
Nicoletti, G. et al. 73
Nitsch, V. 3, 6, 7, 40, 87–8
Nitsch, V. and D. Schumacher 6, 7,
    38, 40
North Korea, sanctions against 115
Norway
    bilateral trade to GDP ratios 13,
        102, 104
    distance effect in economic trade 12
Nossal, K. 136

O'Brien, D. 2
Oldersma, H. and P. van Bergeijk 14,
    17, 36
Olson, R. 44
Oneal, J. 185
Ottaviano, G. and T. Mayer 92

Pape, R. 125, 140
Pen, J. 109–10, 120
Pevehouse, J. 34, 46
Picchio Forlati, M. 169
Pindyck, R. and D. Rubinfeld 108,
    112
Pisu, M. 92
Polachek, S. 5, 6, 18, 25, 31–3, 34
Polachek, S. and C. Seiglie 44
Polachek, S. and J. McDonald 31
Poland, bilateral trade to GDP ratios
    13
policy making
    and empirics of economic
        diplomacy 179–81
    without perfect knowledge 179–84
political economy
economic sanctions, expected utility
    of positive and negative 164–8
and public choice aspects, economic
    sanctions 120–3
Pollins, B. 6, 31, 37–9, 137
Pomery, J. 47
Porter, M. 92, 147, 153

Portugal
  bilateral trade to GDP ratios 13,
    102, 104
  distance effect in economic trade 12
  Methuen Treaty 2, 25, 69–70
producers
  and free trade and no-trade decision
    making 55–7
  MNEs 15–16

Rae, D. and M. Sollie 10
Ratnapala, S. 25
Reekie, D. 117–18
Reuveny, R. 46
Riberio, A. 11
Ricardo, D. 1–2, 24–5
Richardson, L. 31, 32
Richardson, N. 46
Robinson Crusoe Fallacy 124–5, 133
Rodriguez, F. and D. Rodrik 71
Roemer, J. 41
Rose, A. 5, 6, 7, 38, 40, 83–5, 91, 101,
    102, 103, 105, 179–80
Rosecrane, R. 24
Ruffin, R. 47
Russia, state visits, importance of 87

Sachs, J. and A. Warner 71, 72
sanctions *see* economic sanctions
Sandler, T. 169
Sandler, T. and K. Hartley 186
Sayrs, L. 31, 32, 46
Schelling, T. 148, 149, 156
Schiavo-Campo, S. 23
Schneider, F. and B. Frey 42, 44
Schneider, G. and G. Schultze 34
Schneider, G. et al. 42, 91
Schrödt, P. 150
Schultz, C. 120
Schumpeter, J. 25, 27, 69, 184
Scolnick, J. 136
Seeler, H. 117
Segura-Cayela, R. and J. Vilarrubia 85
Shone, R. 154
Sideri, S. 20
Simon, J. 169
Sinderen, J. van 35

Skylakakis, T. 18
Smeets, M. 120, 136
Smith, A. 140, 166
Smith, Adam 2, 24, 28
smuggling 129, 130, 132, 145
South Africa
  bilateral trade to GDP ratios 102,
    104
  sanctions against 16, 115, 118,
    142–3, 148, 168
South Korea
  bilateral trade to GDP ratios 13
  distance effect in economic trade 12
Spain
  bilateral trade to GDP ratios 13,
    102, 104
  country-specific knowledge and
    comparative advantage 92
  distance effect in economic trade
    12
  terrorism and tourism 41
specialization, and trade and conflict
    25, 27, 30
Spero, J. 24
Spindler, Z. 135
Srinivasan, T. 29, 47, 70, 169
state visits
  and economic diplomacy 3, 7
  and international networking 3, 7,
    86–9, 108, 178, 181
  motivation for 88–9
  see also economic and commercial
    diplomacy, agenda for;
    economic diplomacy
Straathof, B. 77
Strange, S. 4, 23
Subramanian, A. 47
Summary, R. 6, 38, 39, 83
Sweden
  bilateral trade to GDP ratios 13,
    102 104
  distance effect in economic trade 12
Switzerland
  bilateral trade to GDP ratios 13,
    102, 104
  distance effect in economic trade
    12

terrorism
and economic diplomacy 7, 17
and globalization 34
and tourism 40–1
and trade decline 40
Thailand, bilateral trade to GDP ratios
102, 104
Thompson, P. 162
time factors, and economic sanctions
123–4, 128, 131, 134, 145–6
Tinbergen, J. 23, 35–6, 46, 96, 149
Tolley, G. and J. Wilman 30
tourism
and international networking 85
and terrorism 40–1
trade barriers, and commercial policy
and economic diplomacy 77–8,
97
trade benefits, and commercial policy
and economic diplomacy 71–7
trade and conflict 23–46
capital flows, conflict and
cooperation 42–5
and capitalism 26–7
and colonization 26–7
conflict and co-operation, beyond
binary measurement of 37–41
conflict, net frequency of 32–3
conflict and trade, causality of 31–5
and diplomatic activity, costs and
benefits of 32–3
East-West trade and *Détente* 36–7,
85, 96, 139, 147–8, 180
and economies of scale 26–7
European policy experiment 34–5
FDI and political instability 42–3,
44, 108, 180
hostile and cooperative diplomacy,
and bilateral trade variance
39–40
and institutional characteristics 43,
80
and international free trade theory
24–7
international political economy 24
international trade relations,
political dimension of 24–8
and Marxism 26, 27, 28
and multilateral institutions 44–5
national defence tariff theories 23,
24, 28–31
and national security 24
and New International Economic
Order (NIEO) 27–8
policy responses to threat of market
disruption 29, 30–1
and protectionism 27
and specialization 25, 27, 30
and sphere of influence effects 41
terrorism *see* terrorism
and trade intensity of manufactured
goods 41
trade relations management,
differences between countries
38
trade-politics relationship, empirical
findings 35–41
trade flows, bilateral *see* bilateral trade
flows
trade liberalisation, and economic
sanctions 119–20, 183
trade uncertainty and trade disruption
47–66
anticipation of future trade
disruption 62, 63
autarky to free trade time path 60–1
and decentralized decision making
55–7
dynamic analysis 59–61
and economic sanctions 57–8, 61,
63
endogenous uncertainty 57–9
exports and comparative advantage
58–9, 62
free trade and no-trade utility
functions model 51–3, 55
optimal specialization and trade
inclination parameter 58–9
and political economy 63
private decentralized decision
making 30–1
production, consumption and
specialization model 48–50, 58
protectionism 64

responsiveness of trade parameter
    58
specialization and endogenous trade
    uncertainty 58–9, 64, 182–3
study model 48–54
study model extension 54–63
trade interventionism 64
trade uncertainty reduction 63–4
trade uncertainty and specialization,
    impact of 50–4, 62
in unitary actor economy 53–4
transportation costs 10, 41, 79, 97, 98,
    100, 136
Tsebelis, G. 124–5, 140, 167
Tunisia, bilateral trade to GDP ratios
    102, 104
Turkey
    bilateral trade to GDP ratios 13,
        102, 104
    distance effect in economic trade 12

Uganda, bilateral trade to GDP ratios
    102, 104
UK
    bilateral trade to GDP ratios 13,
        102, 104, 106
    country-specific knowledge and
        comparative advantage 92
    distance effect in economic trade
        12
    economic sanctions against
        Rhodesia 61
    export premium percentages 74
    Methuen Treaty 2, 25, 69–70
    sanctions against Argentina 125
    and trade intensity of manufactured
        goods 41
UN
    sanctions against Iraq 115, 120,
        134 139, 149
    sanctions against North Korea 115
    sanctions since 1990 137, 147, 160
uncertainty
    and expectation of sanction 149,
        158, 159–60, 167
    trade uncertainty and trade
        disruption

    see trade uncertainty and trade
        disruption
Ungar, S. and P. Vale 167–8
Uruguay, bilateral trade to GDP ratios
    102, 104
US
    bilateral trade to GDP ratios 13,
        102, 104
    border effects 77
    China economic engagement 163
    conflict and cooperation measures
        for trade 39
    country-specific knowledge and
        comparative advantage 92
    distance effect in economic trade 12
    financial sanctions against Iran 115
    food aid as positive economic
        sanction 162
    sanctions and bilateral trade flows 9
    state visits, impact of 3, 87–8
    TFP growth 75
    and trade intensity of manufactured
        goods 41
    trade missions and exports,
        relationship between 89–90
    trade shares 4

van der Ploeg, R. and S. Poelhekke 43
Veenstra, M.-L. van 100, 112, 176,
    180
Venezuela, bilateral trade to GDP
    ratios 102, 104
von Neumann, J. and O. Morgenstern
    53, 149, 153, 154

Wacziarg, R. and K. Horn Welch 72
Wagner, J. 92
Wallensteen, P. 116
Waltzer, M. 150
Wang, Z. and L. Winters 36
Weck-Hannemann, H. and B. Frey 28
Weede, E. 46
welfare reduction, and economic
    sanctions 119, 120, 122, 123, 183
Went, R. 26
Wilkinson, T. and L. Brouthers 89, 92
Wolf, T. 127, 157

Wolfe, R. 15
Woolcock, S. 14–15, 17, 173
World Bank lending behaviour 44–5
WTO 15, 28
    and export credit schemes 82
    and free trade commitment 64
    trade uncertainty reduction 64, 73

Yakop, M. 6, 85, 86, 105, 112, 176
Yakop, M. and P. van Bergeijk 7, 38,
    40, 84, 95, 101, 103, 105
Yanikkaya, H. 91
Yeats, A. 146

Printed and bound by CPI Group (UK) Ltd, Croydon, CR0 4YY

23/04/2025

14660962-0005